FORTUNE ADVISER
1998

FORTUNE ADVISER 1998
First Printing 1997

FORTUNE ADVISER STAFF:
Executive Editor: Thomas A. Stewart
Editor: Joe McGowan
Designer: Laura Ierardi, LCI Design
Copy Editors: Edith Firoozi Fried, Charles J. Attardi
Editorial Operations: David V. Rile

Special thanks to: Rosalind Klein Berlin, Geoffrey Colvin, Therese Eiben, Carol Gwinn, Joan Hoffman, Joseph Napolitano, Eileen Naughton, Rik Kirkland, Carolyn Sampson, and David Sloan

To order FORTUNE Magazine, please call (800) 621-8000.

ISSN 1096-1070
ISBN 1-883013-19-4

FORTUNE ADVISER 1998

By the Editors of FORTUNE
and Joe McGowan

FORTUNE BOOKS
TIME INC. HOME ENTERTAINMENT
1271 AVENUE OF THE AMERICAS
NEW YORK, N.Y. 10020

CONTENTS

◆◆◆

CHAPTER ONE

◆◆◆

THE FUTURE IS NOW

THIS ISN'T YOUR FATHER'S STOCK MARKET

BY MELANIE WARNER

◆◆◆

In a market with a total capitalization greater than the U.S. GDP, celebrity mutual fund managers, and rules that are constantly broken, these are exciting— and weird—times to be an investor.

◆◆◆

A funny thing happened to hedge fund manager James Cramer back in June. He was a guest on a CNBC stock show, talking about how he liked "Lilly," trader shorthand for drug giant Eli Lilly. Two days later he received three E-mails—one from an investor who thanked him for recommending "Louie," taken to mean Lucent Technologies, a stock that had gained two points since Cramer's appearance; another thanking him for plugging "Big Nose Louie," old Wall Street parlance for Beneficial Loan, which also had jumped two points; and a third from an admirer who got it right and bought Eli Lilly, watching it gain almost five points. "In this market you're not only a genius when you get it right, you're a genius when you get it wrong," mused Cramer, who blamed the misunderstandings on his Philadelphia accent and tendency to talk at a frenetic pace.

Indeed, these are weird and amazing times to be an investor in the stock market. Just when you think the market can't possibly go up any higher because price-to-earnings valuations are near the all-time high or because for the first time ever the total capitalization of the market is larger than our national GDP (gasp!), the Dow blows through another 1,000-point milestone, as it's done five times in the past three years.

This market's become impossible to predict. More than a few esteemed market pundits have nearly lost their shirts by daring to call the top. They issue bearish pronouncements expounding on how it will all end, only to watch stocks roar ahead. (Some analysts have been calling for a downturn for so long that when or if they turn out to be right, it's possible that no one will care.)

Such is the madness of trying to be a market seer when so many of the rules of the game have changed. It used to be, for instance, that a 100-plus daily drop in the Dow could send people running for the hills. Today the market nosedives and everyone thinks it's a buying opportunity, sending the Dow back up the next day. There are even some once fundamental principles about the market and economic cycles that are no longer true. Just about every market professional over age 40 was schooled in the logic that you buy certain groups of stocks when the economy is growing and certain other groups when things are in a slump. Chemical and food stocks, for instance, once held to be on opposite sides of economic cycles, are now rallying at the same time—in this market everything goes up.

But perhaps the strangest symptom of this exuberant bull market is that people like James Cramer have assumed the unlikely status of mini-celebrities. Cramer manages just $270 million in assets and is small potatoes compared with other money managers who oversee billions of dollars, much of it in retirement accounts. As the mutual fund industry continues to swell to astronomical proportions (in mid-1997 there was $4 trillion in funds—more than total deposits in commercial banks), the folks managing these collective fortunes have found themselves wielding newfound power and enjoying a newfound, well … sex appeal.

It hasn't always been important for us to know what mutual fund managers think and what kind of people they are. Suddenly they're on TV offering up thoughts on everything from the stock market and the balanced budget to NAFTA and world peace. They pose for stylish magazine photos, the sort once reserved for people who actually lead stylish lives, rather than spending the better part of a day glaring at computer screens. They share information about themselves—we read, for instance, that 34-year old Arieh Coll, manager of Fidelity's Trend Fund, asked his parents for a subscription to *Value Line*, the stock-investing bible, at age 13 and that Gloria Santella, manager of Stein Roe Capital Opportunities, does volunteer medical work in the Philippines.

Michael DiCarlo, manager of John Hancock Special Equities fund, landed on the cover of the *New York Times Magazine* for an in-depth 7,500-word profile, and Cramer was lionized along with Mira

Sorvino and millionaire porn publisher Bob Guccione in a recent *GQ*. And why not—mutual fund managers, equipped with large arsenals of stock, are calling the shots on Wall Street and in corporate boardrooms. If computer geeks can become the rich technorati of Silicon Valley, fund managers can be the sexy new Wall Street titans. After all, mutual funds are now as ubiquitous as home computers, with one-third of all households owning money in one.

There's been much attention devoted to the new empowerment of individual investors, and while it's true that there are greater information resources available to the small guy than ever before, it's not your neighbor's 500-share trades that move the market. The market moves because mutual fund managers buy or sell large blocks of shares. It's your money they're managing, but *they're* making the decisions on what to do with it. When a hot health care company like HCIA loses half its market value on one day, it's because so-called momentum fund managers like Gary Pilgrim of PBHG sold their entire position after the company warned of an earnings disappointment in a conference call before the trading bell. Individual investors could find out about the conference call later in the day in wire stories, but at 9:30 A.M. the stock opened down 60%.

When a small computer equipment company called Innovex shoots up five points with no real news, it's because Jeff Vinik, former star manager of Fidelity's $56 billion Magellan fund and now a hedge fund manager, decides to buy a 9% stake. Wall Street insiders often figure out who's buying large chunks of shares, but the investing public doesn't know until the person files a 13G with the SEC. With such large chunks of ownership in a company, fund managers either have the cooperative ears of management or try to shake things up the way corporate raiders did in the Eighties. The biggest champion of such rabble-rousing is Michael Price, who runs Franklin Mutual Series and in 1995 incited the merger of Chase Manhattan and Chemical Bank. [See Chapter Two, "Michael Price: The Scariest S.O.B. on Wall Street."]

The lesson for individual investors in all this is that to really understand the manic moves of this market, you have to know the fear and greed of mutual fund managers. Unfortunately, to keep up with them you need the same information they have. So unless you're willing to blow $1,200 a month to have a Bloomberg machine in your kitchen or to start making friends with Wall Street analysts, there's not much of a chance of winning the short-term trading game. Individual investors can glean some insight on how people like Pilgrim and Price work by reading fund prospectuses, magazine articles, etc., but the key is not to play their game at all.

The great thing about this market is that you can win by playing it safe, buying for the relative long term and on a company's fundamentals, not because a bunch of zealous institutional investors with too much of other people's money to spend have hopped on a stock and made it hot. These investors need quick, flashy rides to boost their market performance, which is published daily for all the world to see. But individual investors have the luxury of stepping back and taking the short-term pain, watching from a safe distance, for instance, as Intel reaches an all-time high and then tumbles almost eight points the next day. Of course, it's not easy. It takes a strong stomach and a certain amount of wisdom to take the bumps. But hang on and enjoy the ride, because the market's madness isn't over yet.

ELECTRONIC COMMERCE: FROM PEPPERONI PIZZA TO SPORT-UTILITY VEHICLES

BY MICHAEL H. MARTIN

◆◆◆

Consumer confidence, improved technology, and a few visionary companies are transforming the "no-shop zone" Web into a multibillion-dollar marketplace. Ignore it at your peril.

◆◆◆

Bill Gates calls the Web the consumer market's first step toward "friction-free capitalism." He imagines being able to say to a PC: "See what kind of a deal you can get me on that blue Donna Karan ensemble

Hillary was wearing on Jim Lehrer last night, tailored the way I like it, delivered by six o'clock next Friday." A short time later, your intelligent agent replies, "Madame, Saks in Singapore has the DK for $799, but for $825, Labels por Menos in Havana will ship you the outfit plus a bottle of Dom Pérignon for your brother's birthday, which, you may recall, is next week." (FORTUNE, February 5, 1996)

This imaginary scenario appeared in a column entitled "Why the Web Is Still a No-Shop Zone." The idea was to point out the huge gap between the reality of online shopping and the sugar-plum visions of such digital burblings as Bill Gates's *The Road Ahead*. Most of the article was devoted to describing the extreme difficulty most of us encounter in finding anything on the Internet worth buying.

While we're still nowhere near being able to boot up personal shopping software to hunt down bargains, the prospects of electronic commerce are brighter than ever. Most of the predictions about electronic commerce have proved wrong, except one: It is a reality that consumers and businesses ignore at their peril.

The big news is that most online sales are not consumers shopping while they surf, but rather businesses buying from one another. Cisco, which makes equipment for office computer networks, sells $5 million worth of networking gear on its Website each day, much of that to FORTUNE 500 companies. The company is on track to exceed $1 billion for the year. Computer maker Dell sells more than $2 million worth of PCs on the Web every day. Those figures are probably understated: Lots of customers use the Web to select their Dell or Cisco products, and then place their orders over the phone. It's no wonder that industry giant Compaq felt compelled to announce a new direct-sales strategy even though it risks alienating its network of computer retailers. Nor is electronic commerce restricted to high-tech goods like computers. General Electric uses a Web-based trading system to buy online more than $1 billion a year of products like molded plastic fittings and machine-tool parts from suppliers. The system helps speed up procurement and saves GE a bundle in the process.

What should really make your mouse-hand itch, though, is that consumers are coming around. Last year more than 200,000 of the 15 million cars sold in the U.S. were ordered online. Chrysler expects sales with an Internet component to constitute fully a *quarter* of its U.S. sales in less than four years. Millions of Web surfers are logging on to sites like Auto-By-Tel to punch up information about automobiles from various manufacturers, and the options available. Potential buyers can arrange financing and place their orders right online. Dealers contact them with a no-haggle price to buy or lease a new or used car. Customers can comparison-shop without having to fend off hard-charging salespeople, while manufacturers bypass the middlemen standing between them and their customers demanding a piece of every sale. (Of course, many salespeople are aghast at the prospect of being cut out of the action.)

When it comes to creating an online storefront from scratch, no Internet retailer is more closely watched than Amazon.com, a Seattle-based online-only bookseller. With a few mouse-clicks, Web-surfers can search, browse, and purchase books from a database of over 2.5 million titles. Most titles are discounted 20% to 30%. Once a customer decides on a book, he selects hardcover or paperback, gift wrapping, and mode of shipment. Payment is by credit card, submitted via telephone or via the Web—the transaction is safeguarded by encryption. Amazon requests the books from publishers and packs and ships them. Most orders are delivered within five days. Pay extra, and you can speed things up by a day or two.

Don't mistake Amazon's operations for glorified catalogue sales. Customers can sign up to be notified of new releases or receive recommendations based upon what they've already purchased. And the virtual storefront opens up some remarkable new marketing possibilities. Say you're fascinated by vintage cars, and you create a Website to share information with like-minded folks. Connect your site to Amazon's with the one-mouse-click-gets-you-there "hyper-links" that make the Web work, and you'll get a commission of up to 15% on each purchase made by anyone who follows that link and buys a book. Some of Amazon's 11,000 "associates" have earned thousands of dollars without ever touching a book. In the works are customized storefronts—a regular customer who tends to buy computer books will automatically be presented with the latest Microsoft programming manual, while a mystery fan might see a tout for the newest Patricia Cornwell thriller.

Other industries in which online sales have proved surprisingly strong include financial services—online stockbrokers undercut even Schwab's prices—and travel agents. By selling direct to travelers via company Websites or in partnership with online travel services like Expedia or Travelocity, airlines seek to cut the typical 10% commission paid to agents. And though it's rarely mentioned in the business press, the privacy of online sales means that sex sites are often ahead of the curve when it comes to selling video clips, customizable service, and live video-, er, "conferencing."

In fact, most of the mechanisms that will make electronic commerce work are now well established. Standardized software makes electronic storefronts open to anyone with a Web browser, some 43 million and growing in the U.S. alone. Digital IDs from companies like VeriSign and GTE work like electronic fingerprints that incorporate a mailing address and credit card data. The IDs, files that are encrypted on your computer's hard disk to protect them from prying eyes and tampering, are far more difficult to forge than a signature. On the process side, Visa and MasterCard have committed to a standard protocol for secure credit card purchases that makes using your credit card number on the Internet safer than using it at the restaurant next door.

Other important building blocks for Internet commerce are also falling into place. CyberCash and DigiCash are just two of several companies seeking to enable something called "microtransactions," small purchases that aren't practical with credit cards because of processing costs. One scheme combines a month's worth of minipurchases into a single charge on your credit card bill. Others function like digital currency. Money is transferred from a buyer's electronic "smart card" or hard drive to that of the seller. When your "wallet" is empty, you'll simply refill it at an automated teller machine or online. Giants like IBM and startups like InterTrust in Sunnyvale, California, are working on technology that would prevent the unauthorized copying of digital content, which is easily duplicated and redistributed electronically. Such technical fixes could eventually resolve many of the intellectual property issues raised by digital media and curtail the billions of dollars lost to copyright piracy each year.

We're still a long way from Gates's vision of humans barking orders to computers that continually scour the globe for worldwide bargains. But think about it. Not so long ago, lots of us were excited about the fact that Pizza Hut let people in a few U.S. cities order pizza over the Web. Now we can order up sport-utility vehicles. We've come a long way.

THE WAGES OF MEDIA SYNERGY

BY TIM CARVELL

◆◆◆

A couple of years after the megamergers, mediaglomerates are finding that achieving the magical phenomenon of synergy isn't as easy as wishing upon a star.

◆◆◆

Two years ago, amid much fanfare and dozens of turgid Ken Auletta stories, the media world collapsed in upon itself. Over the course of one long, hot summer, it saw more inbreeding than the British royal family has seen in centuries—Disney wed ABC, Westinghouse grabbed CBS, Time Warner courted Turner Broadcasting, and Seagram snagged MCA. Billions of dollars changed hands, and by Labor Day, the landscape of media power had been reconfigured so completely that, one imagines, even L.A.'s famously status-conscious maitre d's were having a little trouble figuring out who outranked whom.

As each week brought a new megamerger, Wall Street and the press applauded the results. The reason for such widespread optimism rested in the captivating concept of synergy, the magical process that would make these new companies amount to much, much more than the sum of their parts. Synergy, the line went, meant that as new divisions were plugged into the existing companies, sparks would fly between them as they realized fantastic cost savings and cross-marketing opportunities: The production house's shows would flow straight to the network, which would promote the studio's movies, which would tie in with the record label's soundtrack, and so on.

But as with so much involving the media business today, the hype was a good deal more entertaining than the follow-through. Two years after that summer of love, the limitations of synergy have become woefully apparent. For while these companies have indeed realized some gains from their new alliances, they have also had to contend with unforeseen consequences, ranging from the usual internecine battles that accompany any union to the fact that in certain cases, the mergers extended companies well beyond their core competencies. Nowhere have these stresses and shortcomings of synergy been more apparent than at the company whose merger was most lavishly applauded in the summer of '95: Disney/ABC.

When Disney bought itself a network, the popular thinking was that the company was well on its way to its greatest triumph yet; after successful forays into producing feature films through its Touchstone division, the savvy revival of its animated film franchise, and its purchase of the classy independent studio Miramax, Disney had gone as far as it could in extending its reach in films. Now the studio's manifest destiny was carrying it to television, purchasing the network that already carried some of the studio's hottest shows, among them the top-rated *Home Improvement*. A hot brand name with a proven track record, venturing into a medium that opened new distribution channels for its content—the strategists of synergy were practically rubbing their hands with glee.

Flash forward to June 1997, and what must surely stand as one of the worst months ever for a media company. While the company has realized some gains from its merger—most notably in the form of boosted profits from ABC's cable division—the month stands as a prime example of the pitfalls of synergy. June begins with Disney shuffling executives at ABC, which nobody at the company can quite figure out how to run. Skilled though the Mouseketeers are at the movie business, they have found dealing with the messy realities of affiliates, production companies, and advertisers to be far more complex than they imagined. Their star programmer, Jamie Tarses, is effectively demoted before her new season can begin, even as production companies charge that Disney unfairly favors its own shows over their product. Then the Southern Baptists announce that they have decided to boycott Disney theme parks and products, charging, among other things, that one of the few decently rated shows on ABC, *Ellen*, promotes homosexuality with its newly lesbian lead character.

Meanwhile, the company's struggling Hollywood Records division ships 100,000 copies of *The Great Milenko*, the latest album from a Detroit-based hip-hop duo who call themselves the Insane Clown Posse; six hours later Disney comes to its senses, realizes that obscene clowns rapping songs like "Fat, Sweaty Betty" and "I Didn't Mean To Kill Him" don't blend in with the Timon and Pumbaa plush toys, and yanks the albums from stores. And to cap things off, the company's announcement that it won't sell advertising time to competing animation studios during its *Wonderful World of Disney* unleashes a spate of negative press. Synergy, it seems, is a sword that can cut both ways.

Disney's is, perhaps, an extreme example of the dangers facing mediaglomerates today—after all, few companies have such a squeaky-clean image to worry about—but the problems Disney faces are reflected in the woes of other media companies whose reach may have exceeded their grasp. Time Warner's merger with Turner, for example, seems to have worked out better than Disney/ABC, in part because Turner's cable holdings like CNN and TNT formed a logical extension of Time Warner's TV and news-gathering properties. But the company has still had to contend with Ted Turner's acid critiques of its "gangsta rap" albums and racy movies, as well as his reputed antipathy toward the company's fledgling broadcast network, the WB.

Interestingly, the less touted, non-synergy-intensive mergers like Seagram/MCA have met with more plaudits over the past two years. This was due, in part, to the fact that expectations for them were much lower. But it was also due to the fact that the suits at non-media corporations have turned out to be better at delegating control of their media baubles to seasoned hands—as MCA did with Creative Artists Agency co-founder Ron Meyer—rather than trying to patch their acquisitions into the existing corporate hierarchy.

None of this is to say that synergy is unattainable—for certain companies, in certain instances, it can and has proved enormously lucrative. Sony, for example, has realized huge gains from coordinating terrific soundtracks to cross-promote with its hit movies. But the past two years have made everyone a touch more clear-eyed about this mystical phenomenon. Simply slamming together two successful companies is not enough—there must be a vision of where the two can go together, and a management team with enough political and business acumen to take them there. The mistake Disney made was not in acquiring ABC; it was in believing that the task of integrating the network into the corporate structure would be an easy one.

Tellingly, since that long, hot summer of 1995, there have been few media mergers, and none on the scale of a Time Warner/Turner or Disney/ABC. It is almost enough to make one hope that the media chieftains have learned from their mistakes. Then again, as the miraculous careers of Charlie Sheen, Tom Arnold, and even Andrew "Dice" Clay have proved, Hollywood's skill at learning from its mistakes is matched only by its propensity for making them all over again.

WHY WALL STREET IS CAUGHT UP IN A FEEDING FRENZY

BY ANDREW E. SERWER

◆◆◆

The Hunters and the Hunted: With
stock market values much smaller than
those of commercial banks, Wall Street
investment firms are ripe for takeover.

◆◆◆

The investment banking sharks, who formerly spent their days helping clients devour other companies, have themselves become prey. By mid-1997 four big-name firms—Morgan Stanley, Dillon

Read, Alex. Brown, and Robertson Stephens—had been bought out, and Montgomery Securities was in talks with both NationsBank and Dutch financial giant ING. More deals are almost certain to happen. "Rightly or wrongly, there's now a belief on Wall Street that bigger is better," muses Paine Webber CEO Donald Marron over lunch in a room crawling with dealmakers at New York's "21" Club.

Why are so many of these firms merging? Much of the reason is that U S. commercial banks now can move into the securities business. But there are a number of other factors, including the raging bull market, which is producing an enticing stream of profits at Wall Street firms. Of course the good times won't last, but you'd never know it from the premiums paid in recent deals. "Astronomical," growls veteran Wall Street analyst Perrin Long. "Way out of whack." And in the wake of each takeover, stock prices of the remaining, unacquired firms spiral ever higher.

As for the deals consummated in 1997, each reflects one of the several forces behind this unprecedented round of consolidation. Take Morgan Stanley's selling out to Dean Witter. What was once an unthinkable step down the prestige ladder for Morgan Stanley became a logical move given the changing fortunes of Wall Street's two broad lines of business. Back in the 1980s, investment banking firms such as Salomon Brothers and First Boston were king, while retail brokerages like Smith Barney and Prudential were déclassé, never mind much less profitable. Not anymore. The average return on equity for investment banks declined from 50% in 1981 to about 20% in July 1997, whereas the figure for retail brokerages has climbed to around 20%. The reason is that the investment banking business suffers from overcapacity, while the retail business is booming thanks to the growth of 401(k)s and asset management.

Swiss Bank's purchase of sleepy Dillon Read signals another trend: foreign banks wading onto U.S. beaches to build their investment banking businesses. The conventional wisdom among European bankers is that to be a global player in financial services, you must be a force in the U.S. securities markets. Deutsche Bank, with its high-profile talent raids on U S. firms, and NatWest, which in 1995 acquired the merger boutique Gleacher & Co., are other examples of this trend. So far, though, the foreigners have been too skittish to make a major acquisition. Nor have they struck fear into the hearts of Wall Street's elite. "We've seen this movie before," sighs Steve Rattner, heir apparent at Lazard Frères. "It's very, very hard to build or buy into this business. Not one new player has broken into the top tier of investment banking over the past 15 years." Buttressing Rattner's point: NatWest's head of investment banking, Martin Owen, resigned after his division reported a $130 million trading loss and generally subpar numbers.

The buyouts of Robertson Stephens by BankAmerica and Alex. Brown by Bankers Trust, on the other hand, are products of deregulation—the most powerful consolidating force on the Street. The disintegration of the provisions of the Glass-Steagall Banking Act of 1933 that separated commercial and investment banking is blurring the distinctions between the two businesses. As of March 6, 1997, the investment banking affiliates of commercial banks can derive up to 25% of their revenue from underwriting and trading, up from a 10% threshold.

Commercial bankers have longed to enter the investment banking business, since traditionally banks lose corporate customers to Wall Street when these companies need to do stock or bond offerings. "We've got to offer a full range of services," says Ken Thompson, managing director of the capital markets group at First Union. "After all, the investment bankers are coming in our business." In the spring of 1997, the bank, based in Charlotte, North Carolina, considered buying a sizable Wall Street firm—Lehman Brothers and Salomon were said to be on the radar screen—but decided to pass soon after the Bankers Trust–Alex. Brown deal was announced. First Union bankers say lofty premiums such as those Bankers Trust paid (some 2.7 times book value) helped dissuade them.

That a commercial bank in Charlotte can even consider buying world-renowned Salomon Brothers might seem strange—until you look at their respective market capitalizations. Says Marron of Paine Webber, whose company is always on the short list of takeover targets: "The U.S. banks are in the strongest position they have ever been in." Big commercial banks could easily digest many Wall Street firms, and the betting is that some of them will.

But buying a Wall Street firm is easy. Making the merger work, that's the hard part. After all, the assets are fickle: princely paid investment bankers who will simply walk if they aren't happy. As Sanford C. Bernstein analyst Sallie Krawchek puts it, "Wall Street is littered with the carcasses of those who have tried to set up shop here."

ALL LINES ARE BUSY: TELCOS SCRAMBLE FOR THE LONG-DISTANCE MARKET

BY HENRY GOLDBLATT

◆◆◆

The long-distance telephone business, once dominated by AT&T, is now highly competitive, leaving the field wide open for a host of new players—from upstart niche carriers to deep-pocketed infotech companies.

◆◆◆

You don't need to look beyond AT&T to realize how bloody the telecommunications industry has become. Over the past year, the $52 billion company was marred by a messy management shakeup that ousted CEO-heir apparent John Walters; a failed merger with SBC Communications that would have provided AT&T easy entry to lucrative local phone markets; and a plummeting of the company's share of the long-distance market to below 50%, compared with 90% in 1984.

To say the least, it was a challenging year for AT&T. And things weren't much different industrywide. AT&T's major long-distance rivals—MCI, Sprint, WorldCom, Frontier, and Excel—all saw their net income decline at some time in 1997. The situation didn't look as bad for long-distance companies when lawmakers passed the Telecommunications Act of 1996. The much heralded law opened the $100 billion local telephone market and the $80 billion long-distance market to competition. Suddenly callers could get their phone, cable, and Internet service all from the same company, and the provider of these services might be anyone from traditional phone companies to cable companies or electric utilities. All this competition, so the theory went, would drop long-distance and local phone rates, increase the number of phone calls placed, and grow profits for the biggest and leanest companies.

Well, things haven't worked out exactly as planned. Even as telephone use grows and revenues climb, an overcrowded and fiercely competitive market—more than 800 companies contend for your long-distance telephone business—is pushing prices down and squeezing the profit margins of the top long-distance carriers. Furthermore, upstart niche long-distance companies are cutting into the market by reselling—at bargain prices—network time they buy in bulk. And Internet and video telephony technologies promise to fan the competition by attracting powerful entrants like Microsoft and Intel.

While little competition has come from expected sources like cable companies and electric utilities, the long-distance carriers have faced scrappy new opponents that have siphoned off some of their most profitable customers. The largest phone companies have been assailed by smaller companies specializing in specific services like dial-around or call-back. You might recognize them from those stickers they've mailed you, emblazoned with a five-digit code. Dialing the code allows customers to circumvent their presubscribed long-distance carrier at rock-bottom rates.

These smaller carriers, realizing the difficulties and cost of full-scale marketing campaigns, have successfully poached customers through grassroots efforts. Companies like Startec Communications in Bethesda, Maryland, have targeted immigrants at community fairs, telling them they can save fistfuls of money when they call their relatives abroad. According to Atlantic-ACM, a research firm in Boston, niche companies have taken a $1.2 billion bite out of the long-distance industry and have thrived in international long distance, where AT&T, Sprint, and MCI enjoy their biggest margins.

Other innovative competitors have carved niches in the business market, targeting especially price-sensitive customers like those with small and home offices. The challengers range in size from U.S. Long Distance, a company with $180 million in revenues that offers small businesses bundled plans with local and long-distance service, calling cards, and Internet access, to WorldCom, a $4.5 billion long-distance carrier that has until now focused exclusively on the $43 billion business market. These carriers are expected to enjoy continued success at the expense of the Big Three, since they can choose their customers by exclusively targeting very select niches rather than having to worry about serving all types of customers with different packages.

New technology is also upping the long-distance ante. Over the next five years, the way you conceptualize a phone call will change drastically. Internet telephony, for example, allows users to make phone calls over Internet lines dirt-cheap. Companies like Lucent Technologies, spun off from AT&T earlier this year, Northern Telecom, and New Jersey–based VocalTec are developing servers that convert your voice into data packages, and route them over the Internet.

To place an Internet-telephony call, you dial the local or toll-free number of your nearest server, which converts your voice into a data package that travels over the Internet. When it reaches the server of the party you called, the data package is reconverted into voice and travels over local telephone lines to its destination. So far, carrying calls over Internet lines is virtually free, so callers pay only for the local connections on either end. MCI and GTE are testing these servers, and deployment is expected in 1998.

Other technologies will enable callers to incorporate video and data into multimedia-type communication. For instance, during a phone call, you will press a button to send pictures of the kids to your parents, all the while maintaining a normal conversation. Companies like Microsoft and Intel are working on products that could make this type of communication available to consumers in the next couple of years. For the traditional phone companies, this means competition from deep-pocketed sources that are more technologically able. "The telephone companies are investing a lot of money in traditional technologies," says Bryon Van Dussen, an analyst with the Yankee Group in Boston. "At some point the return on that dollar will slide. If they fail to invest in new technologies early enough, they might be caught unawares."

In the short term, the big phone companies are offering an array of services to attract and retain customers in this competitive market. Recognizing that consumers don't want to write separate checks for their long-distance, local, Internet, and cell-phone services, carriers are offering bundles, or suites, of services at cut-rate prices in order to attract and retain customers. Callers can also expect to see more straightforward, flat-pricing plans, such as Sprint's "Dime-a-Minute" rate, with which the company has had enormous success.

Which telecom company will be the victor? Only deft management, skillful navigation of regulatory hurdles, proper resource allocation, and a bit of luck will tell how this guerrilla war among the telecom players will unfold. One thing's for certain: It's going to be a fierce battle.

CHAPTER TWO

◆◆◆

COUNSEL FROM TITANS
OF COMMERCE

THE HAPPY CHAIRMAN: SANDY WEILL

BY CAROL J. LOOMIS

◆◆◆

*Travelers Group's CEO has transformed
a collection of unspectacular
businesses into a financial services
powerhouse. Here's how.*

◆◆◆

In a corner of Sanford I. Weill's wood-paneled office at Travelers Group Inc. in lower Manhattan, there hangs a neon sign—yes, neon—given him by one of his executives. It's a VACANCY/NO VACANCY sort, capable of a two-way message: "The Chairman Is Happy" or "The Chairman Is *Not* Happy." And which gets the nod? Bet on the first version. This is a guy who's ten years into a corporate adventure—first called Commercial Credit, then Primerica, and now Travelers—that would make any boss light up.

Travelers' 1996 revenues of $21.3 billion rank it No. 40 on the 1997 FORTUNE 500 list, and its profits of $2.3 billion put it higher still, 32nd. Moreover, in those respects, and in total market value, Travelers outranks a certain other financial services company, American Express. Weill used to hang out there as president and, in his words, "deputy dog." You don't think Weill, a cash-strapped kid out of Brooklyn originally, likes surpassing American Express? Get real. Or how about the fact that Travelers has been placed in the 30-stock Dow Jones industrial average (of which American Express is a long-standing member)? When Weill learned that Travelers had made that blue-chip club, he had a "Wow" reaction, says a Travelers executive: "He was ecstatic."

Small wonder. This is an unlikely outcome for a man who just over a decade ago was unemployed and batting .000 in his job applications; he'd tried to nab a division of American Express, and then the whole of BankAmerica, and had failed both times. Then, when he finally connected, he bought what looked like dregs—first, a small-loan business, then a sleepy brokerage firm and an outfit that sold term-life insurance across kitchen tables. From this start, a bare ten years ago, Weill builds a company with $2.3 billion in profits? One person marveling is General Electric's Jack Welch, who says of Weill: "He's been fantastic. He took air and turned it into this big, successful thing. It's been remarkable."

Naturally, his stockholders appreciate this talent. On a dollar basis, Weill's stock has moved: The shares that carried the name Commercial Credit in 1986 and are now called Travelers rose by about a multiple of ten, to a price of $51 in March 1997. Along the way, Travelers ran up a $33 billion increase in market value—some of that from issuing new shares to make acquisitions, but most of it from the climb of the company's stock price. If you compile a list of CEOs who held their jobs at the end of 1986 and still have them, and then figure who's added the most market value over this period, Weill makes the top ten. Above him are Roberto Goizueta of Coca-Cola; Jack Welch of GE; Bill Gates of Microsoft; John Reed of Citicorp; Maurice "Hank" Greenberg of American International Group; Hugh McColl of NationsBank; Michael Eisner of Disney; and Warren Buffett of Berkshire Hathaway. Not a bad crowd to be running with.

This chairman's a nut about creating shareholder value. It can't hurt that he's got a whopping stake in this company himself. Weill instinctively thinks as an owner, not as a hired hand dealing with other people's money. Famous for loving to make deals, he's equally known for buying shrewdly. Once into an acquisition, the owner in Weill is sure to cut the stuffing out of its costs—and when he's well along in that process with one company, he'll probably buy another. He'll spend cheerfully for assets that land on the balance sheet. The costs that run through the income statement—visionary spending, say, on new projects that may never pay off—he'd just as soon skip.

A BLOOD OATH, FRIENDS, AND FAMILY

He will, though, pay up for talent. Weill's tack is to load managers with options and restricted stock, and then pressure them to retain all the equity they get. Both his management team and Travelers' directors have sworn—internally, this is called the "blood oath"—not to sell any Travelers shares (except to finance the costs of exercising options and any resulting tax bills). Imprisoning most of an executive's net worth in his company does tend to focus him on what's best for shareholders.

Then again, if an executive persists in not focusing, Weill slides him out of his job, often by moving somebody in beside him to take over authority. An offender seldom gets fired: Weill hates confrontation and besides, being a sociable type, he tends to become pals with not only the people working for him but their families as well. So the executive who's not performing stays on, becoming a member of the group known inside as Friends of Sandy's. Do the big salaries these people draw really equate with delivering shareholder value? Weill bristles a little: "I think I'll just stand on our results for the shareholders."

The "I" in that sentence conveys a lot about how Travelers operates. This company, like any large organization, needs a fine executive team, and has built one. James Dimon, Travelers president and Weill's right-hand man for the past 15 years, justifiably gets his name in lights in what's sometimes called the "Sandy and Jamie show." But fundamentally, this is Weill's company. Says an executive who once worked closely with Weill: "There is *nothing* of significance that goes on in Travelers that he doesn't personally have a hand in. He's involved in every detail of that business—in *everything.*"

He's even got his family working in the shop. His son, Marc Weill, is chief investment officer of Travelers. His daughter, Jessica Weill Bibliowicz, ran Smith Barney's mutual funds operation until June 1997, when she left to become president and chief operating officer of a smaller New York firm. The chairman's wife, Joan, has been doing unpaid corporate duty for their 42 years of marriage. As wives of CEOs go, she is an unusually close adviser. At dinners masquerading as pure social events, she looks over people he's thinking of hiring—sometimes giving them a thumbs down, he says. She listens endlessly to his ruminations about the business. She's even a featured speaker at Travelers events. We're not talking spousal breakfasts, but rather main-tent appearances at big company gatherings. She is a particular hit at the huge, revival-type conventions of the Primerica Financial Services division, that part of Travelers still selling term insurance across kitchen tables.

For all this, Joan Weill doesn't usually make the press. But she did get there in a downbeat way in 1990, because of disclosures she'd made earlier to her psychiatrist about two big deals of her husband's that she feared might disrupt their lives. The first deal was Weill's 1981 sale of the brokerage firm he had built, Shearson, to American Express, and the second was his ultimately unsuccessful assault on BankAmerica in 1986. Hearing these pieces of news, the psychiatrist bought Shearson's and BankAmerica's stock and also wised up a broker who engineered other trades. Caught years after the fact, the psychiatrist was fined, sentenced to five years of community service, and ordered to take an ethics course. Mrs. Weill was not charged with wrongdoing. In fact, she brought a $5 million suit against the psychiatrist, which was later settled out of court.

"SANFORD WEILL, 53, EXP'D MGR, GD REFS"

It is unsurprising that Joan Weill agonized over the BankAmerica assault. That was a part of the difficult 13 months in 1985 and 1986 when her husband was unemployed—though by then fat in the wallet—and looking impatiently for the right way to get back into the financial services business. He'd gotten out of it by leaving American Express, after having failed in a bid to buy its troubled property and casualty insurance operation, Fireman's Fund, which he'd personally been parachuted in to rescue. With him out the Amexco door went Jamie Dimon, a smart, confident Harvard business school graduate who had been Weill's assistant for three years.

Back then the two, plus a secretary, holed up in five painfully quiet rooms in Manhattan's Seagram Building, sometimes catching sight of other animated beings only when breaking for lunch. Mostly they pored over the documents of financial services companies and talked to dealmakers. BankAmerica got in Weill's sights because it was a laggard—you can buy laggards more cheaply than leaders—and pretty soon he was making it brassily clear to the incumbent CEO, Sam Armacost, that he'd be happy to replace him. The board support that Weill had counted on failed to solidify, and he was told to get lost. So he went back to reading and talking to dealmakers.

FORTUNE then played a part in his liftoff by publishing an article called "Sanford Weill, 53, Exp'd Mgr, Gd Refs" (May 12, 1986). Reading the piece, two financial officers of Commercial Credit, of Baltimore, had a "Eureka!" reaction. Without breathing a word to their CEO, the two came to Weill to urge that he buy the company from its owner, Control Data. Weill already knew that the parent was eager to sell, because Commercial Credit had been shopped to American Express when he was there. His visitors, though, told him things were getting untenable. Control Data was losing money and Commercial Credit, tarred by its parent, was in danger of losing its access to the capital markets. Also, Commercial Credit had diversified itself aimlessly and unprofitably, having strayed into such losers as leasing in Israel and Latin American loans.

Weill listened. Maybe he wouldn't have earlier, when he was thinking grand thoughts like BankAmerica. But now he'd spent ten frustrating months on the sidelines. Besides, he has always been an opportunist. As he peered through the fog surrounding Commercial Credit, he saw a solid core not visible to all: a lending business that made good money and, on the side, a property and casualty operation, Gulf Insurance, that would return Weill to a business he knew.

Before long Weill had worked out a deal with Control Data, which sold 82% of Commercial Credit to the public in November 1986 at $20.50 a share while Commercial Credit itself raised money by issuing a new chunk of shares. Weill, taking over as CEO, personally invested $7 million, and Dimon, who at age 30 became the company's chief financial officer, scraped up $425,000 for stock—"a lot more money than I had, I'll tell you." What they got for this commitment was a company that in 1986 made $46 million on $1.1 billion in revenues. Core profits from small loans and Gulf were about $25 million, and the new bosses saw opportunities for getting that to $75 million pretty quickly. None of it could exactly be called thrilling, says Dimon. "But it was a start; it was a platform; it was life."

It was also hard, intensive work. Dimon literally moved to Baltimore for a while, and Weill, along with an executive team, encamped there each week from Monday to Friday. In time the Israeli leasing operation, the Latin American loans, and other diversions disappeared from the books, and so did innumerable inefficiencies in the core operations.

SMITH BARNEY "CHANGED EVERYTHING"

Two years later, in 1988, Weill had strengthened the business enough to reach out again, buying Gerald Tsai's Primerica Corp. for $1.5 billion in cash and stock. Out went tangential businesses like mail-order merchandisers Fingerhut and Figi. Weill focused instead on financial services, including the term-life operation then known as the A.L. Williams business and now called PFS.

But the Primerica prize that really mattered to Weill was Smith Barney, the vehicle that put him back in the brokerage business that is his undying love. He was a broker himself, gets an eternal kick out of schmoozing with brokers, and can't for long keep his eyes off the stock prices running across the screen in his office. He also has a chart of Travelers' stock price in his head, consultable at any moment. Recalling that Primerica was tough to digest and that the stock market in 1990 didn't like financial services companies anyway, he says, "Our stock dropped then to $17—no, $16.87." And then a wry, "Not that we watch."

It was also in 1990 that Weill made his first try at recapturing Shearson from American Express, which had controlled the firm since buying it from Weill. That effort foundered, but in 1993 Weill succeeded, going on to merge Shearson with Smith Barney. Weill speaks of the acquisition with near reverence, saying it "changed everything." Smith Barney alone, in a really good year of the brokerage cycle, had the ability to make $150 million to $200 million, he says. The Shearson purchase, taking into account both the revenues added and the efficiencies gained, created a firm capable, he figures, of exceeding $1 billion. Smith Barney in fact made $889 million in operating profits in 1996, which was 37% of Travelers' total. Smith Barney's return on equity was over 30% that year.

Out of this event that "changed everything" and that in effect put the finishing touches on that earnings-growth record of 28% comes the obvious question of what Weill plans to do for an encore. If he's thinking another 28% decade, he's not saying that. His announced goal is to double earnings every five years, which would translate into a growth rate of roughly 15%. Doing even that would be first-class performance: In the 1997 FORTUNE 500, only 67 companies increased their earnings at a rate of 15% or better over the past decade. And most started from a small base, as Weill himself did with Commercial Credit. Today, though, he's riding an elephant in the top 50 of the list. Making that creature lumber along at a 15% rate is a different, and much tougher, kind of job.

Logic says that good lumbering won't occur without at least three things happening. First, Travelers is going to have to do well in insurance. Second, the company's executives must pull off the usual management challenge: cut costs, raise revenues. Third, you just know that Weill is going to make more acquisitions. That's his pattern, his thing, his *shtick*.

RAISING REVENUES BY "CROSS-SELLING"

The centrality of the insurance job is signaled by the company's newest name: Travelers. Weill has long held Gulf Insurance, of course, and next came the A.L. Williams business that got rechristened PFS. But then Weill remade the map of Hartford, buying the whole of Travelers Insurance in 1992 and 1993 for $4 billion and tacking on the property and casualty operations of Aetna in 1996 for another $4 billion. All that has been reorganized into three divisions. In a flash after buying "old" Travelers, Weill sold its health insurance business for close to $900 million. Weill then put all the P&C operations into a company now called Travelers Property Casualty (nicknamed TAP) and sold off 18% of it in 1996 to public and private investors.

The other two insurance segments are PFS and Travelers Life & Annuity. PFS, whose term policies can compete directly against Travelers Life's whole-life policies, could have been an albatross for Weill but instead turned out to be a quintessential example of what makes him so successful. PFS's huge sales force of 90,000 is not on Travelers' payroll. These people are independent contractors, paid instead through a "pyramid type" of structure, in the manner of Mary Kay and Amway. In the A.L. Williams days, which continued for a while after Weill bought Primerica, the sales force tended to be conspicuously out of control, so aggressive in behavior that it was continually under investigation by regulators. But then Weill moved

THE WEILL KINGDOM

◆◆◆

Travelers Group still gets good earnings from its roots, Commercial Credit, but by 1996, 90% of its profits came from businesses added on.

1996 OPERATING EARNINGS

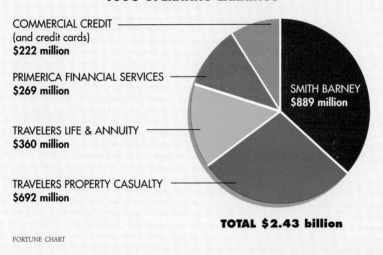

COMMERCIAL CREDIT
(and credit cards)
$222 million

PRIMERICA FINANCIAL SERVICES
$269 million

TRAVELERS LIFE & ANNUITY
$360 million

TRAVELERS PROPERTY CASUALTY
$692 million

SMITH BARNEY
$889 million

TOTAL $2.43 billion

FORTUNE CHART

his own executives into authority and pushed for more training, more discipline, more professionalism in general.

That brought on extreme pain, including a sharp falloff in both the number of salespeople and sales of new life policies, which in dollar terms tanked in three years by 56%. But Weill kept changing PFS's management team, looking for the right leadership, and by 1993 the operation was back on an upward track in sales. By then it was also gaining real respectability.

Beyond all that, PFS has become the main strike force in an aggressive drive by Weill to raise revenues by "cross-selling." The PFS salespeople, for example, are merchandising loans "manufactured" by Commercial Credit; auto insurance policies underwritten by TAP; and mutual funds created by Smith Barney. PFS's distant sibling Travelers Life & Annuity is also into the cross-selling game in an important way. It manufactures annuities that are sold by Smith Barney and encourages the firm's brokers to search among their clients for small-company owners who might want to sign up for Travelers Life 401(k) programs.

Many financial services companies, among them American Express when Weill was there, have bombed at cross-selling. One man who's noticed that Weill is succeeding on the second try is Peter Lynch, whose Magellan fund bought into Commercial Credit when Weill took it over in 1986 and who today still keeps Travelers in the portfolios of charities he helps run. Says Lynch: "Sandy doesn't shout a lot when he gets criticism. He just goes out and does what he says he's going to do."

Of course, he sometimes flounders too, and that's been highly visible in Smith Barney's continuing push to cure its biggest revenues shortcoming, which is weakness in investment banking. Weill tried to fix that in 1993 by hiring a Morgan Stanley top gun, Robert Greenhill, to run Smith Barney. Getting Greenhill and his crew was hugely expensive—and hugely disappointing. Weill wanted to see Smith Barney gain the investment banking status of a Merrill Lynch, but with a minimum of spending. Greenhill had a more expansive vision. In early 1996, Weill ended the arrangement.

Jamie Dimon is now head of Smith Barney and taking a different, definitely non–star system, tack about investment banking. He says the firm's equity strengths—in research, distribution, and trading—are unarguably large, and that the job is simply to get everyone in the place pushing to get that recognized. He's focusing both on midsize deals rather than giants and on industries in which Smith Barney analysts and bankers have special expertise, such as health care, technology, finance, and media/telecom.

Balanced against Travelers' need to do well in insurance, and the challenge of cutting costs and raising revenues, is the ever present question of what Weill might buy next. He says he has no ambitions of broadening into any new areas, being happy with the types of businesses he's in—mainly securities, loans, and insurance. He's convinced that Travelers, and particularly Smith Barney, needs to grow overseas. Is there an ultimate clue to when Weill will make his next move? Maybe it's his weight. That's right: One friend of Weill's has a theory that the chairman puts on major pounds when he's about to acquire something and then sheds them when it's in the bag.

What does the chairman say about this theory? Early in 1997, he laughed and disclosed his commitment to slimming down. But by September, Traveler's had sealed a deal to acquire Wall Street powerhouse Salomon Inc. for $9 billion. One thing is for certain: Regardless of what the scale says, this is a man who will keep right on making deals.

RALPH LAUREN: THE EMPEROR HAS CLOTHES

BY SUSAN CAMINITI

◆◆◆

By seizing the middle ground of fashion,
Ralph Lauren has become the
best-selling designer in the world.

◆◆◆

On a brilliantly sunny summer afternoon, we're in a Manhattan office building trying to figure out where Ralph Lauren will sit. Actually, we're in Lauren's small, all-white office on Madison Avenue, and with two large chairs and a big cushy couch laid out before us, the answer is far from obvious. Rather than chancing some giant faux pas by claiming his favorite spot as our own, we bravely ask: "Mr. Lauren, is there a particular place you'd like to sit?" His response: "Wherever the light makes me look best."

That's Ralph. For nearly 30 years Ralph Lauren has earned a handsome living showing Americans (men especially) how to look good, using himself as the model. And therein lies a puzzle. Somehow Lauren, who thinks it's fine for men to wear black velvet slippers in the office, has become the designer of choice for guys to whom the mere mention of velvet slippers causes first one and then the other eyebrow to be raised. Men with no tolerance for velvet slippers in the office, at home, in the tool shed, or on the moon.

And yet mainstream guys bought $2.7 billion in suits, shirts, ties, and other Ralph Lauren garments in 1996. Add in women's clothes, eyeglasses, perfume, bedsheets, dinner plates, leather couches, and the rest, and consumers around the globe spent some $5 billion on Lauren goods—making him the best-selling designer in the world. Somehow Lauren—faux cowboy, relentless Anglophile—has come to occupy the kind of solid middle ground that Brooks Brothers did in the 1950s: He is the default fashion choice for men who don't care a whole lot about fashion but nevertheless want to look good in office clothes.

Let other designers urge kilts and capes and corduroy plus fours upon an impressionable public. Lauren stands manfully above the fray, upholding simple, classic good looks. Risky dressing? Not for Ralph. He is the nation's leading proponent of safe slacks. "Ralph's world is not unapproachable or scary," says Neil Kraft, former head of advertising for Calvin Klein. "Everything is done with the promise of good taste." And derivative idealism. When Lauren creates the look of an English country home, the panache of a Savile Row suit, or the luster of some Western belt, his version is always a little cleaner, a little brighter, just a touch more polished. He doesn't sell socks; he sells his very mildly fevered dream.

Could Martha Stewart have existed without Ralph? He blazed the trail of "lifestyle" merchandising, selling not just items but his own personal context—at premium price—at a time when such things weren't done. He was the first to sell not only the suit you wear to work but also the pajamas you wear to bed and the sheets you sleep on. "When people buy his products, it gives them the feeling of having class and stature," says Martha Stewart. "They're buying a piece of his world." Since June 1997, when Polo/Ralph Lauren went public, people can buy a piece of Ralph's company too.

PART MAGIC, PART MACHINERY

◆

The price of admission to Lauren's world is relatively high, as befits a business with aspiration at its soul. A Polo suit might sell for $900; a woman's blazer for $1,200; a leather sofa, $9,000. Even so, by 1996 there were enough customers to sustain 116 freestanding Polo/Ralph Lauren stores, 62 discount outlets, and some 1,300 boutiques inside department stores all over the world.

How does Lauren keep coining money? His accomplishment depends partly on magic, mostly on machinery. The magic part he expresses as a question: "Did you ever see a man or a woman walk into a room, and they look great, but you don't know exactly why they do? You just know that you want to look like that?"

The Lauren machine is driven by licensing. No fewer than 26 companies pay to make, ship, and advertise Lauren's goods. Lauren provides the design and creative talent, getting in return a cut of sales (about 6%) plus minimum guaranteed payments. Polo/Ralph Lauren still manufactures its top-of-the-line men's and women's clothes, but the bulk of its profit comes from these licensing agreements. For example, Cosmair, which makes Lauren scents, put an estimated $20 million in Lauren's pocket in 1996 alone, according to fragrance industry experts. He sews not much, but damned if Ralph don't reap!

Other designers have gone down the licensing road, of course, and quite a number have lurched into a ditch when they let their licensees get control of their brand. That isn't likely to happen to Lauren: His need to protect everything bearing on his company's image, and his own, is palpable, unsleeping, electric, scary.

Lauren grasped early the importance of protecting his brand. Back in 1967, as he struggled to build a business out of his line of wide men's ties, he refused to sell to Bloomingdale's. The retailer wanted him to make the ties narrower and take his name off the label. "We're talking a quarter of an inch. That's all they wanted," Lauren explains. "And as for my name being on them, well, no one could care less who Ralph Lauren was. But I said no. When I left the store, I thought, 'What am I, crazy?' I was dying to sell Bloomingdale's, but I didn't because I really wanted to do what I believed in." Months later, Bloomingdale's came knocking on Lauren's door. It saw how briskly competitors were selling his ties and agreed to carry them exactly as Lauren had designed them.

Emboldened by this early success, Lauren next designed a line of men's shirts, then turned his attention to suits, favoring wide lapels—to go along with his ties—and natural shoulders. It wasn't long before Lauren branched off into women's clothes. In 1971 he

WHO'S BEHIND RALPH'S $5 BILLION EMPIRE?

◆◆◆

The world's most successful designer earns the bulk of his profits from 26 licensing agreements.

APPAREL AND ACCESSORIES:
◆ **Infants/Toddlers** Schwab
◆ **Polo Jeans** Sun Apparel
◆ **Chaps Men's Clothing** Peerless Clothing
◆ **Gloves** Swany/Elmer Little
◆ **Chaps Men's Sportswear** Warnaco
◆ **Small Leather Goods/Belts** RL Leather Goods
◆ **Scarves** Echo
◆ **Underwear/Intimates** Sara Lee/Playtex
◆ **Lauren** (Women's apparel) Jones Apparel Group
◆ **Men's Tailored Clothing** Pietrafesa
◆ **Women's Jewelry** Carolee Design
◆ **Eyewear** Safilo/ Optique du Monde
◆ **Hosiery** Hot Sox
◆ **Fragrance** Cosmair
◆ **Handbags/Luggage** Wathne
◆ **Footwear** Rockport/Reebok

HOME COLLECTION
◆ **Sheets, Towels, Bedding** WestPoint Stevens
◆ **Bathroom Rugs** Newmark
◆ **Table Linens** Audrey Table Linens
◆ **Flatwear** Reed & Barton
◆ **Paint** Sherwin-Williams
◆ **China, Crystal, Home Fragrance** Pentland
◆ **Wallpaper, Fabric, Rugs** Folia
◆ **Blankets, Pillows, Bedding Accessories** Pillowtex
◆ **Furniture** Henredon
◆ **Area Rugs** Shyam Ahuja

opened the first Polo/Ralph Lauren store in Beverly Hills. More stores soon followed.

ONE BRAND, MANY THEMES

◆

In 1983 Lauren branched out from clothing and started his home collection of sheets, towels, flatware, and furniture. Rather than simply putting out new colors or patterns like others in the field, Lauren created products that revolved around lifestyle themes, like New England Cottage and English Countryside. The Serape collection, for instance, features aged solid-oak tables and chests as well as distressed-leather chairs and couches tooled, as the brochure reads, "in the tradition of fine leather boot making."

A recent addition to the home line is Ralph Lauren paint, produced under license by Sherwin-Williams. Isn't that just paint with a big designer name on it? That's exactly what it is. "Look," says Mort Kaplan, head of Creative Licensing, a firm that brings together licensing partners, "I'm sure the paint is good, but azure blue is azure blue is azure blue. The difference here is that Ralph Lauren stands for something. He knows how to package it, how to set it up in stores so it conveys his image." Walk into any Home Depot that sells the paint, and you'll see what Kaplan means: Behind each mixing counter stands a Ralph display, all lit up. Brochures group paint hues by theme—Safari, Desert Hollywood, Santa Fe—and show not just paint swatches but evocative bits of Laurentian context: a horse, a sideboard, a pair of satin gloves. Lauren's home furnishings business rings up retail sales of $535 million a year worldwide, vastly outselling any other designer's.

Ever since his first in-store shop opened in Bloomingdale's in 1971, Lauren has insisted that retailers sell his goods his way, in boutiques set up with his props and fixtures. Most of the time he gets what he wants. Says Kenneth Walker, who installed Polo in-store shops: "Ralph's people are hard but fair. They don't throw hissy fits, but they know exactly what they want." And they walk when they don't get it. In 1996, when Bergdorf Goodman's men's store in New York refused to build a Polo boutique to the company's specifications, Lauren pulled his business from the store.

There wasn't really any breakthrough that thrust Lauren's clothing into the nation's fashion consciousness; the closest his work came to making a splash was when Diane Keaton wore his clothing in *Annie Hall*. Lauren did runway shows, but rather than making the models look like hookers from space, he dressed them in clothing you could wear to the office. From one year to the next, changes were of degree, not of kind. In retrospect, he was formulating the Ralph Doctrine: clothing that isn't shocking, just incrementally nicer, with snob appeal prominently in the weave.

That's Lauren's same m.o. today, of course. It's those incremental touches, however, that make Ralph Ralph. Some suits in his high-end Purple Label line, for example, sport a tab on the top of the left lapel. "That's a wind tab," explained a salesman in Lauren's New York flagship store. A wind tab? "That's so that when you're walking home from church across the moors on a windy day, you can pull that lapel over and button it to a corresponding button on the jacket collar." A suit like that costs up to $2,500.

How does Lauren come up with those touches like a wind tab? In New York City and elsewhere, Lauren's scouts comb vintage clothing shops, looking for garments (or for details on garments) that they think Ralph might like. Some of them he does. After experiment and prototyping, an old green-striped broadcloth shirt from the 1930s, say, may get a new lease on life.

Lauren surrounds himself with seasoned executives, most of whom have been with him for years—a rarity in the fashion business. They understand what Lauren wants, usually without his having to spell it out. Says Buffy Birrittella, senior vice president of women's designs and a 25-year veteran of the company: "When Ralph says he wants something white, I know what kind of white he means." As we said before, it ain't all science.

THE EARLY YEARS

If Lauren himself isn't the epitome of the WASP image he sells, just who is he? Lauren was born Ralph Lifshitz in the Bronx. His father was an artist who painted houses for a living; his mother raised the kids (Ralph was the youngest of four). He played stickball, dated

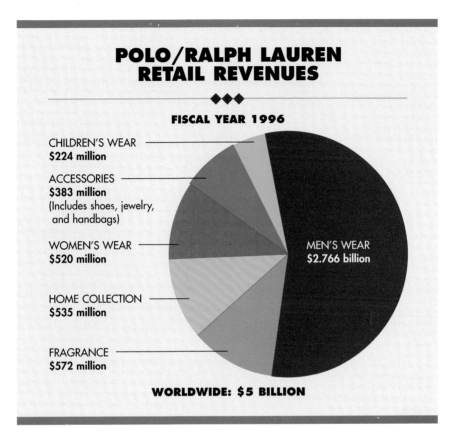

POLO/RALPH LAUREN RETAIL REVENUES

◆◆◆

FISCAL YEAR 1996

CHILDREN'S WEAR
$224 million

ACCESSORIES
$383 million
(Includes shoes, jewelry,
and handbags)

WOMEN'S WEAR
$520 million

HOME COLLECTION
$535 million

FRAGRANCE
$572 million

MEN'S WEAR
$2.766 billion

WORLDWIDE: $5 BILLION

girls, did all the normal stuff. He didn't grow up sketching clothes, and he didn't go to fashion school. "I don't know, from the time I was 12 years old I looked cool," he explains. "My father was a painter. Maybe I got some sense of color from him. I do know that whatever I had on, other kids would say, 'Hey, where'd you get that?'"

As he got older and worked after school, Lauren would use his paychecks to buy expensive clothes. Even then his fashion eye spotted the best. "If I saved $100 to buy a suit, which in those days was a lot of money, my parents would say, 'Why didn't you go to this place? It's cheaper.' And I would say no."

Lauren pursued a business degree at City College in Manhattan, taking night classes, but dropped out after two years. He worked as a salesman for two glove companies and then for tie manufacturer A. Rivetz & Co. While at Rivetz, Lauren started designing his wide ties, and before long he decided to go into business for himself. In 1968, Norman Hilton, a clothing company executive, backed him with a $50,000 loan. Lauren called his company Polo Fashions, a name that he and his brother Jerry liked because it connoted money, style, and a sort of international mystique.

By the early 1970s sales were nearly $4 million, and the company was expanding too quickly. Lauren bought out Norman Hilton's stake and hired a boyhood chum as his treasurer and CFO. The friend turned out to be "somewhat in over his head," Lauren says, and the business, though booking lots of orders, was hemorrhaging money.

To save the company, Lauren poured in his life savings—$150,000—and hired one of Hilton's key executives, Peter Strom, to help run it. Strom liked Lauren and agreed to come aboard if Lauren gave him a 10% equity stake in the business. "When I joined the company, it had 800 accounts, was doing about $5 million in sales, and wasn't making a dime," recalls Strom, who retired from Polo in April 1995. "I thought we'd be lucky if we ever broke $20 million in sales," he says. "Ralph loves to remind me that I said that."

A question of authenticity has dogged Lauren much of his career. Chatting with him late one sunny afternoon at his Colorado ranch house, it's clear he's weary of the charge that somehow his work, and by extension his life, are phony. "I slept in a room with two brothers growing up," he recalls. "I couldn't wait for one of them to move out so I could have half the drawers. That molded me. But do I want to live like that today? No, I don't. So is it phony, then, to say I want to live out west, or I want to live in the country? If you're born in the Bronx, does that mean you have to stay in the Bronx?

"I've tried to do things honorably in my business. I think I've added something to America. I don't rip people off. I don't downgrade children," he says, getting in a parting dig at Calvin Klein. "I try to give people a clean, aspirational quality, with no bullshit. Where's the negative in that?"

To which we answer: There isn't one. Our economy is kept wound by aspirations of the sort young Ralph held (hell, old Ralph holds). No wonder business people like to buy his clothing: In Lauren, they recognize a brother under the skin.

MICHAEL PRICE: THE SCARIEST S.O.B. ON WALL STREET

BY ANDREW E. SERWER

◆◆◆

When Wall Street's foremost value
investor takes a big position in a
company, he sees to it that the stock
moves, or else.

◆◆◆

John Teets was a CEO with big problems. The company he ran, an unwieldy conglomerate called Dial, was flagging: Profits were down; morale was low; its brands were tired. More ominous yet, an anonymous letter, purportedly written by a longtime Dial executive, was making the rounds. The letter accused the CEO of "utilizing [Dial's] assets as if he owned them outright," including a company-owned New York penthouse and a Gulfstream jet. It claimed that Teets had used corporate assets to buy into the Arizona Diamondbacks, the new Major League Baseball franchise. It accused him of committing serious sexual improprieties (which Teets "categorically" denies). "I think it is time Mr. Teets paid the piper," the letter concluded. But even that wasn't Teets's biggest problem. No, his biggest problem was that Michael Price—legendary mutual fund manager, value investor, and in recent years, stalker of underperforming CEOs—had taken a 9.9% position in Dial's stock, worth more than $250 million.

Once upon a time, back in that bygone era known as the 1980s, there were few things more terrifying to a CEO than the knowledge that a corporate raider—a T. Boone Pickens, a Carl Icahn, a Jimmy Goldsmith—was buying up the company's stock. Here in the 1990s, with the raiders largely extinct, it's Michael Price who can instill that kind of fear.

With good reason. It was Price who grabbed control of Sunbeam and helped bring in a new CEO, Paul Kazarian. Two CEOs later, when Price again became unhappy with the company's performance, he saw to it that "Chainsaw" Al Dunlap was brought in to turn things around. This was a move that practically guaranteed large layoffs, but one that so excited investors that the stock price bumped up more than 50% when Dunlap's hiring was announced last summer. Price was also almost single-handedly responsible for one of the biggest deals of the decade: the merger of Chase Manhattan and Chemical Bank, which resulted in the loss of some 12,000 jobs. But the $10 billion deal was a windfall for Chase shareholders, including, naturally, investors in Price's funds. Chase's former CEO Thomas Labrecque is still with the company, but he's no longer in charge. Chemical CEO Walter Shipley is running the merged bank.

And sure enough, it was pressure from Price, more than weak sales or anonymous letters, that caused Teets to announce his resignation. Trying to get the stock price up, Teets split the company in two. One of the new entities, which contained Dial's service businesses, was called Viad. But this didn't deflect Price, who strongly voiced his disapproval of the way the split-up was structured. A week after Price filed a 13D with the SEC blasting the split-up and calling into question the company's lavish perks, the Dial board met to respond. The next day the company issued a press release. John Teets, it said, would retire in early 1997.

A RAIDER YOU CAN RIDE WITH

It's tempting to view Michael Price the way we used to view Pickens or Goldsmith—as no more or less than an 1980s-style corporate raider. And on the surface, the comparison is an easy one to make. He has in common with the raiders of yore a fearlessness—and a kind of calculated ruthlessness—in taking on big, powerful targets and bending them to his will. He shrugs off the potential public relations backlash when thousands of people lose their jobs after a Price-instigated restructuring. He harbors the same withering contempt for his targets that the raiders did, and like them, he uses the press deftly, conveying a swaggering, larger-than-life persona. He's also rich as sin: His passion is polo, where the primary piece of equipment is a $40,000 pony.

But in more important ways, he represents something new. Unlike the raiders, Michael Price is a mutual fund manager, which is to say that the pool of capital he uses to take large positions in companies—and force change upon them—comes not from wealthy institutions but from small shareholders all across the country. In other words, this is a raider with whom you and I can go along for the ride. Also unlike the raiders, Price is not in this game to take the money and run; he's in it to take the money and stay. Price is a value investor, and he views what he is doing as a way of "unlocking value" in a company; as it's unlocked, he wants to be around to reap every last penny of his reward.

Finally, and most fundamentally, Price is both the personification and the beneficiary of a sea change in the way many Americans now view the relationship between CEOs and shareholders. If for most of the postwar era the CEO was the supreme entity within a corporation, today it is widely accepted that the shareholder is boss and that his interests must come first. As Michael Price has shown repeatedly, woe be to the CEO who doesn't view his chief task as enriching shareholders.

One reason Price gets his way is that many investors simply agree with what he's trying to accomplish. And what exactly is that? He doesn't bother hiding behind the sanctimonious rhetoric of the 1980s raiders—that they were trying to take over the companies and show the world how they should be run. He admits flat out that all he's trying to do is get the stock price up. And if his tactics are a little rougher—all right, a lot rougher—than those of most other mutual fund managers, well, it works, doesn't it?

Long before he became known as a high-profile saber rattler, Michael Price was one of the best-known value investors in the country. Among the cognoscenti, that's still what he primarily is. More to the point, it is still how he sees himself. "When most people look at the day's stock tables, what do they turn to first?" Price asks. "The day's most active stocks. Why? Who cares about volume? I look at the day's biggest decliners," he says. "I love to read about losses."

That, of course, is the essence of value investing: Find Wall Street's lumps of coal—the distressed companies, the bankruptcies, the castoffs—and sell them only after they've been squeezed into diamonds. Always, the goal is to find hidden value in a company that others either can't see or can't unlock. "We like to buy a security only if we think it is selling for at least 25% less than its market value," Price says. Of course one thing that separates Price from most other value investors is that he more than occasionally gets involved in speeding along the process of squeezing the coals into diamonds. He and his lieutenants contend that when that happens, it's just another form of value investing. "Look," he says, "I'm just trying to find cheap stocks and realize the value." If unlocking that value means ousting a CEO, so be it.

THE EARLY YEARS

Michael Price learned his trade at the feet of a celebrated value investor, the late Max Heine. Price, who grew up on Long Island, in Roslyn, New York, went to work for Heine, his father's stockbroker, in 1975, a few years after graduating from the University of Oklahoma. Max Heine, a German-Jewish refugee, had set up Heine Securities to invest his friends' money. The firm's single mutual fund, Mutual Shares, had about $5 million in assets.

Heine was an avuncular sort, with a thick old-country accent, a gentle nature, and a genius for security analysis. He was also a classic value investor. Just as Warren Buffett learned about investing from securities guru Ben Graham, so did Price learn from Heine, who set about passing on his investing principles to his new protégé. Recalls Price: "Max taught me that if you really wanted to find value, you had to do original work, digging through stuff no one else wanted to look at." Price caught on quickly. By the early 1980s, as Price was becoming the dominant presence at Heine Securities, he and Heine worked out a deal whereby Heine remained the principal owner of the firm (he had 99 shares to Price's one), but the profits were split more or less equally between the two men. And in 1986, when Heine was 75 and ready to retire, he worked out another deal with Price to ensure that the latter would wind up sole owner of Heine Securities. They agreed to continue splitting the profits so long as Heine was alive—and they also agreed on the sum Price would pay for the firm when Heine died. The size of the payment would depend on when Heine died. (If he died in 1986, Price would pay the estate $8 million; if he died in 1987, the price would be $6 million; in 1988, it would be $4 million; after that, $2 million.)

Less than two years later, Heine was dead—hit by a car in Arizona while crossing a road. So according to the schedule, Price was able to buy his mentor's firm for $4 million. Price says he actually shelled out somewhat more than that because he continued to pay Heine's share of the firm's income to the estate for some undetermined period. But even so—and even though the assets of the firm were only a fraction of what they are today—it was still a rock-bottom price. A value, you might say.

A VALUE GODFATHER

One thing you can never accuse Michael Price of being is avuncular. It's another fall day, and Price is in his Short Hills, New Jersey, office—a single floor of a modern building in a nondescript office park: a value investor's office. Although Price is less involved in the day-to-day decision-making than he used to be, he still sits at the head of a T-shape trading desk in front of his 12 traders. Flanking the traders are the brains of the operation, his analysts, led by four senior people. Price doesn't really do much actual research these days. Instead he acts as a kind of value godfather, a sounding board for his analysts.

One of the things that quickly become clear is that while they may not be growth investors, Price's people are certainly traders. They spend their days buying and selling stocks, just like everyone else in the fund business. They are trading for all five Mutual Series funds. All five funds are value funds, of course, for that is the only kind of investing Price believes in. Like Heine, Price has passed on to his acolytes a style of investing that requires digging and original research, relying on primary documents rather than Wall Street analysts. He and his staff tend to talk fast and talk complicated, launching into discussions about debt restructuring, cash flow, and lawsuit valuations, always searching for value they can unlock one way or another.

If old-fashioned value investing is what made Price's original reputation, it's his public, pointed—and usually successful—forays into underperforming companies that have made him notorious. Surely it

THREE WHO LOST CONTROL

Michael Price is not a patient man. One of his favorite lines: "You have exactly 30 seconds to tell me why." Meet a trio of leaders who took too long.

◆ **Roger Schipke** CEO, SUNBEAM. Signed on in 1993, by way of GE. When Sunbeam's fortunes began to deteriorate, he lost his job. And "Chainsaw" Al was brought in.

◆ **John Teets** CEO, DIAL. Tried to be proactive by spinning off some Dial businesses into a new company. It wasn't enough. Price got mad; Teets resigned.

◆ **Thomas Labrecque** CEO, CHASE MANHATTAN. Resisted Price's message to "unlock the value" at Chase. The result: Labrecque is COO, not CEO, following the Chemical takeover.

is no coincidence that the assets in his firm have nearly tripled in the past three years—which is to say, in pretty much the same time that he was becoming known as a rapacious shareholder who doesn't take no for an answer. Price denies that there's anything new about his shareholder-activist persona. While that's true enough, Price doth protest too much. What changed in the 1990s was both the size and the scope of the Price attacks—and the astonishing ambition they revealed. It was one thing, after all, to go after a Sooner Federal Savings & Loan, as Price did in 1981, quite another to take on Chase Manhattan.

A number of factors coalesced in the 1990s that helped propel Price along his current path. For one thing, as his funds grew larger he needed to buy stocks with larger market capitalization in order to have the same impact on the funds. For another, the overheated bull market has made it increasingly difficult to find old-fashioned value stocks—stocks that would eventually "unlock their value" without Price's having to turn the key personally.

Finally, a 1992 change in the rules governing institutional share-holders helped unleash Price. The old law prevented stockholders from sharing information with one another without going through expensive and onerous proxy filings. The new laws specifically allow groups of shareholders to communicate without triggering the proxy requirements. And large shareholders can also now publicly announce how they plan to vote on issues without having to file a proxy—a previously muddy point of law. In his battle with Chase, Price clearly took advantage of this new regulatory environment.

PRICE'S CHASE BLITZKRIEG

The Chase battle, without question, made CEOs sit up and take notice. When Price forced the sixth-largest bank in the country, a white-shoe institution if ever there was one, to merge with Chemical, the message was heard in the far corners of corporate America: If you find yourself in Michael Price's cross hairs, watch out—he uses real bullets.

The origins of Price's Chase blitzkrieg go back to early 1994, when Price's banking analyst Ray Garea set his sights on Michigan National, a smallish, poorly performing bank in Farmington Hills, Michigan. Price bought 5.5% of the stock and soon declared the best way to realize the value of the bank would be to sell it. A year later, Michigan National sold out to the National Australian Bank for $110 a share. Price's take: close to $50 million.

And then Garea picks up the story: "It was a Friday, and we had just finished Michigan National, and Michael asked me—he was kind of kidding—'So, Ray, who's the next target?' And I looked at him, and I said, 'I think we should do Chase.' And he looked at me like I had lost my mind." Garea told Price that the stock, which he figured was worth $60, easy, was trading at $33. "I don't believe you," Garea recalls Price saying. "Give me some stuff to look at over the weekend." "On Monday morning," says Garea, "Michael walked in, and I could see it in his eyes from down the hall: We were going to do Chase."

With $120 billion in assets, Chase was a huge institution. But it also had had an undistinguished record over the past few years, and its stock had lagged behind other bank stocks. Garea continues, "I told Michael that if we were going to do Chase, he needed to understand that he had to be aggressive; otherwise nothing would happen." And so it began. Price already owned a smattering of Chase stock; now he started buying heavily. From February 13 to March 3, he and Garea quietly bought about 3.7 million shares of Chase. Garea put in a call to Chase's head of investor relations, Bill Maletz, requesting a sit-down with the bank's CEO, Tom Labrecque. "Why do you want to see him?" asked Maletz. "Because we own a fair amount of stock," replied Garea. "How much?" asked Maletz. "Over $100 million," said Garea.

Several weeks later, Price and Garea met with Labrecque and Maletz. The script was a familiar one: Price told Labrecque he thought the stock was undervalued; the Chase CEO agreed but said he felt that within two years it would be substantially higher; Price replied that the time frame was too long. He and Garea suggested selling various businesses or spinning off divisions. Labrecque said no; in fact, he said, he wanted Chase to continue to be an important global bank. Price was unimpressed. "What does financing car loans in New Jersey have to do with lending in Kuwait?" he says. After the meeting, Garea turned to Price and asked, "What do you think?" Price didn't pause. "I think we should buy more stock."

All through March and early April, Price and Garea bought another 7.2 million shares, giving them a total position of some $375 million. By the time they were done, Heine Securities owned 11.1 million shares, or 6.1%, of the bank's stock. That, of course, meant the firm had to file a 13D, since the holding had passed the 5% threshold. This Price did on April 6, at which point the whole world knew what he was up to. Almost immediately the stock climbed from $38 to $41 a share.

It was at this time that Price really swung into action, demonstrating just how much you can do these days with 6% of a company's stock. Taking advantage of those new SEC rules, he began contacting major shareholders, such as the brokerage firm Sanford C. Bernstein and Dallas money manager Barrow Hanley Mewhinney & Strauss. "We found out that Tom Labrecque visited these people too, but every time, he was a week behind us," says Price. "I think that's when he realized he had a problem." Meanwhile, Price's allies began buying the stock, which helped Price's bargaining position.

By the middle of April, rumors were flying. One of the most widespread was that NationsBank was looking to acquire Chase. The rumor gained steam when NationsBank CEO Hugh McColl confirmed that Chase looked attractive. On April 18, in this over-heated atmosphere, Chase held its annual meeting. It was a long, drawn-out affair, but finally, after nearly two hours, Price rose to speak. "Dramatic change is required," he reportedly said, addressing Labrecque. "Unlock the value, or let someone else do it for you."

A week later, Price and Garea held a second meeting with Labrecque. Again the Chase CEO refused to make any commitment to change anything. But in fact he was about to take some action—though it was too little, too late. In May he brought in a cost-cutting consultant. In June he announced plans to slash expenses by some $400 million. Meanwhile he had retained Goldman Sachs, Chase's longtime investment banker. Whether he knew it nor not, he had just put Chase in play, as they used to say in the 1980s. By August the stock had climbed to $53.

This time the price run-up was being driven by a new rumor—that Chemical Bank was poised to buy Chase. And the rumors were true: Labrecque had decided to sell to Chemical (though Chemical would keep the more prestigious Chase name). On Sunday, August 27, Labrecque phoned patriarch David Rockefeller at his house in Seal Harbor, Maine, to give him the news. The next morning the deal was announced. In a stock swap, Chemical would give Chase shareholders 1.04 shares of Chemical stock—then worth about $60—for every share of Chase they owned. Price couldn't have been happier. "We love this merger," he was quoted as saying at the time. But even after the merger, value remained a top priority. Price met with Labrecque and Chemical CEO Walter Shipley several times to ensure the new bank would continue to make moves to boost its share price. It has.

And then came Price's best deal of all: the sale of his firm, in October 1996, to Franklin Resources, a family-controlled firm with $169 billion in assets. Franklin is a hugely successful marketer of load mutual funds, which it sells through brokerage firms. It has also proved it can successfully acquire other fund companies: Its 1992 purchase of the Templeton Fund Group, led by the legendary investor Sir John Templeton, is widely considered a model for the rest of the industry.

When the mating dance was over, Price, who had bought Heine Securities for somewhere around $4 million in 1988, was selling it eight years later for $628 million—with additional incentives that could well bring the final total to more than $800 million. It's all going directly to Price, since he's the sole owner of Heine Securities.

The buyout of Price's firm raises two significant questions, though. The first is whether he will continue to run the Mutual Series funds. Certainly Franklin and Price would like to give the impression that Price will rule over his kingdom for years to come. Whether he will remains to be seen.

The second question is whether he will still be willing to unlock value by rattling the cages of America's underperforming CEOs now that he is part of a larger institution. It's a sticky question because most big-fund families shy away from such behavior. For his part, Price insists that his funds won't stop, as he puts it, "asserting their rights." So far, at least, that seems to be the case. Not long ago, Price began buying stock in Dun & Bradstreet. He's spoken with management to air his complaints. He's contacted other shareholders.

There he goes again.

BILL GATES'S GREATEST POWER GRAB

BY DAVID KIRKPATRICK

◆◆◆

Microsoft's CEO wants all your business, and he's starting to get it with new software for corporate networks.

◆◆◆

In the movie *Volcano*, an eruption threatens to destroy Los Angeles. Inexorably, with shocking speed, the lava engulfs the city, forever changing the landscape. The coast, as the slogan has it, is toast.

This is a story about another eruption, one that's altering the landscape of computing. Windows NT, Microsoft's new operating system for your desktop PC and the corporate network it runs on, is beginning to take over. NT has been bubbling since its introduction in 1993—but only now is there evidence that the software is likely to help Microsoft seize large chunks of the corporate computing market and dominate them as thoroughly as it does the market for desktop PCs. In 1996, sales of NT software for network servers exploded 86%, vs. 12% growth for other software that runs corporate networks. In 1997, according to Montgomery Securities, Microsoft will license NT software to another 7.4 million corporate users. Sales of NT and BackOffice, the suite of applications that runs on NT, will exceed $1.8 billion, up from $591 million in 1996.

Behind this eruption is a Vulcan named Bill Gates, who is stoking it for one reason only—to ensure that Microsoft keeps growing explosively. Forget Internet browsers; forget MSNBC; forget multimedia, Slate, and the Microsoft Network. "NT," says Gates, "is the centerpiece of what we are doing." The PC business, after all, represents just over half of the $550 billion worldwide market for computing software, hardware, and services, according to McKinsey & Co. Gates's strategy is to extend Microsoft's hegemony from the desktop into the windowless rooms housing the servers, minicomputers, and mainframes that are still central to business data processing. If he succeeds, Microsoft could dominate information technology well into the next decade.

The easiest way to understand NT is to compare it with Windows 95, the operating system that runs virtually every PC sold in the past two years. Windows works in the background to keep your PC performing smoothly; it makes sure software applications get appropriate attention from the microprocessor, keeps track of all your files, and knows the difference between your CD-ROM drive, your modem, and your printer. NT provides similar housekeeping services for a network of computers—it keeps track of the devices on the network, helps assure smooth delivery of data and applications from servers to desktops, and controls who gets access to which files. NT and Windows 95 are closely aligned—if your company switches to NT, you'll have new software installed on your PC, but what you see displayed on the screen won't change much at all.

Comparing NT with Windows 95 is also the easiest way to understand why the newer product seems unstoppable. As it has done before, Microsoft is combining product innovation with marketing power and financial muscle to take over a market. It has thrown billions of dollars of R&D into improving NT, which in its earliest version was a typically unreliable, bug-ridden Microsoft mess. Now, however, many corporate information managers think NT is becoming the technological equal of Unix, the server operating system that for years has been the backbone of many corporate networks. To get NT into all the right businesses, Microsoft is working closely with PC makers that sell heavily to corporations—Compaq, Hewlett-Packard, and Digital Equipment—and with Intel, of course. Like earlier versions of Windows, NT is a wedge that will enable Microsoft to sell profitable applications software, in this case the BackOffice suite. Says Gates: "We are a very predictable company. What we did with Windows on the desktop, we're doing with Windows NT on the server. What we did with Office on the desktop, we're doing with BackOffice on the server." When combined with BackOffice, NT is far more profitable, per user, than anything Microsoft has done with Windows.

The eruption of NT is good news for Microsoft's closest allies. For others, NT may well stand for Nasty Trouble. Companies using NT may no longer need Novell's flagship product NetWare, which was until recently the de facto standard for connecting computers on an office network. Preferring to get the bulk of their key network software from one vendor, some corporations may snub IBM's Lotus Notes and choose Microsoft's competitor, Exchange, which is part of BackOffice. And Sun Microsystems' servers and workstations are threatened by lower-priced PCs running NT and powered by Intel's Pentium Pro.

No one is saying that these companies or their products are toast. NT is a relatively young technology, and financiers, engineers, and others who need high-powered networked computing at their fingertips may stick with their present suppliers. If Windows crashes your PC, you just reboot; if an NT server crashes, your whole network goes down. A trading house could potentially lose millions. And unlike Sun, Novell, or IBM, Microsoft has little experience supporting corporate customers' most essential computing operations. But Microsoft does have $9 billion in cash, lots and lots of patience—and Bill Gates.

THE ROAD TO NT

Few successful computer companies have seen their products vilified as much as Microsoft. For 15 years, as the company has racked up one victory after another, jealous observers and rival executives have carped that Microsoft is nothing more than an overbearing marketer popularizing work bought or appropriated from others.

With NT, Gates finally has a chance to mute the naysayers. Built by Microsoft programmers virtually from scratch, NT is perhaps the most important step toward a goal long envisioned by Gates, co-founder Paul Allen, and other forward thinkers: shunting the world's biggest computing tasks from mainframes to cheaper, smaller machines. The shift started in the 1970s as minicomputers took on some of the work of mainframes. The 1980s brought so-called client-server networks that used Unix, an operating system invented at AT&T's Bell Labs. Unix networks took over services like database access, order entry, and accounting for small companies and departments of large ones.

Gates has long wanted the next phase of this evolution to bear the Microsoft stamp. Around 1982 he and Allen approached Bell Labs with a proposal to jointly develop, standardize, and promote Unix (there are currently 36 major versions of Unix, and getting applications to work on several is a chore for developers). But after serious negotiations, says Allen, Microsoft was "stiffed": AT&T, which then owned Bell Labs, decided it could do without the help of puny Microsoft.

The seeds of NT were planted soon after, when Microsoft teamed with IBM in an ill-fated effort to develop the OS/2 operating system. By 1990 the partnership had fallen apart, and Gates shifted scores of programmers to building Microsoft's own Unix killer: NT, which stood for New Technology. Gates has developed it with Microsoft's hallmark intensity, throwing money, marketing expertise, and gallons of Jolt cola at the project. With Windows gaining almost universal acceptance among PC users, and knowing that corporate buyers want as uniform a system as possible, Gates and his team made a critical decision: NT would look like Windows and run existing Windows applications.

In 1997, Microsoft is expected to spend about $1 billion on operating-systems R&D. Most of that is related to NT, which Gates wants to endow with something called scalability, a geeky buzzword for the ability to tackle really big corporate computing jobs. So far, Microsoft has shown that NT is muscular enough to handle workaday tasks like departmental database management and accounting. That's a vast market in itself. But the company aims to prove that NT can also run complex applications— hotel reservations systems, say, or real-time stock trading systems—on the same scale as Unix networks hosting hundreds or thousands of users. Jim Allchin, who oversees all NT and BackOffice work at Microsoft, says he will meet the challenge: "It's just a matter of time before no customer would even consider buying a proprietary Unix system. To be clear, though, my sights aren't just set on Unix, but on the mainframe."

Allchin has a long way to go. For instance, Sun's top Unix machines run 64 processors simultaneously—enough computing power to handle many large-scale corporate tasks. NT currently can't efficiently manage a server with more than eight processors. Closing the gap will likely take years and is a top Microsoft priority, according to Gates.

All the same, there's enough of a market at the lower end of server processing that NT is already outselling the Unix competition. According to Dan Kusnetsky at International Data Corp., the market watcher in Framingham, Massachusetts, Microsoft sold 732,000 server copies of NT in 1996, while all versions of Unix combined sold only 600,000. This fiscal year Microsoft will likely sell 1.2 million copies of NT server software at a cutthroat $625 each. Microsoft is also expected to sell 6.2 million copies of NT's desktop edition, for about $85 a pop—up from $35 a seat for Windows 95.

THE COMBINATION PUNCH

One reason Gates can offer NT at such low prices is that the operating system is but the lead of a two-punch strategy for capturing the corporate network market. The knockout punch is BackOffice: a fearsome assemblage of built, bought, and borrowed computer code that will bring Microsoft into direct competition with almost every

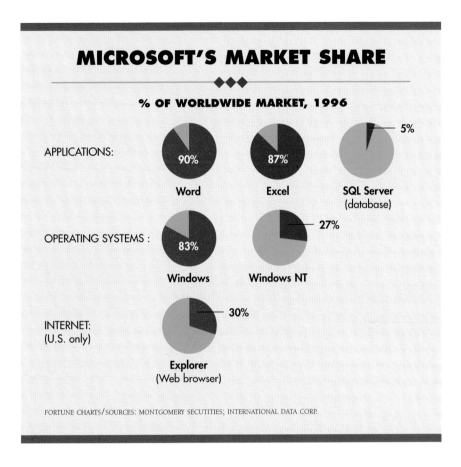

MICROSOFT'S MARKET SHARE

◆◆◆

% OF WORLDWIDE MARKET, 1996

APPLICATIONS:

Word 90%

Excel 87%

SQL Server (database) 5%

OPERATING SYSTEMS:

Windows 83%

Windows NT 27%

INTERNET: (U.S. only)

Explorer (Web browser) 30%

FORTUNE CHARTS/SOURCES: MONTGOMERY SECUTITIES; INTERNATIONAL DATA CORP.

major software company on the planet. Its parts include Exchange, a groupware program aimed at Lotus Notes, which, according to Merrill Lynch, brought IBM $2 billion in software and services revenues last year; SQL Server, a database aimed at Oracle's estimated $2-billion-a-year flagship product as well as at products from Informix, Sybase, and IBM; systems management and transaction-processing software; modules to connect NT servers to mainframes; and more.

Gates is using the NT and BackOffice combination to assault IBM, Novell, and Oracle in much the same way he used Windows and Microsoft Office to kayo WordPerfect and Lotus 1-2-3 on the desktop. NT customers get to buy the whole BackOffice bundle as one superdiscounted package. The threat to Oracle and other companies that create enterprise software for Unix is hard to overstate.

With its billions of dollars in cash, Microsoft can afford a bloody price war. But the rise of NT poses another, potentially greater threat—that Microsoft may lure away key software and consulting allies on whom all Unix software makers depend.

As they reengineer their businesses, many corporations have turned to customized, enterprisewide applications created by developers like SAP, Baan, and PeopleSoft. Their software automates manufacturing, finance, logistics, and human resources. The stuff is costly, complex, and so crucial to the businesses that use it that installing the software properly can require armies of consultants and months or even years.

To serve customers in the fragmented world of Unix, SAP must offer 34 versions of its manufacturing-automation software. One, for example, is painstakingly tailored to Oracle's database on Sun's version of Unix. Another iteration for Oracle's database runs on IBM's version of Unix. No wonder the Microsoft solution, by contrast, seems attractive—SAP and other software firms need only adapt their software once to serve most NT customers. Even though NT has existed for only four years, 27% of SAP's 10,000 corporate customers now use it.

As NT spreads into more companies, some of the hottest applications developers are forgoing Unix and building products that work exclusively on NT. Says Deborah Willingham, who heads Microsoft's Enterprise Customer Unit: "The more customers on the platform, the more business logic there is for applications companies to develop for it. It's the same success loop that happened years ago on the desktop with Windows." Gates explains the shift to NT in simple terms. "It's all volume," he says. "What NT represents is that the PC model has won out. It's just a superior economic model."

THE ADORING SUITORS

◆

Unsurprisingly, Microsoft's key partner in perpetuating this volume strategy is Intel. Just as NT is cheaper than Unix software, the computers that run NT tend to be servers and PCs that are cheaper than the heavy-duty Unix boxes made by companies like Sun Microsystems and Silicon Graphics. Even though they are lower priced, the NT-based computers incorporate powerful microprocessors. Windows 95 does much of its work in 16-bit-long chunks of data; NT processes information in chunks of 32 bits at a time.

Enter Intel, whose new Pentium Pro chips are 32-bit microprocessors. Says Pat Gelsinger of Intel's desktop product group: "We made a pretty fundamental decision to make NT the centerpiece of our business computer positioning. When we introduced Pentium Pro, we said it was the best processor for NT. Period."

With Intel backing them up, the leading PC makers are salivating over the prospect of delivering the hot rods that will drive corporate computing in the future. The opportunities are huge. According to IDC, computer makers sold $3.8 billion of NT-based servers in 1996; but the worldwide market for large-system hardware totaled $53.6 billion.

Saying that the PC manufacturers want to ally with Microsoft doesn't begin to express the intensity of their courtship. These companies are behaving like a giddy bunch of college football players infatuated with a gorgeous but petulant debutante all the jocks want to bring to the dance. Some of the boys find that occasionally Miss Microsoft flings a drink into their face, but they quickly head back to the bar for her refill. Every one of the biggest PC makers—with the notable exception of IBM—insists that Microsoft likes it the best.

Digital CEO Robert Palmer created his joint "brand" back in August 1995. At the time, it seemed to the world (and to Digital executives) that Microsoft had chosen Digital as its hardware partner for its heavy assault on corporate computing.

Why would Gates want an ally as saddled with troubles as Digital? Microsoft lacks what is perhaps the most important asset in today's corporate computing market—a service organization. Complex global corporations require extensive hand-holding, consulting, and support services for their computer operations. When a company like Sun Microsystems, Hewlett-Packard, or IBM installs a large-scale network for a customer, it often leaves employees on-site to ensure that the system runs smoothly. Microsoft has but a small services operation, mostly dedicated to answering phone calls from PC users who can't figure out how to do things like transfer an Excel spreadsheet into a Word document.

There were only four computer companies with the global service infrastructure Microsoft needed to deliver NT to corporate customers—IBM, HP, Digital, and Sun Microsystems. Sun was clearly out of the question as an ally because it had no NT-related business. IBM and HP both had big Unix businesses that NT might cannibalize.

That left Digital, a company with a 22,000-person service and support force with old ties to many of the world's biggest corporations. Microsoft so desired access to that manpower that it included in the deal a payment of more than $100 million to help defray Digital's costs of training engineers and software developers. So far, the alliance has been a success, especially for Digital. According to Robert Bismuth, Digital's vice president for strategic alliances, well over one-third of Digital's $14.5 billion in 1996 revenues came from hardware, software, and services related to NT.

How nice. But Miss Microsoft has a wandering eye. Sure, Digital carried the ball for a few early scores, but the championship is looming. Suddenly a beefier boyfriend, a running back by the name of Hewlett-Packard, looked appealing. "This powerful combination will make HP the leader in Windows NT ... enterprise solutions," said HP CEO Lew Platt at a joint press conference with Gates, where the companies announced a strategic partnership. When Gates spoke to press and analysts, he called the HP alliance "the most comprehensive set of initiatives we've ever undertaken." And he showed how little he worried about Digital's sensibilities when he referred to that company as "DEC," a moniker from the past that makes current management wince.

The Microsoft linkup represents a sharp swerve for HP. It has a $6.5-billion-a-year business selling Unix servers. Nevertheless, CEO Platt phoned Gates after the Digital alliance was announced and asked what HP could do to have a similar relationship. Gates replied: Show more enthusiasm for NT. In 1997 HP will sell $1.1 billion in NT servers, ten times what it sold the year before, estimates Montgomery Securities.

The computer maker wariest of a close relationship with Microsoft is IBM. Big Blue's dilemma is that in addition to PCs, it sells loads of mainframes and Unix servers. Even more important, it competes with Microsoft in software. IBM is the only company squared off against Microsoft with a BackOffice–like suite of NT applications: It sells Notes (E-mail and groupware), DB2 (a database), and software for systems management, transactions, security, and more.

The product that most impedes cooperation between IBM and Microsoft is Notes, the prize IBM acquired when it paid $3.5 billion for Lotus in 1995. Says Gates: "Inside Microsoft, I always said that as soon as IBM realizes OS/2 has failed, we're going to have a great across-the-board relationship. Now what prevents IBM from approaching us at all on a deal like the one we've done with HP is their ownership of Notes."

Microsoft would love NT to have IBM's wholehearted support. After all, no company can match IBM's access to and influence over corporate customers. But a far-reaching alliance is unlikely anytime soon. As Aaron Goldberg of the Computer Intelligence research firm points out, IBM isn't happy when another company's product has a key place in a customer's infrastructure. "IBM's all about account control," he says, "and NT is an opportunity for somebody else to exert influence on the account."

IT'S NOT A ONE-SIZE-FITS-ALL WORLD (YET)

If there's a Tommy Lee Jones character in this saga, it's Scott McNealy, the CEO of Sun. When he surveys the computer industry around him, he sees a bunch of wimps rolling over as the NT conflagration approaches. He dismisses HP, for instance: "Either you're a car manufacturer or you're a dealer. And HP's becoming a dealer. They'll resell Intel, Oracle, Unix, Netscape, Microsoft—anything anybody will give them. They're out of the computer business."

McNealy wants the computing landscape to include a diversity of products that don't absolutely depend on Microsoft. "There will never be one of anything. There's always more than one cola, ketchup, car, whatever," he says. "Besides, there's a very interesting bunch of people out there who are scared to death of Microsoft. If NT were to become the only answer, SQL Server becomes the only answer and Exchange becomes the only answer. So where can companies like Oracle, Sybase, Informix, and even IBM consolidate? What are they going to do, rally around the Mac OS?"

Obviously not. McNealy's answer is that they will rally around products and software created by Sun. On the high end, he thinks Oracle and other developers can profit for many years by continuing to write software for high-octane Unix servers. He says that customers who demand top performance, who can't afford to gamble on a relatively young piece of software like NT, will stick to Unix. Novell CEO Eric Schmidt says there's an even more basic reason to stay with Unix: "There's a simple test. I can crash NT in a few minutes, and I can't crash my Unix machine. NT will lack the fundamental stability and scalability of Unix for at least three years, maybe longer."

Gates believes there's little chance Microsoft can be thwarted by network computing, improvements in Unix, or NT's technological shortcomings. Remember what happened on the desktop, he says. "Customers wanted somebody who integrated the user interface and made all the software work together. That is just more attractive than having piece parts that people buy separately."

He acknowledges that there are "tough technical problems" Microsoft must overcome before big customers will move lock, stock, and barrel over to NT and BackOffice. He also admits that this will take a "long period of time," so much so that in an interview he drew out the word "long" over several seconds. Then he smiled and added: "But we are very patient people."

HOW BOB WRIGHT AND GE MADE NBC NO. 1

BY MARC GUNTHER

◆◆◆

NBC's CEO was derided as one of GE's dim bulbs. But he's made the Peacock Network fly—hiring great managers and routing the competition.

◆◆◆

Traditionalists at NBC were appalled. General Electric CEO Jack Welch had announced that he was changing the name of the landmark RCA Building at 30 Rockefeller Center to the GE Building.

This was in 1988, two years after GE acquired NBC in its purchase of RCA, and unhappy network staffers feared the venerable old Peacock Network—famous for Huntley-Brinkley, Milton Berle, and *Bonanza*—was being destroyed, morphed into just another cog in the GE machine. Even NBC's own late-night star, David Letterman, loved to take nasty on-air jabs at Welch and his boys from Fairfield.

It turns out that those worried NBC staffers were wrong—and a good thing too. Since then, Robert C. Wright, the GE-trained lawyer chosen by Welch to run the network and the man once maligned as an industry know-nothing, has transformed the company into the powerhouse of the TV business. He has deftly expanded NBC beyond broadcasting into cable, new media, and global television, creating a diversified media company with strong prospects for growth. He has put together an all-star team of executives, probably the best ever to run a network. And he has driven NBC to its fourth consecutive year of record growth, with more than $5 billion in revenues and an estimated $950 million in operating profits in 1996.

From *Today* at dawn through *Tonight* at bedtime, NBC is clicking. The network dominates in entertainment and sports and has all the momentum in news with shows like *Dateline* and its *Nightly News*. And Wright, derided for years as an uninspired cost cutter, is finally getting respect. What's not well understood, though, is the story of how Wright reinvigorated NBC. The secret: Wright did exactly what his critics told him not to. He imported GE's hard-driving culture to NBC, staying the course with Welch's unyielding support—and occasional nudging. He did so even as experts warned that television is a uniquely creative business, where rules that govern the rest of the corporate world don't apply.

That, it appears, simply isn't true. Welch says: "People say, Jack, how can you be at NBC, you don't know anything about dramas or comedies ... Well, I can't build a jet engine, either. I can't build a turbine. Our job at GE is to deal with resources—human and financial. The idea of getting great talent, giving them all the support in the world, and letting them run is the whole management philosophy of GE, whether it's in turbines, engines, or a network."

Wright and his senior executives now run NBC the GE way. They think strategically, globally, and long term. They hire strong, self-confident people. They promote speed and simplicity. They decry bureaucracy. These may sound like management bromides, but they explain why NBC owns the rights to the Olympics through the year 2008, why NBC has mounted a successful cable news network when rivals Disney and Rupert Murdoch could not, and why NBC beat its rivals to the Internet and expects now to become a programming force in Europe and Asia.

From the start, Wright moved into new businesses to create a hedge against the decline of broadcasting. In early 1997, broadcasting still represented the bulk of NBC's revenues and profits, but that business is in a long, slow, seemingly inexorable decline. In 1986 broadcasting had 92% of viewers; ten years later it had only 67%.

It's not just that the audience is shrinking. Prime time, especially, is a cyclical and unpredictable arena. A recession hits, and ad revenues wilt. Pick a few dogs, and, with a click of the wand, viewers will desert you in droves. "That's the horrible part about the business," says Wright. "You can't will the audience to fall in love with your shows." And even hit shows don't stay hot forever. Already NBC blockbusters like *ER* and *Friends* are in decline.

NBC GOT THE LIGHT-BULB PEOPLE

◆

Wright's journey so far has been anything but smooth. When the Big Three TV networks changed hands in the mid-1980s, the conventional wisdom was that NBC got a rotten deal: ABC was sold to Capital Cities, a broadcasting company; CBS went to Laurence Tisch, who promised to rebuild; and NBC wound up with the light-bulb people. The reaction of NBC News anchor Tom Brokaw was typical. "My heart sank," he recalls. "GE people were engineers and accountants. They came from a different gene pool."

More than the GE factor was working against Wright when he was named NBC's CEO in 1986. The CEO he replaced, Grant Tinker, was a classy, stylish former producer, well liked by colleagues. By comparison, Wright was a stiff, colorless outsider whose best qualities—his brainpower, integrity, and decency—weren't immediately apparent. NBC, meanwhile, was in its best shape in years, thanks to prime-time programming wiz Brandon Tartikoff. NBC's employees wanted to be applauded, but Wright came bearing bad news.

Sure, he would say, the ratings are great for now, but NBC's costs are too high, and viewers are fleeing to cable. This was a message few at NBC wanted to hear. But Wright felt obligated to deliver the unpleasant news. Doing so was a cornerstone of the GE way, preached often by Welch: Face reality (even when it's uncomfortable), communicate candidly (even when it stings), and embrace change (it's an opportunity, not a threat).

Professionally, Wright was a product of GE and protégé of Welch, his close friend, who'd brought him back to GE in the early 1970s after he'd left briefly to practice law. He toiled in GE's plastics and housewares divisions, but then left again to spend three years in Atlanta as president of Cox Cable in the early 1980s. In the mid-1980s he returned to run the ultimate station of the GE cross: GE Capital. Though Wright had never worked in broadcasting, he was hardly the TV neophyte his critics believed, having witnessed at close hand the growth of Ted Turner's cable empire while he ran Cox.

Personally, Wright was well armed for the cold rebuff he received upon arriving at NBC. He is a man shaped by close family relationships and a strong sense of self. Like Welch, Wright was the only son of a stable, hard-working, and religious Irish Catholic mother who believed in him at every turn; his father, an engineer by trade, was an entrepreneur who, Wright says, "was always looking to be a millionaire but never made his fortune." Wright got a Catholic education, at Chaminade High School on Long Island and at Holy Cross. The other crucial relationship in Wright's life is his longtime marriage to college sweetheart Suzanne Wright. Because the couple is very much a team, the NBC transition was tough for both of them. She remembers inviting several senior NBC executives to their Connecticut home and being stunned at how chilly some of them were.

But tensions were running high at the office, as Wright pushed his two-pronged strategy: Cut costs and find ways to get into cable. Neither course of action was popular, but Wright had no choice, particularly on the cost side, where Welch was pressuring him along with the rest of GE to eliminate layers and root out waste. The bureaucracy was so bad, recalls Dick Ebersol, then a producer and now president of NBC Sports, that "someone who wasn't qualified to produce a bowel movement could slow you down for months."

JACK WELCH, THE TV CRITIC

◆◆◆

GE's CEO takes a special interest in NBC. He loves Seinfeld, *hated* The Single Guy, *and tracks every ratings point.*

Jack Welch was excited. He'd just had a fax machine installed in his home—this was nearly a decade ago—so every morning before breakfast, he could read the overnight Nielsen ratings for his new acquisition, NBC. "It's great," he told the network's top programmer, Brandon Tartikoff.

Tartikoff winced. He'd been living and dying with the overnights for years. "I go to sleep every night with a knot in my stomach like I'm in the sixth grade and my report card's coming out the next day," he said. "And you think that's great."

The daily report cards are just one of the things General Electric CEO Welch likes about television. GE bought NBC in 1986 because the company wanted a cash flow stream at a time when its manufacturing businesses were coming under pressure. Welch now sees NBC as a core part of GE's information businesses, which in 1996 accounted for $11 billion of the company's $79 billion in revenues. In 1995, NBC alone brought in 5.6% of GE's revenues and 7.6% of its profits. No wonder Welch takes a special interest in the network. What are some of his favorite shows? Welch never misses *Seinfeld*, and he loves *Frasier* and *Law & Order.*

Wright attacked NBC's bloated work force, cutting it from 8,000 to fewer than 5,000 full-time jobs, saving close to $120 million a year in overhead.

To many, Wright was foolish to curb spending on profitable broadcast operations so he could invest in risky cable deals. But

Wright believed fervently in cable and pressed on with his cable portfolio, buying stakes in regional sports channels and such networks as Court TV, Bravo, and American Movie Classics. Nearly all now make money. But his biggest cable gamble was CNBC. NBC created this business news channel in 1989 and later ensured its survival by outbidding Dow Jones and Westinghouse to buy a money-losing rival, Financial News Network, for $155 million, far more than it was worth. Since then NBC has pushed CNBC into 60 million homes, despite lackluster programs.

EXECUTIVES WITH ENTREPRENEURIAL DRIVE

Far from getting credit early on for his cable strategy, Wright instead took a beating in the early 1990s when NBC's prime-time ratings tumbled. To make matters worse, the collapse came just as the TV advertising market fell into its worst slump in two decades. Says Wright: "The hundred-year flood hit on the day we were having our boat repaired." NBC's profits plummeted from a peak of $603 million in 1989 to just $204 million in 1992.

Wright was partly to blame for the problems. GE had taught him to find the strongest person possible for each job, but here he faltered. The entertainment and news division heads Wright brought in initially had neither the businesss skills nor the broadcast know-how to run major network businesses. What's more, Wright had limited some of their spending authority. The upshot was that, during the toughest of times for all the networks, NBC's entertainment and news divisions were in the wrong hands.

Wright, having lost patience with his own division heads, decided that what he really needed were executives with entrepreneurial drive. Early in 1993 he hired Don Ohlmeyer, a sports and entertainment producer who ran his own production company, to take over NBC Entertainment. Ohlmeyer had made millions on his own, but he longed to become a major player in Hollywood. An outspoken, fiercely competitive bear of a man, Ohlmeyer demanded full control over entertainment and more freedom to spend money on programming. To run NBC News, Wright hired Andrew Lack, an ebullient and innovative CBS News producer. Like Ohlmeyer, Lack had an entrepreneurial spirit; he'd worked in advertising, produced a TV movie, and created the pseudo-hip CBS News magazine *West 57th*.

That Ohlmeyer and Lack were producers as well as executives was no accident. To run NBC Sports, Wright had already hired Ebersol, another executive who was as comfortable in a control room as in his office. After appointing Ebersol, whose production credits included *Saturday Night Live*, a professional wrestling show, and Bob Costas's late-night NBC talk show, Wright realized that having executives around with an instinctive feel for TV production— something he lacked—was probably a good idea. It's called show business, after all.

Wright gives his three top executives lots of running room and demands that they move fast—tenets of GE management. Consider, for example, how NBC engineered a stunning coup—the $1.25 billion Olympic rights deal for Sydney in 2000 and Salt Lake City in 2002. Wright summoned Ebersol and Randy Falco, who organized NBC's Olympic coverage, to a meeting in August 1995, immediately after the Disney-ABC and Westinghouse-CBS mergers were announced. With the industry in flux, Wright and Falco came up with the unprecedented idea of launching a preemptive bid for two Olympics, which up until then had been auctioned one at a time. Welch, reached on Nantucket, gave the go-ahead—and a GE jet to fly the two to Sweden that night to present their plan to International Olympic Committee officials. "We had an answer within two minutes," Ebersol says. By the weekend, they also had a deal with the IOC. Says Welch: "Drive speed for competitive advantage ... we breathe that." Later, Ebersol and the IOC negotiated an even grander deal, a $2.3 billion package that gives NBC the rights to all the Olympics through 2008. By the time ABC, CBS, and Fox woke up, the game was over.

The entrepreneurial spirit is also alive at Andy Lack's NBC News, which boasts the best collection of assets of any TV news operation. *Today* has a dominant lead in the mornings. *Dateline* has grown into a commercial, although not a critical, success, and NBC's *Nightly News* is mounting the first serious challenge to ABC's *World News Tonight* since the late 1980s. NBC's most significant victory was the successful launch last year of MSNBC, the 24-hour cable news network and Internet site jointly owned with Microsoft.

Wright negotiated a favorable deal with Microsoft that enabled NBC to create the news channel with no cash outlay.

Of all the aggressive managers Wright installed, Ohlmeyer produced the most dramatic results. When he took over entertainment in 1993, Ohlmeyer tore down internal barriers in the division, organizing a daily 2:30 P.M. "war room" meeting of his department heads where they develop strategy, identify problems, and brainstorm. The goal is to promote teamwork, eliminate second-guessing, and bring the best brains to bear on issues—part of a concept GE has enshrined as "boundarylessness."

So far the results have been impressive. The network's promotion machine is awesome; just look at how NBC's "Must See TV," an oxymoron if ever there was one, has become part of the lexicon. Under Ohlmeyer, NBC was the first network to eliminate commercial breaks between programs, leading viewers seamlessly from one show to the next. *The Tonight Show* with Jay Leno, overcoming a rocky start, has won the late-night battle with CBS's David Letterman, Welch's old nemesis. In daytime, a perennial weak spot, NBC still trails its broadcast rivals, but the Peacock Network has made impressive gains in ratings and profits since Ohlmeyer took command.

Still, Wright's taking nothing for granted. Much as he pushed into cable a decade ago, he's now making risky, long-term investments in Europe and Asia, where NBC lags behind Murdoch and CNN and ESPN. With a little help from friends at GE—the same executives in charge of selling jet engines and medical equipment abroad are now trying to peddle some TV ad time—NBC is distributing four networks: CNBC Asia, CNBC Europe, NBC Europe, and NBC Asia. The idea is to get a foothold in markets that could soon explode. That's also the thinking behind a host of NBC investments in new media like NBC Desktop, an online financial service. Here, once again, no one can accuse Wright of complacency.

It would be folly to underestimate Welch and Wright. "Success is addictive," Wright says. "We don't want to lose it. We feel we worked hard to get here and, dammit, we want to stay." At GE, managers have to be No. 1 or No. 2 in their markets, or the business gets closed or sold. That's something Wright, with his fighting Irish spirit, is not likely to let happen.

SEARS:
ARTHUR MARTINEZ'S
REVOLUTION HAS BEGUN

BY PATRICIA SELLERS

◆◆◆

The retail icon's CEO wants to sell
Sears' powerhouse brands—to anybody,
anywhere, any way he can.

◆◆◆

Is retailing a good business? You'd expect Sears Chief Executive Arthur Martinez to have a ready answer to the question. He's been in retailing, after all, for most of his career. He's the man who brought Sears back from its near-death experience five years ago. And Sears Roebuck, for goodness' sake, is almost a synonym for retailing. But at an interview with FORTUNE, the normally smooth-talking CEO falters. Martinez (pronounced MAR-tin-ez) hems and haws, raises his eyes to the ceiling, crosses his arms in front of his barrel chest, and—finally—smiles and says: "The retailing business is middle of the pack at best."

That less-than-rousing reply explains a lot of things. First, it reveals how profoundly Martinez's thinking about his company and his business has changed over the past few years. It is also the key to understanding how he plans to reinvent Sears. Again. Martinez's new plan is to transform Sears, the retailer, into a top-echelon consumer-brands and services company. To do so, he is rejecting all retail models of how to run a company. He is copying—unabashedly—key strategies of standout consumer companies like Coca-Cola, Walt Disney, General Electric, and General Motors' Saturn division.

The Sears he envisions will no longer revolve around the "Big Store," the traditional Sears department store. Instead it will be built around the powerhouse brands that Sears owns—brands like Craftsman (America's leading tool line), Kenmore (the No. 1 appliance brand), DieHard, and Sears itself. Martinez believes that no other retailer and few other companies of any kind boast such strong brands. To get these brands to consumers, he'll open small stores—thousands of them—far from America's shopping malls. He will invest big money in outlets that won't even bear the Sears name. And he will build, he says, a $10 billion service operation—which isn't retailing at all.

SEARS' TURNAROUND DRAMA

If Martinez can make it happen and make it pay, Sears' transformation will be the stuff of future management texts—one of the most sweeping and surprising corporate makeovers ever. It will also be one hell of a third act in the Sears turnaround drama.

You may be familiar with the story. Act I begins in 1992. Arthur Martinez, the low-profile but charismatic vice chairman of tony Saks Fifth Avenue, trots into down-market, downtrodden Sears, which is in the process of losing $3.9 billion. As CEO of the Sears Merchandise Group, he is the first outsider ever to head the retailer. His assignment: Restore the health of the Sears stores while the old, embattled management pares the conglomerate to its rotten core. Sears unloads its financial services businesses—Allstate insurance, Coldwell Banker real estate, the Dean Witter brokerage, the Discover credit card—and sells its famous headquarters, the 110-story Sears Tower. With no time to waste, Martinez shuts 113 unprofitable "big stores" and cuts 50,000 jobs. He even terminates the well-known Sears catalogue, the origin—and some argued, the soul—of the retail giant.

Act II is a nervous time for Martinez. He is in charge of Sears' stores, and they are out of date, out of touch, and apparently out of ideas to win back shoppers from rivals like Wal-Mart and J.C. Penney. Many people wonder whether the company will even survive. Martinez decides that Sears doesn't have a clue as to who its target customer is. So he chooses one: the Middle-American mom. He packs the aisles with women's apparel. He advertises "the softer side of Sears," promising "We're not who you think we are."

It worked—and much faster than anyone dreamed possible. The "dinosaur" turned into a cash cow. Sears earned $1.3 billion on revenues of $38.2 billion in 1996. The profits didn't come just from cost cutting, either. The stores have consistently gained market share from competitors in virtually every category of merchandise.

Martinez rose to CEO in 1995, and Sears' reputation ascended too. In FORTUNE's survey of the most admired companies, Sears was once the least admired in the category of innovation—dead last among hundreds of companies. This year, Sears was rated the most innovative general-merchandise retailer.

The greatest testament to the turnaround is the stock price. Since Martinez arrived at Sears, the shares have outperformed the big-brand companies that he's trying to emulate, including Coca-Cola and Disney (assuming investors held on to Sears shares that became Allstate, and Dean Witter shares, when those businesses were spun off as separate companies). "Only now," Martinez says, "have we earned the right to think about growth."

THE TYRANNY OF BRICKS AND MORTAR

Sears still has its problems. Store profit margins are mediocre. Customer satisfaction lags behind Wal-Mart's and Nordstrom's levels. Sears' international business is floundering. A chain of furniture stores is a loser. But these are minor compared with Sears' big problem. The company is still stuck in retailing—which Martinez is so ambivalent about. "I want to go beyond the tyranny of bricks and mortar," he says. Tyranny, Arthur? "Yeah, the store is the tyranny of retailing. You're making 20-year, 40-year asset decisions. For all practical purposes, it's a forever kind of decision."

Not that Martinez is giving up on department stores. In early 1997 he had 821 of them in shopping malls across America, and he intends to invest heavily enough to keep them fresh looking. He explains, "That's Job No. 1, as Ford would say. If we ever got into a situation again where the full-line stores aren't healthy, it would be deadly. It would undercut our entire growth program."

That growth plan is radically different from anything Sears has done before—so radical, in fact, that it seems to be a reversal of what Martinez has accomplished so far. Consider: The guy who revived the Big Store now says the store of the future is a small box. (Of 380 new Sears units scheduled to open in 1997, just 22 are department stores; 358 are freestanding specialty outlets.) And Martinez's reputation, remember, has ridden thus far on "the softer side of Sears"; the new specialty stores sell only heavy-duty stuff like tools and auto parts. Call it "the harder side of Sears."

The apparent contradictions surprise even Martinez. Two years ago, he says, he had "no idea" that small stores and service would become Sears' new growth vehicles. But his change of mindset doesn't faze him. "A hallmark of great companies is an ability to recognize the game has changed and to adapt," he says.

So, where did all this new thinking come from? And how is Martinez able to impose it on Sears' sprawling bureaucracy? From his office outside Chicago, the CEO describes the challenge of moving Sears from turnaround to "transformation." He says, "A turnaround is a financial recovery. A transformation is much more. It's all about changing the structure and the approach to the business, and reeducating our people to feel comfortable outside a command-and-control environment. It involves getting them used to risk taking and innovation. And getting the very best out of our people."

Sometimes Martinez sounds as if he's merely skimmed off the best of the last decade's pop management trends: a swing from cost cutting to a "we need to grow" mentality. A shift to selling services. A resurgence of brands. A focus on long-term value creation. Martinez is hot on ever popular EVA, a measurement of capital efficiency that Coca-Cola management, among others, says is the real thing that drives a stock. But Martinez, unlike many CEOs who talk this talk, has actually made these things work. And he has the results to show for it.

His success, in part, is innate: He's the kind of guy who sets a goal and reaches it. The only child of a Brooklyn fish wholesaler, Martinez graduated from high school at age 16. He used an ROTC loan to put himself through college, did his Army tour, and went on to Harvard business school. And he's not shy. By sheer force of will, for instance, Martinez recently persuaded Disney CEO Michael Eisner to speak at Sears' annual gathering of its top 200 managers in Phoenix. "You gotta understand, I don't do these kinds of things," says Eisner, who had never met Martinez before the Sears boss invited him. "Arthur got me there. He wrote me. He called me. I went because he seemed to be a man on a mission." So impressed is Eisner with Sears' revival that he jokes he may be miscast as Martinez's role model. "I think I'm gonna watch what Arthur does and copy him from now on," Eisner says.

INVESTING IN SPECIALISTS AND BRANDS

◆

But the main reason Martinez has been able to change Sears is that he changed the people. Most of the senior executives are Martinez recruits, and most had no prior experience in retailing. "We used to be so inbred, it's a wonder we all didn't have one eye in the middle of our foreheads," says executive vice president Bill Salter, a 32-year Sears veteran. "The most important thing Arthur has done is bring in specialists in their fields."

Case in point: marketing honcho John Costello. An alumnus of Procter & Gamble, Pepsi, and Nielsen Marketing Research, where he was president, Costello is Martinez's chief brand evangelist. A brand, he preaches, signifies a relationship with the customer. It is a company's most valuable asset. It's also the main differentiator, the best defense against price competition, and the key to customer loyalty. "Competitors can copy your features and benefits, but they can't steal your brand," Costello says. Before Martinez arrived, Sears viewed all its brands—Kenmore, Craftsman, DieHard, Weatherbeater (paints), and the Sears brand—"as tools to sell more merchandise, instead of as assets we need to invest in," Costello says.

Martinez and Costello got intrigued with Disney as they were casting about for a compelling, explicit way to extend Sears' brands. "The retail models are lousy," the CEO says. Not only are most retailers poor brand managers; these companies typically grow by putting up more and more stores. When their look-alike units have sprouted in every major market across America—wham!—the companies hit the wall on growth.

Unlike the retailers, Disney had found the secret of renewal. "Here was a consumer business whose brand franchise had weakened," Martinez says. Eisner joined Disney as CEO from the outside in 1984. He has invested heavily in Disney's brands, from Mickey Mouse to Quasimodo, and in the core of the company, animation. Eisner has extended the brands into big-budget movies, TV, all sorts of theme parks, merchandise, even retail stores. Martinez says he foresees a similar growth strategy for Sears. The Disney model of brand extension, he says, "is based on deep and imbedded customer relationships."

Thus Sears is doing lots of brand research. In 1997 alone, the company will survey some two million consumers. "We ask the customer, 'Where does Sears have authority to compete?'" Martinez says. "We expand into areas only where the customer permits us." Customers, for example, "permit" Sears to sell them hardware, appliances, lawn and garden supplies, automotive gear, and electronics. So, Sears' off-the-mall specialty stores sell this heavy-duty stuff.

Craftsman is Sears' sturdiest brand. And the best vehicle for moving it beyond the traditional retail box is Sears' freestanding hardware stores. In fact, this business is a veritable minilab of the new and emerging Sears.

The company tried the hardware-store idea about a decade ago but abandoned it—in part because the department store folks disapproved. Martinez, though, thinks the small hardware store is Sears' most exciting retail format. "It's an elegant concept," he says, "because it's a flanking strategy around arguably the best-managed retailer, Home Depot." Not that Martinez expects Sears' small (20,000-square-foot) hardware outlets to hammer Home Depot. He simply wants to win over a few million shoppers that the Depot doesn't satisfy. "Our customers, particularly female customers, are often put off by the very thing that the category-killer retailers stand for: incredible selection," he says. "There's some evidence that these stores have gotten too big, too overwhelming, and too confusing to shop. Too frightening."

Yes, Bernie Marcus is watching. The CEO of Home Depot, the king of big-box hardware retailers, once viewed Sears as a dying company. ("Sears and IBM believed their own bullshit," he told FORTUNE.) Marcus has since changed his tune and now says that Sears is his fiercest competitor.

Martinez is stocking Sears' hardware stores with new and fresh management talent. Last year, for instance, he discovered a chain of hardware stores in California that were more productive and more profitable than his own. So he bought the company, Orchard Supply Hardware Stores. "This is our potential Saturn," Martinez says. The CEO's view is that Orchard, like GM's quasi-independent small-car company, is a model of innovation, customer friendliness, and healthy corporate culture. He wants the Orchard organization to pollinate the rest of Sears.

CAPITAL-EFFICIENT BRANDS

———————◆———————

Another small-store innovation that flouts the old rules is Sears' fastest-growing retail format: "dealer stores." These outlets sell tractors and TVs in outposts like Eagle Pass, Texas, and Thief River Falls, Minnesota. Actually, the concept was born out of failure in 1993, when Martinez closed Sears' 2,200 catalogue outlets in rural areas. "Our problem wasn't our inability to generate revenues. It was our inability to make money," Martinez says about the catalogue stores. "We wanted to find a capital-efficient way to keep the Sears brand in small-town America."

The tiny (5,000-square-foot) dealer stores require almost no capital investment from the company—just $10,000 or so for a big, blue Sears sign over the front door. Reason is, Sears doesn't own or operate the outlets. Entrepreneurs do. Sears supplies the merchandise (a limited line of tools, appliances, electronics), contributes quite a bit of advertising, controls the pricing, and monitors the quality. The local proprietors supply the bulk of the capital and the sweat equity. They earn commissions on the goods they sell. These owners are not franchisees, since they pay Sears no fees. The dealer-store concept is unique. "It's collaborative," says Martinez. The dealer stores show the value of "getting beyond the tyranny of bricks and mortar," as the CEO says.

The winning strategy has been to locate the dealer stores right across the road from Wal-Mart—that's right, the retailer that once almost killed Sears. The dealer stores compete quite nicely by offering higher-quality merchandise and higher-touch service than Wal-Mart. Steve Titus, who heads the business, explains, "The key is finding owners who really like people. The best owners have sincerity off the charts, and if they told a lie, they'd fall over." Today Sears has 472 dealer stores. Martinez expects the chain to double in size in three years.

Sears' most promising growth vehicle is Sears Home Services, and it requires no physical building at all—just thousands of service workers with thousands of trucks to carry them to customers' homes. This new division encompasses a jumble of offerings, from appliance repair to pest control, that Martinez believes can earn higher returns than Sears' stores.

Jane Thompson is the home-services chief. Martinez says he followed Michael Eisner's management credo—Move by instinct—when he assigned her to head the business. Thompson originally told Martinez she'd like to run Sears' $4-billion-a-year tire and auto-parts empire. Martinez said no. He wanted her to get her fingernails dirty in home services instead. "Jane had no experience in the business, but I knew she would come at it from a marketplace perspective," Martinez says. "We have plenty of operators at Sears. We don't have enough people who think about the business from the outside in."

Thompson's challenge is to take an orphan operation and transform it into a highly profitable $10 billion business—by 2000, her target. Sears already brings in $3 billion a year in revenues by calling on customers at home—to install their dishwashers, reface their kitchen cabinets, even put roofs on their homes. Trouble is, Sears uses a lot of licensees. Service is inconsistent. Marketing is lousy.

"We're creating a central source for a houseful of services," Thompson explains. She came up with an umbrella brand name, Sears Home Central. And a single phone number for customers to call: 1-800-4-MY-HOME. And a big-budget ad campaign that promotes—what else—"the service side of Sears." The advertising spreads the word that Sears will repair any of your appliances—it doesn't matter whether you bought them at Sears. Thompson says she has chosen to compete in ten different categories of services. Add 'em up, and this is a $160 billion market. And Sears is already the leader, with a brand name consumers trust, and only a 2% share. "As the population ages, spending on home services increases," Thompson says. "We have a great growth vehicle, with no particular competitor to take us on."

The biggest challenge at Sears, however, is not coming up with growth plans and strategies. It is directing 300,000 people to step together—and step lively—as the company reaches in so many new directions. Martinez admits it. "The risk is always executional," he says. Back in Phoenix, where the theme of Sears' conference was "Working in Concert," Martinez invited Steven Kerr, General Electric's chief learning officer, to speak to the Sears executives about "boundarylessness." This is CEO Jack Welch's descriptive term for collaboration across GE's dozens of business units. To transform, Martinez believes, Sears needs to emulate GE. Everybody in the company must shake their not-invented-here fear and snatch the best ideas.

Martinez's new friend Michael Eisner says that recovering from failure is often easier than building from success. Martinez certainly knows this. Though he isn't as sweaty-palmed as he was in 1992, he says he is heeding the lesson of Sears' bungled history: Don't rest a moment, because every strategy ultimately fails. "Today's peacock is tomorrow's feather duster," Martinez tells the people at Sears. A paperweight on his desk, bearing those words, reminds him of that bitter truth every day.

CHAPTER THREE

◆◆◆

MANAGEMENT AND CAREER IDEAS WORTH A FORTUNE

GROWING YOUR COMPANY: FIVE WAYS TO DO IT RIGHT

BY RONALD HENKOFF

*Here's how some shrewd companies
avoid the pitfalls of growing their
companies the wrong way.*

Every half-decade or so, Corporate America rediscovers a concept so astoundingly fundamental that it's a wonder anyone forgot it in the first place. Companies that were recently pronouncing themselves born-again on ideas like quality, efficiency, and speed are now latching on to something very basic and overweeningly simple: growth.

In a survey by the American Management Association, executives at large and midsize companies ranked the quest for revenues as their second-most-pressing priority—after customer service. Companies once obsessed with cutting costs are now urgently trying to boost sales—with new products, new services, and new markets, both at home and abroad.

But there's a harsh, mostly unspoken truth about growth: Getting it right is considerably harder than it looks. Five of the most common ways to grow—overseas expansion, innovation, acquisitions, new distribution channels, and buying market share—are fraught with peril. Buying market share, say, with promotions and coupons can lead to red ink as competitors keep slashing prices to keep pace. For the uninitiated, foreign bureaucrats and antiquated infrastructures can make going global an exercise in futility.

If there's no sure-fire formula for growth, then what can you do? Follow the example of companies like Emerson Electric, Starbucks, USAA, and Cisco Systems. They know how to increase their revenues profitably year in and out. Different as these companies are, they share several fundamental traits. They have stable, experienced management teams, they spend heavily on R&D, and they invest a great deal of energy and money in recruiting and training employees. Above all, they realize that growth doesn't just happen. It has to be planned, nurtured, measured, and rewarded.

BUILD PYRAMIDS

◆

Innovation is on everybody's short list for growth. But new products rarely live up to their hype. Just 42% of the products that hit the market meet the expectations of the managers who launch them. And more than half of those managers admit that their companies skimp on or misspend R&D dollars.

One CEO who's seen the light on innovation is Emerson Electric's Chuck Knight. Three years ago he unleashed creativity in his company by radically changing the corporate culture. In the early 1990s, Emerson, which had been getting much of its profit increases from cost cutting, began to see its revenue growth slow. The marketing and sales forces, constrained by tight budgets, were missing critical opportunities. Innovation flagged, in part because division managers were opting for investments that produced short-term profits. Foreign expansion, long a stated corporate goal, got stuck in first gear as division chiefs, anxious to protect their home turfs, shied away from adventurism abroad.

In 1994, Emerson altered its strategy. It now pursues growth with the same kind of methodical zeal it once used to squeeze costs. The hallmark of Emerson's approach is an annual two-day growth conference conducted by each of the company's 60 divisions. At the conference, Emerson execs, who have a portion of their pay tied to how well they set and meet goals for growth, neatly express their growth plans on a single sheet of paper with two pyramid-shaped illustrations, inevitably known as the twin peaks. The pyramid on the left summarizes the past year's growth programs.

The other pyramid depicts the proposals for the next year, including plans to invest in new products, expand into new markets, and acquire new businesses. The growth conferees weight the proposals by risk, using a formula that accounts for market conditions, capacity constraints, and how long it's likely to be before any investment pays off. Those proposals with the best chance of succeeding—including some that didn't make the cut the year before—fall to the lower parts of the pyramid and are funded first.

Emerson's commitment to growth shows up most tellingly at its largest division, Copeland. The business, with annual sales of $1.3 billion, makes compressors for refrigeration and air-conditioning equipment. So far, Copeland has spent a whopping $300 million to perfect a technology known as "compliant scroll." Elegantly simple in design, the scroll is devilishly difficult to make. The device, which acts as the lungs of a compressor, allows Copeland to produce machines that are smaller, quieter, and more energy efficient than those made by its rivals. The scroll is on a roll, with sales growing at a 40% annual clip.

But the scroll probably wouldn't have flourished if Knight hadn't personally made it clear that he cares deeply about growth. Emerson's CEO realizes his heavy emphasis on cost control was stifling innovation: "It's amazing to think, 'Why the hell haven't we done this stuff before?' Well, we hadn't done it because we didn't have the resources to do it. And we didn't have the resources because we were pounding the shit out of profit margins."

DON'T BRIBE YOUR CUSTOMERS

One time-honored route to growth, known as discounting, rebating, and couponing, is as common as crabgrass. But it can also be just as noxious. Those gimmicks may buy market share, but they're often no more than a quick fix that debases rather than builds the value of your brand. Once your competitor responds with his own discounting, your newly acquired customers are likely to flock to him.

The surest—and ultimately the cheapest—way to increase your total sales is to persuade your existing customers to buy more products. One company that's cracked this formula is USAA. This financial services company is largely run by former generals and colonels. That makes good sense. USAA's main mission is to provide insurance to military officers and their dependents. The company, which is owned by its policyholders, covers a phenomenal 95% of active-duty military officers. How's that for market share?

But USAA has one significant problem. Its niche is shrinking. The Armed Forces commissioned just 17,600 officers in 1995. That's down from 22,000 in 1990. Yet even as USAA's customer base declines, the company continues to grow. In 1995 it reported its best results ever. Revenues increased 7%, to $6.6 billion, and net income surged 29%, to $730 million.

How do you expand in a contracting market? You offer your customers progressively more service. Founded in 1922, USAA has, over the years, transformed itself into a life and health insurance company, a discount brokerage firm, a mutual fund manager, a travel agency, a buying club, and a bank. This financial services supermarket, which conducts all its business by telephone or post, is now the biggest direct-mail outfit in the country.

What makes USAA's growth recipe work isn't just the ingredients. It's the execution. The company answers 80% of all phone calls in 20 seconds, and it provides its employees with the training and technology to do more than one task. An associate selling a customer car insurance, for example, can also help him open a bank account. But what really distinguishes USAA is its career development programs. The company shells out some $2.7 million per year in tuition reimbursement for college courses.

USAA's employees will need that education if the company is to grow in the years ahead. And growth is a priority at USAA. The company recently made the momentous decision to make its niche significantly larger—by marketing insurance not just to military officers and their dependents but also to the nation's four million enlisted personnel (including retirees). In that hotly contested market, USAA will have to do battle with the likes of Allstate and State Farm. CEO Robert Herres confidently declares, "The only real limitation to growth is how well we do our jobs."

GO GLOBAL, GENTLY

It's no secret that the U.S. has turned into a hard-slogging, slow-growth market for many businesses. Nor is it any great revelation that there's a wide world of opportunity in developing countries like China, where GDP has been leaping forward at an average rate of 12% for the past five years. Americans invested a walloping $95 billion overseas in 1995, up from $27 billion in 1990, according to a report by the United Nations. But companies looking for a bonanza abroad are likely to be disappointed and had better prepare for headaches.

Actually, the main message is to prepare, period—with the right local partner and the right local product. Procter & Gamble stumbled for years before it found the right formula for growth in Asia. It once offered All-Temperature Cheer to Japanese housewives, who always wash their clothes in cold water. Now it's doing quite well in Japan, matching its products to local tastes. General Motors recently halted a three-year effort to make American-style pickup trucks in China. Among other glitches, GM insisted on producing a two-door model that seats three, despite the fact that the Chinese clearly prefer four-door trucks that seat six. According to a survey by Andersen Consulting, just 44% of the Western companies operating in China are making money there.

One way to succeed overseas is to know the local markets intimately. For a company like Emerson Electric, China offers exciting potential. For instance, rural villages in China need and can afford Emerson's small electric generators. The company also sees opportunities in the rest of Asia, where newly affluent populations are demanding increasing numbers of air conditioners and refrigerators.

Yet even with huge opportunities in Asia, Emerson faces tough challenges in the region, including coping with its underdeveloped transportation systems and mastering its multiple layers of government bureaucracy. But the biggest hurdle of all is finding the right managers. To jump that, the company woos graduates of top local universities with generous pay and brings them to the U.S. for intensive training. Emerson also sends some of its best homegrown talent to the region, where experience is viewed as a rung on the ladder to senior management.

ACQUIRE ONLY ADDED VALUE

Buying another company is the easiest way to get bigger faster— at least on paper. Merger and acquisition activity, which blew up into a frenzy in the 1980s, is once again racing ahead at a torrid pace, threatening to break the record of $515 billion, set in 1995. But before you call your investment banker, ponder this startling statistic: Just 23% of acquisitions earn their cost of capital, according to a study by consultants at McKinsey & Co.

Corporations that successfully use M&A as a tool for growth know exactly what they want from the companies they're buying—

How often does a company's stock price rise when it announces an acquisition?

How many acquisitions are financially successful?

30% of the time

23% successful

On average, what grade do companies give the financial performance of their alliances?

FORTUNE TABLE / SOURCES: STEVEN KAPLAN; MCKINSEY; JORDAN LEWIS

be it technology, market access, or distribution. They also know—and here's the part that often gets neglected—exactly what value they can add to the deal. When Cisco Systems, for example, goes shopping for an acquisition, it's interested in two things: the right technology and the right culture. The company, which makes hardware and software for computer networks, has grown at a phenomenal rate of nearly 100% per year, reaching revenues of $4 billion in fiscal 1996. About one-fourth of that growth has come from *carefully* targeted acquisitions.

When Cisco paid $90 million for Crescendo Communications in 1993, the fledgling company was doing just $10 million in sales. Three years later, Crescendo formed the nucleus of a Cisco division generating $500 million in annual revenues. "Everyone thought we were crazy," says Charles Giancarlo, Cisco's vice president for business development "What we were buying was a superior technology and a topflight team of people."

Cisco has spent $5.5 billion buying 14 companies in the past three years. But it has quashed twice as many deals as it has consummated, often at the last minute and usually because Cisco decides that the entrepreneurial owners of the target company are more interested in cashing out than in staying with a bigger company and building the business.

CHANGE THE CHANNEL

◆

An oft-neglected route to growth, distribution has become a road to riches for Starbucks. By taking a common product—coffee—and finding uncommon ways to get it to consumers, Starbucks has experienced incredible growth. The chain opened 335 stores in 1995 alone, including two in Japan. The company has 1,020 coffee bars in total, compared with just 50 in 1989. Says CEO Howard Schultz: "Starbucks is not a trend. We're a lifestyle."

But its growth isn't limited to stores. The company constantly searches for new avenues. Starbucks ice cream, produced with Dreyer's, has become the best-selling coffee ice cream in the country. United Air Lines pours Starbucks on its flights, and Barnes & Noble serves it up alongside its *romans à clef*.

Starbucks keeps its channel flowing smoothly by deliberately restricting its growth. The company won't franchise, won't artificially flavor its coffees, and won't join hands with most of the hundreds of would-be partners who bang on its doors each week—stores, restaurants, airlines, hotels, and gas stations, all anxious to piggyback on Starbucks' good name. Why not? Schultz fears that if he grows too fast, he'll lose control over quality and tarnish his company's upscale image. That's why you won't see Starbucks coffee being sold in a 7-Eleven.

And just where will Starbucks be in the not-too-distant future? Says President Orin Smith: "We're going to have to look more at opportunities to grow earnings, at how to manage the bottom line, not the top line. We're looking for efficiencies in manufacturing and distribution. We're reengineering."

Wait a minute. Did he say earnings, bottom line, efficiency, reengineering? One of the most amazing growth companies of the era plans to focus more on the bottom line? But is that really so surprising? The businesses that thrive over the long haul are likely to be those that understand that cost cutting and revenue growing aren't mutually exclusive. Eternal vigilance to both the top and bottom lines is the new ticket to prosperity.

VISION STATEMENTS THAT MAKE SENSE

BY THOMAS A. STEWART

◆◆◆

Most corporate visions are so fuzzy, you
should drive with corrective lenses.
Here's a way to see better.

◆◆◆

Ah, vision. Last thing on Lou Gerstner's mind. Achilles' heel of George Bush. Great topic between rounds of golf on a weekend off-site—justifies the tax deduction without taxing the brain.

Vision is a squishy subject that makes executives squirm. "There is a fine line," a CEO once told consultant Ram Charan, "between vision and hallucination." Visions are Big, Important Stuff everyone's supposed to subscribe to. The easiest way to do that is to drain them of substance so nothing remains to disagree with. Most visions boil down to "Go, team, go!"

Actually, "Go, team, go" implies the right questions: "Where?" and "Who, me?" Forget about "doves appearing from heaven," says Robert Frisch, a vice president of Gemini Consulting; a vision should describe what's happening to the world you compete in, and what you want to do about it. It should guide decisions.

Frisch has a way to develop corporate vision that's very smart. Because it's deliberately "pedestrian," he calls it vision engineering. In the past year he and his colleagues have done it with Bridgestone/Firestone, Norsk Hydro, Sears, U.S. Cellular, and others. It's orderly, sensible, and intellectually engaging.

Often, Frisch says, companies working up vision statements begin by identifying their constituents (customers, employees, etc.), the markets they serve, the pieces of the value chain (manufacturing, wholesale, retail, and so on) they most covet, and how their portfolio of businesses matches them. That's too "inside" for Frisch. It leads quickly into disputed territory: Marketing pushes for new lines of business, manufacturing wants to stick to its last; with no empirical basis for resolving the dispute, the twain never meet, so the train never leaves the station. Other times, visioneers do scenario planning, spinning out visions of the future based on competing assumptions. Useful, Frisch agrees, but it's dessert. The logic of scenarios ultimately leads you to make bets based on uncertainties. Preparing for the unexpected has a place, but it comes after preparing for the expected.

When the executive team enters the room where Gemini is doing vision engineering, they'll find a long table at one end bearing perhaps 100 stacks of cards. Printed on the cards in each stack is a single fact or trend, demographic, social, technological, economic: Baby boomers are reaching 50; work schedules are more flexible; the power of microprocessors will continue to increase exponentially; Americans save less than 5% of personal income. Some are industry specific: A beverage maker's executives found a card stating that store brands are becoming more important. They'll all be true, based on the consultants' research, advice from outside experts, and industry trends the executives themselves have identified.

Now the fun part: Everybody walks around the long table studying the cards, the purpose being to string sets of them together and put headlines on the strings. You might take increased use of credit cards + growing value of brand equity + rising number of Internet users + ability to use technology to do specific market-segmentation. Q.E.D.: It's possible to bypass retailers to sell branded merchandise on the Web.

When everyone has taped a few strings and headlines to the wall, small groups debate, edit, and perhaps combine them. The groups then report to the whole for another round of debate. When this phase—the first of three—is done, the team ought to have half a dozen to a dozen headlines. Each tells a story about something happening in their business world—trends they agree are real and important and that, moreover, have an audit trail back to a set of facts.

Frisch calls them "drivers of change" and grabs a metaphor: "They are waves coming toward the shore. Some are bigger than others, but they are all headed toward us. We can either build a surfboard to ride them, or let them crash over us." Frisch's method has a big payoff: Because leaders aren't just told what experts say but derive and debate the trends themselves, they're less likely to harbor "yes, but" reservations. They get achieved rather than received wisdom.

That was of enormous value to Bridgestone/Firestone, which sold $5.6 billion of tires in the Western Hemisphere a couple of years ago. When Japanese tire giant Bridgestone bought Firestone in 1988, management focused on fixing the manufacturing guts of the place—cutting costs, upgrading quality and plants. Management information systems took a back seat. When those moved to the fore, executives figuratively blanched: A new information system might cost as much as $100 million—an investment that couldn't be made wisely without a vision of the industry's future.

Says Michael Gorey, controller of U.S. tire operations: "We realized we needed to go somewhere, but where that somewhere was, we didn't know." When Bridgestone/Firestone's three dozen top executives gathered for the first of two meetings, Gorey says, "the room was full of factions and functions, each with its own ideas of the major business influences and trends."

It was a triumph, then, when the group agreed on ten key business influences; the list itself is confidential, but not the consensus that technology will reshape how tire companies go to market, compel them to share more information (for example, about inventories) with buyers, and also help the factories forecast and schedule production—in short, a bigger deal than most had realized, with implications that both sides of the house could exploit.

Bridgestone/Firestone's surprise is no surprise. Frisch finds that companies usually identify major forces of change that aren't in any way addressed by their plans. In one stunning instance, a company's executives agreed that their industry was on the road to restructuring—but they had no plans to be the perpetrators rather than the victims of what they all saw coming.

Realizations like that come out of the second and third phases of vision engineering. Phase two asks leaders to figure out how each incoming wave affects each link of the value chain—from R&D to service—for every line of business. These disruptions amount to a list of threats and opportunities, and lead directly to the third phase: a disciplined look at the capabilities and assets the company has or must get if it's to dodge the threats, exploit the opportunities, and ride the waves of change.

You're almost home. Remember the stuff about key constituents, markets, the value chain, and the portfolio? Now's the time to bring that up. With a shared view of the world, Frisch argues, "you can make practical decisions instead of having theoretical discussions." When politics makes its inevitable appearance—for example, when a powerful vice president sees his duchy is threatened—you can battle with facts instead of testosterone.

This isn't soul-stirring stuff. It's better: You get a cluster of opportunities supported by a set of existing and to-be-developed assets, bounded by a realistic view of how your world is changing. Better still, you've also justified the tax deduction.

MAKING DIVERSITY PAY

BY KENNETH LABICH

◆◆◆

Managing a varied work force takes
new skills, but some diversity "training"
has been useless, even abusive.
Now some smart companies are finding
novel solutions.

◆◆◆

Few artifacts of corporate life carry more heft than a new chief executive's first companywide memo. So when Procter & Gamble Chairman John Pepper's initial message to the troops landed, the ripples predictably spread fast and far. The memo's subject wasn't the usual blabber about competitive strategy or cost cutting. Instead Pepper wrote about work force diversity, and declared with gusto that under its new boss, P&G would continue to work hard to promote the careers of people of both sexes, all ages, and many hues.

Pepper's stance was a sign that he and his company are facing up to one of today's most significant management challenges: dealing with the demographic realities of a changing labor force. Academic experts quibble over the hard numbers, but within a decade or so the U.S. work force will be far older and more heterogeneous than ever before. Nearly half of all workers will be women, and more than a quarter will likely be members of minority races. About 40% of the work force will be over 45 years of age—a dramatic jump from 31% in 1996—and only about 15% of new entrants will be the young white males once the main engine of American commerce.

No one really disputes that diversity is an important issue. *Ad nauseam* it's been argued that those companies that understand how to manage a diverse work force will have an edge in attracting the best talent. But there's another, equally compelling reason to take the issue seriously. Simply put, a company with a diverse work force will have an easier time serving markets that themselves are becoming more multicultural. Says Barbara Stern, a vice president at the managed-care organization Harvard Pilgrim Health Care: "With the customer base changing so rapidly, we are talking more and more about a diversity imperative within our company."

CASE STUDIES AND ACCOUNTABILITY

How do you build a diverse work force? First, realize that you'll likely encounter plenty of resistance. Many companies try to surmount cultural barriers to diversity through training. Yet there are gaping pitfalls to avoid here. For several years, the U.S. Department of Transportation provided perhaps the most egregious example of how not to conduct diversity training. In the name of exposing racial and sexual prejudices, employees were subjected to what amounted to psychological abuse. The sessions, finally suspended in 1993, included a gantlet where men were ogled and fondled by women. Blacks and whites were encouraged to exchange racial epithets, people were tied up together for hours, and some were forced to strip down to their underwear in front of co-workers.

In sharpest contrast, the best sort of diversity training emphasizes practical conflict management. No one series of workshops will be ideal for every organization, but the most effective training methods seem to revolve around the daily problems workers face. For example, diversity training at Harvard Pilgrim Health Care includes a heavy dose of real-life case studies. Participants are presented with quandaries like this one: A patient, an elderly white man, must have a blood test. When a black clinician appears to give the test, the patient balks. Does the office manager bow to the patient's wishes or politely assert the company's right to say only the black employee will draw the blood? "The case is about how people can react to cultural and racial differences," says Harvard Pilgrim's Stern. "At healthy organizations, people learn to respond to these differences with sensitivity and respect."

Besides training, senior managers have to wrestle with the question of accountability—just who's responsible for fostering a diverse work force? At P&G, Pepper emphasizes long-term career planning as the best way to retain talented women and minorities. He tells his line managers to map out a multi-assignment path that will enrich budding stars—and to share the plan with the employees in question. "So often, people don't know how you feel about them until it's too late," he says.

WHERE IS YOUR WORK FORCE COMING FROM?

———————————◆———————————

A nother concern, often overlooked, is the physical workplace. Fail to adapt your workplace to your labor force, and you could sacrifice quality and productivity. The growing cadre of older workers presents a hatful of ergonomic problems. In factories, lighting may need to be brighter and warning signals louder. In an office setting, computer keyboards should be large enough to deal with the loss of fine motor skills, and workstations should be sufficiently isolated to cut down on background noise.

Whatever the setting, older workers present a range of special management challenges. In a recent study of over-50 workers commissioned by the American Association of Retired Persons, oldsters at 12 companies of different size, industry, and geographic location rated highly for such things as experience, judgment, and commitment to quality. They scored poorly on flexibility, acceptance of new technology, and ability to learn new skills—the very traits considered most desirable for today's workplace.

But experts have come up with methods to compensate for older workers' reluctance to embrace change. Earl Hunt, a University of Washington psychology professor with an interest in the field, says that training must be adjusted to meet the needs of older workers, who he says learn differently from younger ones. Says Hunt: "The point for management is understanding where the work force is at before you try to move it where you want." Paula Rayman, executive director of the Radcliffe College Public Policy Institute, argues that companies ought to discover ways to better utilize and maximize veterans' store of knowledge. A salesman who has been a road warrior for 30 years may be slowing down—so switch him to a job training new salespeople or working with R&D to develop products for the customers he knows so well.

As the labor force ages, companies may become less inclined to force the fiftysomething set to take early retirement. At Dana Corp., the Ohio auto-parts giant, human-resources officials have actually been looking at ways to entice experienced retirees back to the job. One idea: offering a prorated benefits package to lure older workers back part-time. Tactics like prorating benefits could also appeal to other members of a diverse work force like mothers of school-age children.

Far more than in the past, says Jose Berrios, vice president for diversity at Gannett, astute managers have to concern themselves with employees' lives outside the workplace. You've got to know if someone's performance is slipping because of worries about the quality of the day-care center, or be ready to step in and offer the company's resources if a worker is bedeviled by a troubled teenager at home. Not all of today's workers can isolate family problems from the job. Berrios sees immediate and long-term payoffs for organizations that maintain an enlightened attitude toward work and family issues: "First, it costs a lot more to replace effective employees who are temporarily distracted by personal matters. And in the long run, the companies that handle these problems extremely well will become the employers of choice in an ever tighter labor market."

At the core of managing a more diverse work force, says P&G's John Pepper, is finding a way to make people of every type feel connected to their company. Pepper recalls doing an exit interview with a talented African-American manager a few years back. The job was great in virtually all aspects, said the man, but P&G just didn't seem like a place where he could ever feel comfortable. Says Pepper: "I realized then and there that I, as a white male, had never felt like that. And I also realized that gaining the loyalty of all employees— every one of them—has to be integral to how a company meets it goals. We've never been in a world where we needed it more."

WHY DUMB THINGS HAPPEN TO SMART COMPANIES

BY THOMAS A. STEWART

You've hired the smartest people and you're spending tons on R&D and customer service, yet you keep blowing it. Time to look at how you manage brainpower.

Few people quarrel with the notion that companies must learn to invest in and manage knowledge if they hope to compete in an economy where, more than ever, knowledge is what we buy and sell. But how, they wonder, does one make the case for managing intellectual capital to CEOs and CFOs? And where do we start?

The two questions are cousins, since the best way to build support for any management effort is to start where you'll get early results. Mind you, the forgotten key to succeeding in management is to not stop there; quitting too soon condemns you to the hummingbird style of management, forever flitting and sipping from one blooming idea to another.

But you've got to start somewhere, and here's a way to figure out where: a list of nine symptoms of a "knowledge problem"—something wrong with how your company manages its brainpower. The list comes from David H. Smith, head of knowledge development for Unilever, the giant maker of ice cream, soaps and detergents, frozen foods, and personal products. Smith, who has a background in both information technology and business, was given the task of "helping Unilever act more intelligently"—that is, learn faster and leverage what it knows.

Like Lyme disease, knowledge problems have symptoms that sometimes mimic other problems, more benign or even more malign. But each of the following, says Smith, is a symptom that suggests that you don't manage knowledge well: People aren't finding it, moving it around, keeping it refreshed and up to date, sharing it, or using it.

◆ **You repeat mistakes.** "Your best teacher is your last mistake," Ralph Nader once told me. He, of course, has made a career out of publicizing companies that display this knowledge problem. It's rampant. The nature of icebergs being what it is, for every million-dollar lawsuit there must be tens of millions lost or wasted from repeated mistakes that are dumb but not tortious.

Why does it happen? Fear, I'd guess, is the No. 1 reason: fear of being embarrassed, chewed out, or worse. Many people and companies are so busy trying to hide boners (from the boss, from stock analysts, from customers and competitors) that they tuck away the learning along with the evidence.

You don't, obviously, want to encourage goofs just to learn from them. But the best way to avoid repeated errors is to study failure as assiduously as success. The history of medicine shows that you can learn as much from autopsies as you can from cures.

◆ **You duplicate work.** "Reinventing the wheel" is the inevitable phrase, and most companies spend so much time doing it you would think they were suppliers for Schwinn. A classic example: You inspect the goods before you ship them, and your customer inspects them again after they arrive. Worse, you do the same thing in-house. Usually the underlying cause is a knowledge problem: Customer and supplier either don't know what each expects of the other, or they don't trust each other because they haven't shared processes or results.

People fail to copy success for the same reasons that they succeed in copying mistakes: They're afraid or embarrassed to ask. Sometimes the problem is in systems and structures: They don't know where to look or looking takes too much time or they have no place to store corporate memory. Sometimes the problem is what one might call an overdeveloped engineer's mind: I know Eddie already did this, but I can do it better.

◆ **You have poor customer relations.** If you're not selling schlock, why does a customer get peevish? Probably for one of three reasons, all knowledge problems. First, communication at the point of sale: Either he didn't understand what you were selling or you didn't understand what she was buying. Second, service: If I get the runaround when I have a problem, chances are the people who answer your 800 number are little more than switchboard operators, who don't know what they should.

The third reason is subtler and more interesting. Knowledge work tends to be custom work, or at least customized. That changes the nature of the transaction. You don't sell janitorial services the same way you sell mops. Too often salespeople are in a hurry to hear "yes" so they can write up the order. (Too often their incentives encourage that practice.) Result: You talked about the sale but not the deal.

◆ *Good ideas don't transfer between departments, units, or countries.* This is the most common knowledge problem of all: How do we get people to share ideas rather than hoard them, to accept ideas rather than reject them? There's no easy answer. Here's a starter kit:

Set an example: Great bosses love teaching; great teachers produce great students. Once, interviewing AlliedSignal CEO Larry Bossidy, I confessed not knowing what working capital was. Bossidy positively lit up, grabbed a sheet of paper, scooted around the table, and taught me; his pleasure in teaching turned an interview into a sharing of minds.

Nudge: Nothing will get the troops to use the Lotus Notes database faster than a leader who asks at a staff meeting, "I'd like to hear everyone's thoughts on Kay's posting about the situation in Germany. Bill, let's start with you: What do you think we should do?"

Create incentives: Says Robert Buckman, CEO of specialty-chemical maker Buckman Laboratories: "The most powerful incentives you have are salaries and promotions." Buckman makes sure—and makes it known—that he hands them out based substantially on how well people share and borrow ideas.

Benchmark: Be sure Phoenix knows it has twice as much bad debt as Dayton—and reward both if they close the gap.

Make it fun: When you return from a convention, which do you write up first, your expense account or your trip report? Which contains more creative thinking? Which is read more attentively? One group at Monsanto makes knowledge sharing fun by arming people with snazzy new Kodak digital cameras when they go on trips; when they get back, they show their pictures at the next staff meeting.

◆ **You're competing on price.** No company wants to find itself in a commodity business. What makes the difference? Why could an executive in General Electric's lighting business—light bulbs, for Pete's sake—tell me, in a mock-serious tone, "Cutting prices is not a core value of the General Electric Co.," while some companies making computers—computers, for Pete's sake—are forced to do just that?

The answer is almost always knowledge, or the lack of it. Whatever you sell, you can get out of the price game if you and your customer ride the learning curve together. Everything you learn about a customer—from how he likes pallets stacked to what his plans are—is an opportunity to make it harder for competitors to horn in. The result: margin.

◆ **You can't compete with market leaders.** Sometimes the big guys win because they've got something you ain't got, like prime-rate loans or Super Bowl–size ad budgets. But don't blame your problems on scale until you have explored this question: What do they know that we don't know? Toyota, Wal-Mart, and Southwest Airlines are just three examples of formerly small companies that outwitted bigger competitors.

◆ **You're dependent on key individuals.** Nothing's more dangerous than depending on a few key people. Usually this signals too little teamwork or an absence of ways to encourage star performers to reveal the secrets of their success.

Note, though: The fault may not lie in your stars. Sometimes people have greatness thrust upon them because others are unwilling to achieve it themselves. Hewlett-Packard's CEO Lew Platt says, "You've got a knowledge problem when decisions are made too high in the organization." When things come to Platt's desk that shouldn't, he takes it as a sign that people lack knowledge that would let them think for themselves.

◆ **You're slow to launch new products or enter new markets.** It's obvious that being slow to market is a knowledge problem. But diagnosing its cause can be tricky; as with referred pain, the source may be far from the symptom. It could be a weak lab, a sludge-slowed commercialization process, a rigid budget bureaucracy, failure of competitor and market intelligence, or something else.

◆ ***You don't know how to price for service.*** Do you build the cost of service into your price? Sell a service contract? Bill by the hour, the day, the job? Let someone in the distribution channel handle it? Can you clearly explain why you do what you do, or are you just following industry practice?

The underlying knowledge problem is least self-evident in this symptom. Here it is: If you don't know how to price for service or why to charge one way vs. another, it's a sign that you don't fully understand what your customers do with whatever you sell them. Some customers just buy on price. More often, however, they are buying the solution to a problem. They don't want drills; they want holes. If you know what customers are really paying for, you'll know better who should pay what.

Smith's list is diagnostic, not prescriptive. But each item on it is a knowledge problem with real business consequences that even a skeptical boss will want to fix. It's a start.

SIX WAYS TO SUPERCHARGE YOUR CAREER

BY ANNE FISHER

◆◆◆

*Will you ever get promoted? Yes, if you
understand the new rules of the career game.
The cardinal principle: Forget about titles
and turfs—it's what you know
(and how you use it) that really counts.*

◆◆◆

Let's indulge, briefly, in a New Age visualization exercise. It has a point that even non-Californians can appreciate. Close your eyes, and picture an object that embodies the word "career." If you joined the work force, say, 15 or 20 or 25 years ago, you probably visualize your working life as a predictable series of narrow and distinctly separate rungs that lead straight up (or down)—in other words, a ladder. Well, my friend, the ladder has been chopped up into little pieces and dumped in the garbage pile. A team of sanitation engineers disposed of it at dawn, while you were dreaming.

This development has left lots of people groping for new ways to picture a career path. Is today's career a flexible, expandable web that can be torn down and rebuilt elsewhere? Or is it a toolbox filled with skills that you carry anywhere to ply your craft? Perhaps work is just an ever-widening circle of influence.

Whatever metaphor you prefer, the old days of empire building are gone. You remember, the time when you were rewarded for managing more people. You could sit around, be a good organization man, and practically be handed a new title every few years. But after a decade of well-publicized reengineering, cost cutting, outsourcing, flattening of organizations, and consolidating of industries, the number of managerial jobs has shrunk, and so has the opportunity for old-fashioned promotions.

In the new game people float from project to project, from team to team. Job definitions become blurred, titles become almost meaningless. What matters is what you know, how well you apply it to the business (your "value added," as management wonks put it), and how much you get paid. Those who play this game well are the ones most likely to rise up and grab one of those increasingly scarce—and lucrative—jobs atop the company.

Yes, it's true. Despite all the flattening, companies still have a top level. If you're hoping to get to the top in this lifetime, you need to concentrate on six essential things, all very different from what you used to have to do to get promoted: Love what you do, which entails first figuring out who you are. Never stop learning. Try to get some international experience. Create new business opportunities that could lead to a promotion. Expect more raises and fewer fancy new titles. And—here's the big one—be really outstandingly terrific at what you're doing now, this week, this month.

There's a practical reason for loving what you do: If you don't love it, you won't be fabulous enough to compete with those who do. "The passionate ones are the ones who will go the extra mile, do the extra work, come up with the fresh, outside-the-box idea," says Phyllis Woods, a senior consultant at Drake Beam Morin in Seattle. "So to get ahead today, your first question shouldn't be, 'What are the hot jobs now?' It should be, 'What can I get passionate about?'"

If you're like most of us, you never really had the chance to stop and think about it. Harold Weinstein, CEO of Caliper, a human-resources consulting firm, puts it this way: "Are you sociable, outgoing, self-confident, persuasive? Then what on earth are you doing as a programming analyst? Because you were good at this computer stuff in college? Forget that. You probably ought to be selling computers, not programming them." So, take the time to decide what you're passionate about. Once you know what you really like doing, say Weinstein and others, go for it.

If you're already pretty charged up about your current work but still aren't getting ahead, the problem might not be who you are but rather what you know—or don't know. The specific skills that lead to top jobs change every few years. In 1989, for instance, Korn/Ferry International surveyed hundreds of CEOs around the globe and found that the surest route to the top was through the finance department. The bosses viewed international experience as strictly optional. Marketing was Nowheresville. But in a 1996 survey, marketing took top honors, with 37% of CEOs stressing its importance as a career booster. International expertise came in second, with finance—surprise!—a distant third.

Since, as the Korn/Ferry research suggests, so-called key competencies are hard to predict five or ten years in advance, it makes sense to get as many different kinds of experience as you can. How? Paul Otellini, executive VP and director of worldwide sales and marketing for Intel, is gung-ho on both overseas assignments and broadening one's own skill base at home. He's right. A study by Organization Resources Counselors analyzed the loftiest tiers of management at 20 successful U.S. companies and found that nine out of ten of the top dogs had done overseas stints. Says Otellini: "If you want to understand the global economy, there's no substitute for being there." You don't necessarily have to sell the house and pull the kids out of school. More and more companies are sending U.S. managers overseas for specific projects that last anywhere from three months to a year. That means it's less likely that the people back home at headquarters will have forgotten your name by the time you come back.

As for hopping across functional boundaries to get different kinds of experience, Otellini likens Intel's approach to "a flea market. First, go and find the thing you like doing." Then work for small, temporary teams that come together to work on specific projects, so that a manufacturing person gets to work closely with, say, a marketing expert and a finance guy. If you're hell-bent on hands-on experience in an unfamiliar area (marketing, maybe?), most companies offer ways of getting it. It's up to you to seek out those career opportunities.

You should also seek business opportunities inside your company. There is no better way to kick-start a career than acting like an entrepreneur. If you simply follow the rules, do your job well, and wait to get promoted, it could be a very long wait. Instead, why not help yourself get promoted—either by starting a new line of business, spearheading an acquisition, or providing your company with some important new service?

That's exactly what P.J. Smoot, head of training and development at International Paper, did. When she joined International Paper in 1980, she was in the finance department. While there, she noticed a need for career development and training. So she wrote a proposal to the HR department, where they liked it so much, they hired her to put her ideas into practice. What started as an 18-month assignment has evolved into a full-fledged companywide training program. Smoot, who oversees the progam, has since won six promotions—all because she saw a way to help her company and then acted on it.

Although Smoot is making a lot more money than when she started with International Paper, only two people report to her. She is rewarded not for the size of her empire but for her value to the company. This is called "broadbanding," an increasingly popular trend in compensation. Broadbanding replaces the old career-ladder rungs with wider and more flexible job categories. People are rewarded based on what they contribute to the business, not on what their business card reads. According to the latest research by compensation consultants like Towers Perrin and Sibson & Co., some variation of a pay-for-knowledge plan is probably coming soon to your company.

Depending on your temperament, your energy level, and the limits on your imagination, seeing the old career ladder hit the junk heap either exhilarates you or scares you half to death. (Many people experience both reactions at once.) But some things never change, and here is one of them: If you really want to get ahead, be the best there is at what's in front of you right now—that's right, on your desk or your computer screen this very minute. "Everybody's always looking for a magic bullet, but you know, there isn't any, really," says Gerry Roche at Heidrick & Struggles. "We want to figure out who's doing a really super job running projects day to day. That's who we'll go after for big opportunities elsewhere."

JOB SURFING: HOW TO MOVE ON TO MOVE UP

BY JUSTIN MARTIN

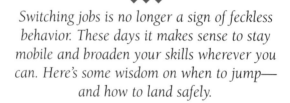

Switching jobs is no longer a sign of feckless behavior. These days it makes sense to stay mobile and broaden your skills wherever you can. Here's some wisdom on when to jump— and how to land safely.

David Friedensohn enjoys running marathons and loves to surf, but jockeying for promotion—well, that's not exactly his idea of sport. He's just not a one-company kind of guy. Over the past decade Friedensohn has worked for four different employers, Citicorp and Viacom among them, and has done a stint as a self-employed consultant.

But don't write Friedensohn off as a fickle job hopper. He could be the poster boy for a new style of career management—one that has evolved in an era of pancake-flat corporate hierarchies. These days, if you find yourself blocked, or no longer learning and growing, you may simply have to change jobs to give yourself a promotion. That's not necessarily an easy task. You'll want to develop instincts to determine when to stick around and when to flee. If you decide it's time to go, a firm grasp of job-search fundamentals, such as networking and using recruiters, will be essential.

First, the question of when to make a move. The key here is to make sure you are divining the clues in your workplace correctly. Look for telltale signs regarding your own fate. Key questions to ask: Am I being given choice assignments? Do others seek my input on major decisions? Am I getting more or less positive feedback than in the past?

Scrutinize your workplace relationships too. As a simple exercise, think about whether your boss actually likes you—not just respects your work, not just depends on you, but actually likes you. Bosses, no matter how seemingly professional, impartial, and meritocratic, still tend to look out for those they genuinely like. And what about your peers? "Popularity counts a lot," says Kate Wendleton, president of the Five O'Clock Club, a job-search strategy firm. "If you get along with your peers, then your promotion would be a popular move."

Always expand the scope of your inquiry. How about the organization itself? What is its reputation with competitors, Wall Street, key customers? Remember, there's a right place/right time factor when it comes to promotions. You can be doing well, but if your company isn't, your advancement may be hindered. Big events such as mergers, restructurings, or a new CEO can be early warning signals that it's time to leave.

Weigh all the factors regularly. Career counselors recommend that you set aside a time, maybe once a year, to assess your situation on a more formal basis. This should be separate from the annual performance review provided by most companies. Think of it as a personal performance review, when you decide whether the outlook is good at your own company or whether it's about time to promote yourself by switching firms.

Don't hold off your search until you've sunk to the deepest level of workplace hell. Often it's good to make a move when you're on top. Success begets success. When your current employment picture is rosy, you just naturally exude confidence. Your judgment tends to be sounder, because you're considering new opportunities from the healthiest standpoint.

The key point is that you have to remain supple, ready to take a leap into the unknown. Consider lateral moves into faster-growing companies. Be willing to take a step backward even, if two steps forward seem likely down the line. Look to big companies for the credentials and professional polish they can provide, but don't rule out going to a smaller firm where you might be challenged by greater responsibility. Always try to be open-minded about your career, thinking about how to expand your skill set. In short, consider all options.

LET THE JOB HUNT BEGIN

And when it begins, you may need to rethink some old job-search notions. Yes, use the three basic sources of information on new jobs—classified ads, personal contacts, and recruiters. But there are some new tricks in the job-search game. Spend some time on the Internet, where you may be able to find dozens of useful job sites. There are multitudes of places to post your résumé, and many companies run job listings at their Websites.

Many folks also don't really understand how to use personal contacts in their hunt. Prime networking venues tend to be social occasions such as parties and dinners, but don't go in with a languid attitude. Talking sports or producing idle weather chatter is not net-working.The trick is to be very directed. You can appear casual, but know exactly what you're after.

It's probably unwise to be too obvious or intense about it; you wouldn't want to seem desperate. But you might do research before-hand by reading recent news clippings on a target company, look-ing at its annual report, or visiting its Internet home page. Show up prepared, with questions in mind about things you want to know: What's it like to work at Company X? Does the big account it just won spell an opportunity to climb on board? Follow-up is crucial too. During that initial conversation, your contact simply may not know of a job for you.

RECRUIT YOUR RECRUITER

For many job hunters, working with recruiters can be very mysterious. To begin, reputable recruiters never charge job candidates for their services under any circumstance. Recruiters work for the client company, which pays them on completion of a successful search. Bear in mind that recruiters tend to be specialists, often working exclusively in one narrow niche like financial services or high tech. If you belong to any professional or trade organizations, check to see whether they've endorsed a particular recruiter. Also, talk to former colleagues who've moved to new companies to find out who placed them. Don't be turned off if the first couple of recruiters you talk to aren't helpful; they may simply be looking for different types at that particular moment.

The goal is to get yourself on the radar screen for future searches, and one good way to do that is to increase your visibility. Write an article for a trade publication, speak at industry conferences—anything to make yourself a target for headhunters. You can stay popular with recruiters by suggesting names of other people at your company who might fit their search criteria. Such helpful acts will not be forgotten.

Of course, you have little control over when recruiters call. That's why it's good to try to form relationships before you actually need their services. The essential rule: Whenever recruiters call, always make time to talk—even if the job they are currently peddling isn't for you.

Conduct your search diligently, using some of the methods described above, and you will likely land some promising interviews. But the battle is far from won at that point. Before any interview, think about the questions you're likely to be asked, particularly the tough ones, and practice answering. For many potential job hoppers, the deal-breaker question may be: "Why do you want to leave your current employer?" Try to accentuate the positive, stressing your desire to move toward the new company over your desire to get away from your current employer.

Once you've made a move, that doesn't mean you can let your guard down. With company tenure averaging around five years, you can expect to change employers a number of times dur-

TEST FOR SUCCESS

◆◆◆

To stay or not to stay—*that is the question. Use the first part of this quiz to figure out whether you're in line for a promotion. If not, the second part will help you determine if it's time to make a move.*

WILL I GET PROMOTED SOON?

If your answer is YES, add...

1. Is your company doing well? Is it posting good financial results, drumming up new business, hiring and promoting others? **10 points____**

2. Do you get choice assignments? Are you put on projects that showcase your talents? Are you pushed to learn new things and increase your skills? **10 points____**

3. Are you popular? Does your boss like you? Do you like your boss? Are you getting along well with your peers? **10 points____**

4. Is your input solicited? Are you included in key meetings? Do people come to you with questions about matters outside your usual domain? **5 points____**

5. Do you have the skills? Can you take the next logical step in your company right now without further training or experience? **5 points____**

6. Are you golden with the grapevine? Do others drop hints that you're in good standing? Hear any rumors that your boss likes your work? **5 points____**

7. Have you groomed a successor? Were you to be promoted, is there someone who could step into your job right away? **5 points____**

If you scored 40 or higher, start thinking about how to decorate that corner office. You're primed for a promotion. 25 to 40—stay tuned. Less than 25, move to part two of this quiz. **Total points_____**

IS IT TIME TO MOVE ON?

1. *Have you stopped learning?* Are you getting stale? Do you no longer get the chance to increase your skills and broaden your experience?

10 points____

2. *Has your status slipped?* Are exchanges with your boss becoming increasingly one-sided? Do you feel you have less freedom to act than in the past?

10 points____

3. *Is your company faltering?* Has it lost market share, taken a major hit on its stock price? Has it been sharply criticized by Wall Street, the press, or its own employees?

10 points____

4. *Are big changes on the horizon?* Has your company merged with another recently? Any kind of major organizational restructuring under way? Have new high-level executives come in from the outside?

5 points____

5. *Are you out of the loop?* Have you stopped hearing gossip? Do you feel you're the last to know about key decisions?

5 points____

6. *Do you dread going to work?* Are you anxious on Sunday nights? Have your eating and sleeping habits changed? Do friends and family comment that you look tired or seem unhappy?

5 points____

7. *Is your salary stagnating?* Are your raises on a downward trend percentage-wise?

5 points____

If you scored 40 *or higher, take a deep breath; then start your search immediately!* 25 *to* 40—*put out feelers. Less than* 25; *your situation may improve, but remain open to outside opportunities.*

**Total
points_____**

ing the course of your career. And in today's competitive climate, companies tend to throw new recruits directly into the fray. You've got to be ready to go from zero to 60 instantly. Happy surfing.

THE GREAT CONUNDRUM— YOU VS. THE TEAM

BY THOMAS A. STEWART

◆◆◆

You're supposed to be a team player.
You're also supposed to look out for
No. 1. How can you do both?

◆◆◆

Squatting between the lines of the "new contract" between employer and employee is an ugly and befuddling contradiction. You know what the new contract says: We, your employer, no longer offer or even imply a guarantee of employment—you're here only as long as we need you. Instead, we offer you employability— stick with us, kid, and we'll reward you well, and when we dissolve the bonds, no hard feelings, no stigma, no problem. Plenty of people will want you because you picked up valuable skills here. Two birds in the bush are worth one in the hand.

That's the deal; here's the contradiction. On the one hand, you're on your own. You're responsible for your career. You're the CEO of "You Inc." in an every-man-for-himself universe of individual initiative and reward; whatever color your parachute is, you sew it and pack it yourself. Ah, but on the other hand, folks here at ol' Amalgamated don't cotton to self-aggrandizement. We want team players, all for one and one for all, because we're a team and we work in teams. Teams may hire their own members, manage their own work, receive rewards as a group, and parcel them out to members according to their collective view of each person's contribution to the group's enterprise. Of the skills you learn here, the most valuable is teamwork.

So it's You Inc. vs. the Team. Says David Witte, CEO of Ward Howell International, an executive search firm: "Do we have a problem here? Oh, yeah, we got a big problem. Talk about individual responsibility—it's absolutely important. But you're part of a team—that's absolutely important. But has anybody married that?" The short answer: No, and maybe the marriage can't be made. But maybe we can find ways to help You Inc. get along in a world of teams.

Mind you, this taffy pull—toward the self, toward the team—is ancient. Under the old dispensation, however, obeisance paid. When the Organization Man subordinated his ego to the group, he got safety in return. Now you can do that and still be on the street when this project is done.

Today's teams are, well, teamier—less a metaphor and more a reality. Gone is the phony "team" where the leader tells the finance guru to run some numbers, the marketing wiz to do some research, the manufacturing maven to come up with cost and capacity data, and everyone to report back two weeks hence. These days team members are likely to work together many hours a day, mucking about in one another's specialties and jointly hammering out the final product rather than slotting together individually made components.

Why does teamwork matter more? First, the content and culture of knowledge work require it. Simple-minded work—may I offer pin-making as an example?—permits a division of labor in which people don't have to work together so long as the pieces of the system fit. But knowledge work—designing a product, writing an ad, reengineering a process—rarely moves systematically forward. It's an open-ended series of to-and-fro collaborations, iterations, and reiterations.

MAKE YOUR TEAMMATES LOOK GOOD

◆

Fly solo on these teams, and you'll be ostracized so fast one would think you'd been caught wiping your nose on the tablecloth at Lutèce. The ethos is to make your teammates look good, not to make sure the boss knows how much you contributed. Him you can fool, but your teammates value only substance. "Shark skills are not appreciated," says George Bailey, a Price Waterhouse consultant who is an expert on teams. "Dolphins beat up on sharks." The cult(ure) of teamwork helps explain why people give themselves self-effacing titles like "facilitator" and "coach" instead of "boss" or "leader."

If knowledge work depends on teams, it makes sense to reward them, not individuals. People who move from project to project cannot be paid according to the number of direct reports they have any more than a road warrior can flaunt her status by the number of windows her office has. Top industrial-design firm Ideo Product Development is a good example. Ideo's performance reviews used to be done by a person's boss and two peers of the employee's own choosing, but that system, offbeat though it was, had to be scrapped a couple of years ago when the company realized that for many employees it was impossible to identify a boss. Now people pick two peers plus one from a slate of six "management types." According to Tom Kelley, people tend to pick demanding evaluators: "The culture says don't pick softies, because this is about improving performance, not about getting ahead."

This kind of teamwork can be very seductive to the individual. At work or on the playing fields of Eton, everyone has experienced transcendental teamwork, a sweet spot of accomplishment and fellow-feeling. When it's working, says Ward Howell's Witte, "the more you contribute, the more other people promote you. It is inspiring." Out at Boeing, people on the teams that make the 777 jetliner weep when one of those babies rolls out of the hangar. "Hot groups," emeritus Stanford business professor Harold J. Leavitt calls them. While they last they can make you think, if your mind inclines this way, that Rousseau was right: In the state of nature we were noble savages, none better than any other, free adherents to a social contract, and if we could only extirpate hierarchy we could return to that paradisiacal place of mutual and reciprocal fraternity.

AMBITION IS GETTING ON THE COOLEST PROJECTS

Teams can do extraordinary work, but it's a dicey proposition to put You Inc.'s fate in collectivist hands. Teams are often inhospitable to oddballs and to some forms of ambition. Says Ideo's Kelley: "I warn recruits, if your needs are to climb the ladder, don't come here. Ambition is about getting on the coolest projects." Peer-oriented meritocracy flourishes at Ideo, says Robert Sutton, a professor at Stanford's engineering school who is writing a book about the company. But, he cautions, it succeeds partly because the work is so complex that the hottest hotshots know they can't go it alone, and also because Ideo sits smack in the middle of Silicon Valley, where a reputation as a great teammate is the ticket to new ventures.

But there are limits. From a company's point of view, teams are of doubtful value as nurseries of executive talent, because no one knows why great teams come together or how to replicate their magic. The experience might happen once in a lifetime. By contrast, Douglas Smith, a consultant and author of *Taking Charge of Change*, says that with the old machinery of promotion and rewards, "when superiors made a judgment to move you up a grade, they could be pretty comfortable that you'd live up to their expectations." As for money, companies can rarely offer significant incentives—the kind that change your life—to reward teamwork. A smallish company of 1,000 people might have a couple of hundred teams, with many people serving on more than one. "How in the world can you ever keep track of it all?" Smith asks.

Companies always say they plump for the pack over the wolf—there's a reason it's called corporate life—but they're really looking for leadership. When Laurie Siegel, director of compensation policy at AlliedSignal, sees a great team, "I will ask, 'Was leadership what made it great?' The answer is always yes. Then I ask, 'Who were the leaders?' and it is always easy to name them." Those are the people AlliedSignal is determined to keep and to create careers for. To be sure, leaders need team skills—as Siegel puts it, "Lone Rangers or political types don't survive at this company"—but they're a means to what AlliedSignal sees as the greater end. Siegel calls it "a culture of individualism that drives team performance," a paradoxical phrase that brings us back to our problem, You Inc. vs. the Team.

So what's to do? First, Smith says, "get a life: You need team skills to succeed." You can find an argument about whether team players are products of nature or nurture, but people compete for status in any group. The "status auction" is more polite in a team culture like Ideo's, says Sutton—it might reward sharing and punish dissers or swaggerers—but it still goes on. Even a natural-born egoist can be a valued teammate and adapt to local rules.

But—second—don't believe everything you hear about teams. Take team-play rhetoric to its limits, and you'd think capitalism had spawned New Soviet Man. Look at the business plan instead. Says Witte: "If you've got a company with a 9% net profit and it needs to get to 11% or 12%, and a couple of divisions are way below average, you want someone to shake up that organization but good. A team player? Not necessarily. But if the strategy is niche acquisitions, improved customer focus, a new service organization—then you need a team builder."

Third, whatever you do, put yourself on what George Bailey calls "the shareholder value team." You ought to be able to tell a convincing story—that is, an honest one—about how your work or your team's work has increased the value of the company. If that story's true, You Inc. will be fine. If it's not, no team can help you.

CHAPTER FOUR

◆◆◆

INVESTMENT STRATEGIES FOR A SECURE FUTURE

REAL-WORLD QUESTIONS AND ANSWERS ON THE NEW TAX LAW

BY SHELLY BRANCH

◆◆◆

What does the new tax law mean for your personal fortune? Here are the questions the experts are hearing—and their solutions.

◆◆◆

As if acting on Pavlovian cue, the financial community immediately responded to the passing of the Taxpayer Relief Act with a mad scramble to pick the "winners" and "losers." However, some of those original hasty interpretations have been subject to modulation. Just ask the CPAs and planners who are busy sifting through the 900-plus pages of the act and finding many shades of "winner" in the process. "When people sit down to do their taxes," says Ed Slott, a CPA in Rockville Centre, New York, and author of *Your Tax Questions Answered*, "they'll see just how complicated all this stuff really is."

In the meantime, plenty of folks have questions. And it's smart to start asking them early: While you can put off thinking about some of the changes until 1998, others are effective immediately. Now that the blitzkrieg of big-picture coverage has faded, it's time to think through how all these new rules apply to you.

With that in mind, FORTUNE checked in with pros on the tax and planning fronts to learn the ten most common real-world questions they're hearing—and what the real-world answers are.

1. I understand that my spouse and I can sell our primary residence and escape taxes on the first $500,000 of gain. If our take exceeds that, we face a maximum capital gains rate of 20%. Is that right?

Not necessarily. "This is a good example of the proliferation of rates," says Harvey Berger, a tax partner with Grant Thornton. If you were entitled to take depreciation on any part of your home—say for a home office or a rental unit—then some of your gain will be subject to a capital gains rate of 25%. Yes, the IRS does seem hell-bent on turning regular folks into math wonks. But that's the most you can complain about, really, since a 25% levy is still an improvement over the old law, which subjected all taxable gains to a maximum rate of 28%.

2. The new Roth IRA—the one that lets me make nondeductible contributions and withdraw the principal and earnings tax-free in retirement—sounds tempting. But does it make sense to roll over my existing IRA into the Roth variety?
Let's start with some Roth basics. If you simply want to contribute to a brand-new Roth IRA, you're eligible if your adjusted gross income is less than $110,000, or if you and your spouse have an income of less than $160,000. Starting January 1, 1998, you'll be able to sock away up to $2,000 a year.

Even if you've already started building a regular IRA, a rollover may be in order. As long as your income is $100,000 or less (that's for an individual or for a couple, strangely enough), you're eligible to roll proceeds over into a Roth IRA—and doing so is often a smart move, says Glen Clemans, a financial planner in Portland, Oregon.

As an example, Clemans suggests looking at the situation of a 40-year-old with $10,000 in a traditional, deductible IRA that's earning him 10% annually. Left intact, his stash grows to $108,347 by age 65, producing a monthly after-tax income of $650. What if that same 40-year-old were instead to roll over the $10,000 into a new Roth IRA, where his account would grow in similar fashion? He'd end up with $903 per month, since withdrawals from the Roth IRA, blissfully, are tax-free.

Of course, upon taking that $10,000 distribution, our 40-year-old Roth investor has a tax bill to settle. Assuming a 28% bracket, that's $2,800. So is it worth it to spend that money in taxes now to net an extra $253 per month later? You bet, since over his lifetime, this 40-year-old stands to save more than $60,000 in taxes he would have paid on proceeds from the regular IRA. (And keep in mind that if you transfer funds by December 31, 1998, the IRS gives you four years to pay the taxes that are due, notes Ray Russolillo, a director at Price Waterhouse.)

WHAT YOU SHOULD DO UNDER THE NEW TAX LAW ...

◆◆◆

AS SOON AS POSSIBLE:

◆ *Review your will.* To accommodate the increased unified estate and gift credit, which gradually rises to $1 million by 2006, you'll want to remove any specific numeric reference to this credit as it appears in your will's trust provisions. For instance, instead of saying, "I leave in trust $600,000 ...," you might say, "I leave in trust the maximum amount under the law resulting in no tax due."

◆ *Strategize on home-sale profits.* If you sold a home between May 7 and August 5, 1997, you're in the neat position of being able to choose which tax rule works best for you. Couples can go with either the new law, which allows them to take up to $500,000 in gains tax-free, or the old rule, which permits them to roll over gains from the sale into a new home, thereby deferring taxes. The latter may work best for those trading up from mansion to palace.

BY THE END OF 1997:

◆ *Change your W-4.* If items like the child tax credit, which goes into effect next year, promise to cut your tab by $2,000 or more, you should at least consider tweaking your withholding in order to take home that extra cash instead of waiting for a refund.

◆ *Weigh the benefits of a Roth IRA,* if you qualify, and

So when does it pay to skip a rollover and the tax hit that comes with it? When you think you will be in a lower tax bracket in retirement. Invest the money you would have paid in taxes, combine it with your untouched IRA, and you come out ahead.

of rolling over sums from an existing IRA into the new account. If you do the latter, remember that the distribution from your IRA might bump you into a new tax bracket, since one-quarter of the amount will be included in your 1998 income.

◆ *Put off tuition payments.* Make payments for 1998 next year, as opposed to in late 1997. Otherwise you may lose the tuition tax credit that goes into effect next year.

BY APRIL 1998:

◆ *Know where you stand.* The glut of new capital gains rates will hit you in April 1998 if you're filing schedule D, so it pays to sort all assets according to type and holding period.

◆ *Use the best form.* You may have filled out the shorter 1040A in the past, but check to make sure it has a place for any new deductions or credits you'll be seeking in 1997 and 1998. Otherwise you might be better off using the longer 1040.

◆ *Quiz your accountant.* With all the changes, you want to make sure your preparer is proficient in the new law. You might try throwing out a few curves ("What's the phaseout for the HOPE credit?"). We're not kidding. As one tax instructor says, "The questions some of these guys ask would scare you to death."

3. If I've already used an installment sale to unload assets like real estate, at what tax rate will my future gains be taxed?
Sellers who have deferred taxes on real or personal property by using an installment sale, under which the buyer pays over a period of years,

stand to score under the new rules. That's because all future payments received are subject to the new favorable capital gains rates, down to a maximum of 20% from 28%—regardless of when the sale began. So whatever the seller's gross profit percentage (that's the amount from each installment that's subject to tax), those who have arranged for payments to balloon over time will reap the big tax savings.

4. If I open up a so-called education IRA for my child, does that limit the amount I can contribute to my regular or Roth IRAs? And what if my kid ends up running off to the circus instead of going to college?

The tax-writing folks must have been weary indeed when they came up with the "education IRA" moniker, since this turns out not to be a retirement account at all (its tax-advantaged status is similar to an IRA's, hence the name).

In any case, you'll qualify if you and your spouse have an annual income of less than $160,000. Assuming you're eligible, you can place up to $500 a year in the account. (It's not deductible.) When your child turns 18, he may make tax-free withdrawals for expenses such as tuition, room, and board. And no, this has no relationship to your own retirement accounts, so you can still contribute the maximum amounts that you and your spouse are eligible to put into regular IRAs.

Now, if Junior runs off to join Cirque de Soleil, you can transfer the account to another child. Either way, beneficiaries must use the account by age 30. If withdrawals are used for any purposes other than education, Junior eats the taxes on the account's earnings at regular income rates, plus a 10% penalty.

5. Is the deduction for student loan interest good for all outstanding college debts?

Actually, no. The deduction for student loan interest is surely good news for some grads, who saw this write-off get snatched away in the 1980s. Unfortunately, not all loans make the grade—a fact that's gone overlooked in most discussions of the measure. Only graduates repaying loans that are five years old or less may take the write-off, which is staggered from a $1,000 limit in 1998 up to $2,500 in 2001 and thereafter. Conveniently for aspiring poets and the like, this is an above-the-line deduction, meaning you won't be required to itemize to get the benefit.

6. I've been too terrified of an audit to think about taking a home-office deduction. Is it safer to do so now?

A 1993 Supreme Court ruling made it tougher for self-employed persons to qualify for this write-off—especially those who saw most of their clients or customers outside of the home office. But because the new law expands the definition of one's "principal place of business," more taxpayers should be able to claim the deduction.

"The [IRS] won't likely be attacking this one as a reflex anymore," says CPA Osofsky, who is careful to point out that these relaxed rules don't apply until 1999. Starting then, the deduction becomes legitimate for anyone who conducts the bulk of administrative and management duties from the home office, even if they don't see clients or customers there. Ideal candidates: salespersons and insurance agents.

7. Is there anything in the act that might push me into paying the dreaded alternative minimum tax?

The AMT, remember, is a separate, arcane tax system designed to strong-arm wealthy types into paying some minimum level into the Treasury. It shouldn't be any surprise, then, that certain outsize deductions are what set off the AMT alarm. But in 1998, even filers in the $70,000 income range could find themselves trapped by the alternative tax.

For when combined, items like the $400-per-child tax credit, plus deductions for local taxes, could pull the less than rich into the AMT. Annoyingly, it is almost impossible to know whether you've fallen into the AMT danger zone without having your accountant run a series of complex calculations (some computer tax programs do it for you). Generally, you might consider yourself AMT bait if your income remains the same from one year to the next, while deductions and credits soar.

8. I stand to inherit a stake in my family's business. Does the new law trim estate-tax exposure?

Sort of. While it's true that starting next year part of a family business may be excluded from a descendant's taxable estate—to the tune of $1.3 million—a closer look at the legislation reveals that there are some major snags.

For instance, the fair-market value of the business must exceed 50% of the entire estate. Also, the firm must remain in the family for at least ten years after the the decedent's demise. So if you opt to sell off Granddaddy's business prior to that, it becomes subject to stiff recapture rules, which state that all the beneficiaries (not just those who inherited the business) may be personally liable for paying estate taxes that could be as high as 55%.

Incidentally, that $1.3 million family business exclusion can't be piled atop the unified estate credit, which also rises under the new law from $600,000 to $1 million by 2006. Considered together, these two items cannot exceed $1.3 million.

9. Are there any breaks in the new tax code that married couples should be aware of?

Fact is, taxes and matrimony have never mixed well, and the new legislation only underscores that unromantic rule. The biggest inequity lurks in phaseouts for the new measures, many of which penalize the wedded state. For example, the phaseout for "education IRAs" begins at $95,000 for single parents and $150,000 for married joint filers—nowhere close to twice the single's rate.

10. There's still a lot of fine print in the new tax code. Whom should I turn to if I have more questions—a tax adviser or a financial planner?

The financial planning implications of the new tax law are being explored in earnest. And surprisingly, professionals on both the tax and planning fronts seem to be deferring to each other. "You probably don't want to change any aspect of your financial plan without at least considering the tax consequences, and vice versa," summarizes CPA Ed Slott.

You can safely ignore the reams of new general "advice" that's sure to come from mutual fund marketers. It's now increasingly important to rely on advisers who get the bigger picture. If your financial planner has been weak on taxes in the past, for example, this might be a good time to search for a new one.

THE SMART WAY TO GLOBALIZE YOUR PORTFOLIO

BY JOHN WYATT

◆◆◆

*If you limit yourself to U.S. shares,
you'll miss out on some of the world's
best stocks.*

◆◆◆

For some time now—at least since 1993, when the world's emerging markets became all the rage—the possibility of making money overseas, big money, has fired investors' imaginations. It's easy to see why: Whole groups of foreign stocks look interesting, from Europe's restructuring plays to small-cap shares in Japan.

Just one problem. Anyone who lost big in Mexico in 1994, or who sat hamstrung in a Japan fund while U.S. shares made out like Michael Johnson, knows there's more to investing overseas than meets the eye. Volatility is higher, and fluctuating currencies add risk. So how, exactly, do you make overseas investing pay off?

A report compiled by SEI, an investment advisory firm in Wayne, Pennsylvania, not only highlights the growing importance of global markets but also offers compelling tips from professional investors on how best to negotiate them. One basic bit of advice—don't delay in spreading your wealth overseas: U.S. exchanges accounted for just 35% of the world's market capitalization in mid-1996 (down from 66% in 1970). In certain industries, U.S. stocks account for only a fraction of the total. Take the auto industry, where the stocks of U.S. manufacturers add up to just 19.2% of the world's auto stock capitalization, vs. Japan's 45.6%. Limit yourself to U.S. shares, and you'll miss out on scores of the world's best stocks.

The arguments for geographic diversification are already well established: Since markets around the globe are driven largely by local factors—say, interest rates—they tend to behave independently of one another and of the U.S. Invest across a number of countries to take advantage of these differences; studies show that investors who do so enhance their portfolio's payoff while reducing risk. That is, you can load up on markets that are more volatile than

America's and actually wind up with lower overall volatility than if you held just American stocks.

Most investors struggle over how much to invest overseas. The average mutual fund buyer puts less than 7% of his portfolio in non-U.S. stocks, according to data from ICI, the mutual fund trade group. The average pension fund manager, in contrast, commits at least twice as much overseas. And after lots of analysis, SEI stakes an even more aggressive foreign claim and recommends an overall international allocation of 30% (20% in the developed markets and 10% in emerging markets). If your stomach starts to turn at that idea, find a number between zero and 30% that you feel comfortable with.

Knowing how best to position yourself in foreign markets is trickier. Not long ago, for example, all you had to know was whether to be in or out of a particular market, like France or Japan. But now these markets have flourishing subsectors, like small stocks or blue chips, or value plays or growth stocks, that can generate different returns from the overall country index's returns. Says Phil Wagner, SEI's director of international equity: "We found that differences in return within markets overseas derive almost overwhelmingly—sometimes 90% or more—from investment styles." The simple translation: Diversify money smartly, and garner bigger returns.

So how do you get smart? One way is to mix and match varying investment approaches and asset classes to complement one another. Japan, for example, is just emerging from a deep recession, and after previous downturns in 1982 and in 1987, small caps trounced big caps as the economy gained steam. But large-cap bargains abound in Europe, where the economic recovery is ahead of Japan's and where corporate management is beginning to show Yankee-like focus on shareholder value.

Fortunately, there are now many mutual funds that pursue specific market sectors, so you can narrow your bets. The total number of mutual funds investing overseas has exploded (over 900 in 1996) and the number of ADRs (which allow you to trade foreign stocks on American exchanges) is also up dramatically.

What should American investors consider when creating an international portfolio? Morningstar suggests they balance geography, big- and small-cap shares, investment styles, and industry

FOREIGN MARKETS
BOUNCE AROUND MORE ...

◆◆◆

Volatility is worse overseas, as measured by standard deviation of monthly returns from 1989 through mid-1996.

11.9% U.S.

17.1% NON-U.S.*

*EAFE and emerging markets.

BUT INVESTING OVERSEAS
DIVERSIFIES RISK ...

◆◆◆

Since overseas markets move differently from the S&P 500, they offset one another in a portfolio.

Perfect correlation with the U.S. market = 1.00*

Britain	0.55
Canada	0.46
France	0.43
Australia	0.42
Germany	0.33
Hong Kong	0.31
Indonesia	0.24
Mexico	0.19
India	0.15
Japan	0.14

*Correlations based on monthly returns from 1991 through mid-1996.

AND VALUATIONS ABROAD
ARE BETTER

◆◆◆

Price-to-book value, at a record high in the U.S., is substantially lower overseas—meaning cheaper stocks.

3.1 U.S.

Price/Book value

2.0 NON-U.S.

FORTUNE CHARTS/SOURCES: SEI; MORNINGSTAR

exposure. Like those at home, foreign funds should be top rated, boast superior performance and proven managers, and have lower levels of volatility than other funds in their peer group. Such an array will bring excitement as groups of stocks soar. And the mix will spread risk to cushion the inevitable spills.

GETTING A FIX ON BONDS

BY AMY R. KOVER

◆◆◆

The oft-overlooked world of fixed income demands a disciplined investment strategy quite different from the world of equities.

◆◆◆

Buying a bond can be the safest investment you make. Or the riskiest. The only thing that separates the two extremes is the bondholder's state of mind. Welcome to the wacky world of fixed income, where very little, it turns out, is actually fixed. Higher prices go with lower yields, and both fluctuate constantly. On Wall Street bond traders make and lose fortunes in an afternoon. Long-term bond owners stand oblivious to the tumult.

There are two diametrically opposed reasons to own bonds. The risky one is a play on interest rates: You buy a bond hoping that rates will fall, leaving you with a tidy capital gain as the market value of the bond rises. That's the business Wall Street institutions focus on, and playing it right can bring huge gains. But you can also experience severe losses, especially since predicting the direction of interest rates is something even the supposed experts have little consistent success with.

The safer side of bonds—and the one more appropriate for most individual investors—is the traditional course of buying and hold-ing to maturity. If that's your mindset, the fluctuations in rates that bounce the market value of bonds around like crazy are irrelevant. While you can't completely ignore how inflation might eat into your purchasing power, you do know that you'll collect your coupon, and at the end of the road you'll get your principal back.

It sounds straightforward, but with so many different types of bonds to choose among—from various issuers, with varying maturities—developing a coherent bond strategy can be quite tricky. What follows is a primer on the risk-reward tradeoffs implicit in different types of bonds and bond funds. We've also included a worksheet that helps investors quantify the extra yield they're getting for each step up the risk chain, to better weigh whether moving up makes sense for their needs.

Naturally, our starting point is Treasuries, the benchmark against which other bonds should be measured because default risk is negligible, trading costs are low, and liquidity is high. You step beyond Treasuries only to get a premium yield, in exchange for taking a greater risk. Municipal bonds, which appeal to individuals in higher tax brackets because they are exempt from federal tax, now enjoy only a narrow advantage over Treasuries compared with historical averages: Long-term Treasuries pay a 1.07-percentage-point premium over comparable munis on an untaxed basis, vs. an average spread of 0.89 percentage points since 1950, according to the Leuthold Group, a Minneapolis research firm. Indeed, the premium being paid for risk is narrow all along the bond spectrum, making Treasuries and insured munis the best relative bargains today.

What about bond funds? They aren't bonds: They don't pay a fixed yield, your principal isn't guaranteed, and their interest rate exposure and average maturity constantly fluctuate. But they can be looked at as an entire bond portfolio. In that context, it is not the fund's current yield that is most important—even though that is the basis on which funds are usually marketed—but rather the historical total return of the fund vs. its peers'. In fact, high yields are often a sign of danger: "There are no free lunches in the bond world," says Mark Wright of the fund research firm Morningstar. "If there's a high yield, it means that the manager is most likely paying out part of your principal and taking on more risk. He's not necessarily earning you more money."

WHICH BONDS TO BUY

◆◆◆

When comparing yields on bonds, one of the key factors to consider is taxes. The worksheet below helps quantify the after-tax yield of different types of bonds with the same maturity, so you can see what you're getting for each level of risk you're taking. The corporate bond section can be filled out twice, to compare a high-yield bond with an investment-grade issue.

TREASURIES

1. *Enter the current yield to maturity* (for rates at auction, call 202-874-4000 or go to www.publicdebt.treas.gov). _____

2. *Enter your federal tax rate,* as a decimal (example: 31% would be 0.31). _____

3. *Subtract* the amount on line 2 from 1 (example: 1 minus 0.31 equals 0.69). _____

4. *After-tax Treasury yield:* Multiply line 1 by line 3. ⇨_____

MUNICIPALS

1. *Enter the yield to maturity* (for rates, check out the PSA/Bloomberg municipal bond index at www.psa.com). _____

2. Muni issues outside your home state incur state and local income taxes. *Enter your combined state and local tax rate for such purchases,* as a decimal (example: 5% would be 0.05). Otherwise enter zero. _____

3. *Subtract* the amount on line 2 from 1. _____

4. *After-tax muni yield:* Multiply line 3 by line 1. ⇨_____

CORPORATES

1. *Enter the current yield to maturity.* _____

2. *Enter your combined state, local, and federal tax rate,* as a decimal. _____

3. *Subtract* line 2 from 1. _____

4. *After-tax corporate yield:* Multiply line 3 by line 1. ⇨_____

We've separated the bond world into its three main components—**Treasuries**, **municipals**, and **corporates**—detailing potential risks, offering trading tips, and giving insights into what a fund might offer over individual bonds.

TREASURIES

---◆---

Risks. The big threat to any long-term bondholder is the combination of rising inflation and rising interest rates. Inflation eats away at the buying power of your principal. Rising interest rates diminish the market value of your bonds, so that if for some reason you couldn't hold to maturity and had to sell, you'd face a loss.

The solution to both these complications is to build what's known as a laddered portfolio of Treasuries—a series of bonds with staggered maturities. For instance, you could buy ten bonds, with maturities from one to ten years. Each year, as a bond comes due, you would buy a new ten-year Treasury with the proceeds. "If interest rates go up, you're glad you've got money coming due to take advantage of the higher rates," says John Combias, a New Jersey financial planner. "If interest rates go down, you've locked in higher rates for ten years." Your portfolio adjusts if rates rise, and if you need to liquidate some portion of your holdings, you'll always have some short-term bonds, where the potential losses will be minimal.

Trading points. The cheapest way to buy Treasuries is from the government's free Treasury Direct program. You simply send in a form to the U.S. Treasury or you can authorize the department to debit your bank account for the exact amount on the day the security is issued. Treasury Direct has a new mechanism for selling that credits your bank account directly for a flat fee of $34 per security. That's less than you'd pay going through a broker.

But cheaper isn't always better. Many people may find the convenience of using a broker right from the start worth the extra expense—especially since fees for trading Treasuries run at only around $40 per transaction. One caveat: Because Treasury Direct restricts you to auctions, it would take quite some time to construct a laddered portfolio.

Fund facts. If you don't have enough money to construct a ladder, consider a low-cost, plain-vanilla fund such as those run by Vanguard. (Always avoid bond funds with high expense ratios and sales loads.) These funds also have the advantage of offering immediate reinvestment of interest, something you can't do with actual bonds.

Another fund option is the American Century-Benham Target Maturity series. These funds mimic zero-coupon bonds, actually terminating at a set date. That makes them ideal for those who wish to play interest rates—net asset values jump around with daily swings in the market—but also for long-term investors with fixed expenses ahead, such as college tuition bills. Unfortunately, just as with actual zeros, you owe taxes each year on the accrued interest, even if you haven't sold your shares.

MUNICIPALS

Risks. Despite all the financial troubles that state and local governments have, they rarely default on a bond. Even Orange County, which went bankrupt after a series of catastrophic derivative investments in 1994, has made good on its munis. The greater risk is a downgrade in credit rating. While it has no impact if you hold until maturity, you would take a shot if you unexpectedly needed to cash out. Just last fall Miami's credit tumbled from investment grade to junk level after the city revealed a major budgetary crisis. Munis are also less liquid than Treasuries.

Trading points. Buying munis individually is not cheap. Minimum investments tend to run around $10,000 each, and a round lot—which is easier to sell—usually costs about $25,000. While there is no broker fee on muni transactions, firms make their money by marking up the price of a bond when you're buying (or marking it down when you're selling). According to a spokeswoman at brokerage A.G. Edwards, such markups on munis can cost an investor as little as 0.03% of his or her principal and as much as 3.5%; the bigger markups tend to come with smaller investments as well as with bonds that are more scarce or longer term, or have lower credit quality.

Fund facts. If you build a ladder of individual munis—at $25,000 per bond—to diversify your interest-rate risk, and also perhaps diversify among locations to limit your downgrade risk, it requires committing a ton of money. Many people don't have that level of resources, which is what makes low-minimum muni funds attractive. They are also more liquid than actual munis. And you get access to a manager who may be able to play the credit-rating changes of a locality to your advantage. "In a bond fund, what you're getting is somebody who spends all his waking hours thinking about how to find the best values in the marketplace," says investment adviser Tim Schlindwein, who puts his own clients into muni funds.

CORPORATES

◆

Risk. Higher rates on corporate bonds may seem enticing, but these days their yield advantage over Treasuries is minimal. Currently a high-grade corporate bond offers a 0.54 percentage point yield-premium to 20-year Treasuries, vs. an average of 0.72 percentage point since 1982. The fact that corporates incur state and local taxes that Treasuries do not further cuts into their apparent advantage.

Junk bonds may look better: The spread between the Merrill Lynch high-yield index and 20-year Treasuries is now 2.3 percentage points. Still, there too the premium is historically narrow: The average spread since 1982 is 3.66 percentage points.

The chance of a default or downgrade is also much higher with corporates, and especially with high-yield bonds. Plus, there's the quagmire of call options—devices that allow an issuer to pay off a loan before the maturity date. Say you buy a corporate bond at par (100) with a call option at 105 for the next year. Then interest rates fall, and the bond's price rallies to 110. If the issuer decides to refinance the debt at the lower rate, it can call the bonds at the lower price, leaving you short $5 per bond. And of course you'll have to find a new place to reinvest your principal—at now lower prevailing rates.

Trading points. As with munis, corporates carry big face amounts (at least $10,000), so you've got to put a lot down to build a portfolio. And they're none too easy to buy and sell. Brokers' markups are similar to munis'—as high as 3.5%.

Fund facts. This is one part of the bond world where funds are usually better for individuals than actual bonds. Professional managers typically negotiate cheaper trading costs and are better equipped to watch the market closely, taking advantage of potential upgrades and downgrades in credit ratings, as well as interest-rate fluctuations. You may well be better off with a fund than on your own.

ADVICE FROM PROPHETS OF PROFIT

◆◆◆

*The former head of the Windsor fund offers
perspective on past bear markets ...
Roanoke's champion small-cap investor
explains the rules he sets—and tells you
when he breaks them ... Westwood Equity's
chief strategist tells about her love affair
with low-risk, neglected companies
that still beat the market.*

◆◆◆

TAMING BEAR MARKETS

◆

John Neff, former head of the wildly successful Windsor fund, is usually described as "crusty," but that's just window dressing. He's an investor with a nose for value, a concern for shareholders, and a unique way with words. When asked to comment on a subject he's not up on, Neff will invariably say, "That's something I'm not qualified to answer," a reply you rarely get from any portfolio manager, much less one whose Windsor fund outperformed the S&P 500 in 21 of the 31 years he was at the helm.

FORTUNE's Lawrence Armour talked to Neff about his experience with bear markets and stock groups he thinks are hot.

As someone who has been through at least two bear markets, what's it like?

The one that's etched most vividly in my memory was 1973–74. It was the most scathing decline I ever faced. That was the era of one-decision stocks, when people were buying big-name growth stocks on a hold-forever basis regardless of price. They pushed the Nifty Fifty to unsustainable 40 to 50 P/E multiples. The market fell 15% in 1973, but we were down 25%—pretty disappointing for somebody who felt he was giving shareholders downside protection.

What did you do?

I retooled the portfolio by moving into allegedly riskier growth merchandise that had low P/E ratios and more intelligent risk/reward ratios. The market was getting hosed pretty good, but we had liquidity because the big stocks were salable. I had a fair hunk of money in solid citizens—AT&T, Safeway, CBS, some electric utilities—so I sold them and loaded up on second-tier growth stocks. They did even better coming out the other side than I would have guessed. It was seven, eight, maybe ten years before the Nifty Fifty got back to their 1973 highs, but we outperformed the S&P 500 by about 10% in 1974, and we just kept going. The S&P was up about 70% in the 1975–76 span. We were up 126%.

What about the 1987 crash?

The difference there was, we went into it with some cash. After the 1973–74 experience, it dawned in my thick skull that when it was hard to find things to buy, maybe not buying and hanging on to a little cash wouldn't be the worst of all worlds. Then, when the market got clobbered—as it inevitably seems to—we could rush back in and pick up stocks at friendly prices. Our mandate was to represent shareholders by being in stocks, but we interpreted that as 80%. That meant you could have as much as 20% in cash if silly season rolled around, and that's what we did in 1987. We had 13% to 14% in cash and another 10% in governments. You could get a 10% coupon on long governments at that point, which wasn't bad, and we figured we could bank 15% if an interest rate move came our way.

What was the emotional feeling? Terror?
Not for us. We were aware how high the evaluations had gotten, and we were nice and liquid. We bought $118 million of stock on October 19, another $192 million the next day. Having cash made it easy to come tippy-toeing back.

Everyone seems convinced that we can't have a bear market again.
They've been right for a long time. We haven't had a good sawtooth since 1990.

Does the it-can't-happen-again school of thought make sense?
No. In the early 1960s, when I was an analyst at National City Bank in Cleveland, the figure we always watched—there's always a figure du jour—was mutual fund cash flow. It was a midget industry then, but that's the loaded cannon we're dealing with today. The boomers have been raised to count on a 16% annual return on the S&P 500. You and I know that's not sustainable, particularly from the levels we've ascended, and when the boomers discover they can't get instant gratification forever, they may have second thoughts about stocks and put their funds elsewhere.

Some people think 8,000 mutual funds are a few too many.
They're right, and it's only these particularly ebullient times that have encouraged all these new offerings. The number will shrink. We've already seen some consolidation of names within fund families, and we'll see more. It isn't only a question of whether you can administer them and catch the public's eye with fancy marketing, but are there 8,000 brilliant managers out there?

What's your view on index funds?
I obviously think I can beat the averages. During my 31 years at Windsor, we did 315 basis points annually better than the S&P. Most [portfolio managers] hit behind the ball. They react to what's already happened rather than anticipating what will happen. Many

also take a husky spot in terms of expense ratios. If you're giving away 100 basis points in expenses, it means you're starting off each year with one foot in the hole.

What groups would you be looking at these days?
Small caps would be one. Another would be emerging countries, which also have had it tough for the past couple of years. The emerging countries—whether it's Thailand, Singapore, or the Philippines, China, India, or the South American countries—grow at about three times the rate of the developed countries. There's obviously more risk, but if you buy a basket of countries or if you use an index fund, you should do all right. When emerging countries are selling at 18 times earnings or thereabouts, vs. 40 to 45 times for Japan, that's an open-and-shut case for me.

I can make a case for housing, starting with long-term interest rates, which I think are probably going to stay around 7% on long governments and 7.8% to 7.9% on 30-year fixed mortgages. At those rates housing is very affordable, and the American public still has a desire to own its own piece of turf. I think housing starts will hold around the 1.4 million to 1.5 million area not only in 1997 but probably in 1998 and 1999 as well.

SMALL-CAP STOCKS AND VOLATILITY

◆

Ed **Vroom** is one of three partners in Roanoke Asset Management, a firm that invests solely in small-cap companies. Roanoke means "money" in the language of the Algonquian Indians of Virginia, and the firm's performance lives up to its name. For the five-year period ended September 30, 1996, it delivered an overall annualized return of 24.1%. This compares with 16.6% for the S&P 500 and 21% for the Russell 2000.

FORTUNE's Lawrence Armour talked with Vroom about small caps, the rules he sets for himself, and when he breaks them.

Is there an inherent risk in small-cap investing?
Yes, it can involve a higher degree of risk, and it almost always means greater volatility. But if done right, it also means higher rates of return.

When you say small-cap investing involves volatility rather than risk, aren't you just playing with words?
No. In July 1996, for example, the overall market declined and small-caps led the way. Roanoke was down 12%. By the September quarter, Roanoke was up 2.8%, which means we recovered all the July drop and then some.

What industries are you looking at?
Health care, technology, and telecommunications. Health care is a $1-trillion-a-year industry that's experiencing profound changes in its structure and in the way services are delivered and paid for. Established companies are losing their franchises, and newer, younger competitors are filling the voids. It's the perfect environment for smaller, entrepreneurial companies.

What do you see for telecommunications?
It's another trillion-dollar industry, and probably more. We haven't even seen the beginning of the fallout from the deregulation bill, but we know that local telephone companies want to get into long-distance, long-distance companies want to provide local service, and cable companies want to do both. Until the dust settles, we're content to be in companies that supply the equipment that makes the networks run.

How about an overview on technology?
The *New York Times* doesn't talk about U.S. Steel's building a new plant or International Paper's developing a new way to deal with pulp. Literally 70% of the business section is devoted to technology-oriented items. The *Wall Street Journal* ran a profile a while back on Hugh McColl Jr., the crusty chairman of NationsBank, who said that technology is the key to the bank's survival. Technology has become an essential part of our everyday lives, and it has to become an absolutely essential part of everyone's portfolio.

Your brand of investing sounds exciting, but it's risky too.
Let's face it, the business risk associated with a ten-year-old company that has $200 million in revenues is certainly greater than the business risk associated with a Coca-Cola. But the returns a smaller company can generate, and its ability to grow at rates much

greater than a Coca-Cola's, offset that incremental business risk. Quarter to quarter, smaller companies are more volatile. But when you look out over a longer period of time, five years and beyond, their volatility becomes almost indistinguishable from larger ones', and the returns remain much greater.

Give me a real-time example.
We bought Oracle five years ago when it was below $10. The company was going through a difficult period, but they had a unique technology that was generating explosive growth, and they were getting their arms around their problems. Oracle has probably increased 15-fold since then, and there were many times when people got nervous and sold, only to see the stock move higher. We no longer hold the stock because Oracle is no longer a small-cap company. But we did very well on it. The important thing in small-cap investing is to never lose sight of why you own a stock, and stick with it as long as the company executes.

That's got to be tough. You know that at some point the market will drop and small caps will get killed. Isn't there a temptation to get out before the roof falls in?
Any portfolio manager who's running serious amounts of small-cap institutional money has to have a defined sell discipline. At Roanoke, a sell is triggered when a stock reaches our price objective or when a holding reaches 7% of a portfolio. The other trigger is a negative change in fundamentals.

What if a stock reaches an objective but the fundamentals change for the better?
That happened with Ascend Communications. One of our larger holdings, it supplies the majority of ISPs—the Internet intermediaries—with dial-up devices that enable people to access the Internet. The stock rose more than tenfold in 15 months, so it met our price objective very early on. But during that time it became an essential part of the Internet, which means its fundamentals are even better than we first thought. You have to understand the dynamics not only of your companies' businesses but also of their markets. You don't want a mechanical discipline that takes you out of the Oracles and Ascends

too early. Ascend breached our 7% rule several times, but it's the leader in a dynamic business and it stays far ahead of the competition.

Is your 7% rule a way to keep the fund from getting too many eggs in one basket?
Yes. The typical Roanoke portfolio will have 40 to 50 different companies, and no new investment can be more than 2.5% of the fund's capital. That way, if we happen to be wrong on a name, it won't kill the performance of the total portfolio.

FAVORING OUT-OF-FAVOR STOCKS

S usan Byrne sure sounds like a loser in today's market: She won't touch Coca-Cola, General Electric, or Microsoft; she's been seeking safety in stocks that pay dividends; she even gets turned off by booming companies if their P/E is above 30. So here's the surprise: Her Westwood Equity fund has been thriving, beating the S&P 500 three of the past four years, including a 27% gain in 1996. The one time she lagged, in 1995, she still managed a 37% return.

Byrne pays painstaking attention to risk in her investing. She lightens up on a position—even winners—if it swells to more than 3% of her equity portfolio. To avoid big losses, she automatically dumps any new holding that falls more than 10% in the first 90 days after she buys it.

FORTUNE's Peter Elkind talked with Byrne about her strategy of beating the market with low-risk, neglected companies that have learned their lessons the hard way.

So you like to invest with executives who have screwed up?
Yes, I do. Mistakes are inevitable. The lack of errors breeds arrogance, which invites really big mistakes. I like to see people who have goofed up, because you learn a lot that way.

Is that what you saw in Dell Computer, which went from $8 a share, split adjusted, when you bought it, to north of $100?
When we got involved, Dell had really disappointed investors because it had mishandled the way it entered the notebook market.

They were in the process of growing themselves into bankruptcy. Wall Street, being the punisher of imperfection that it is, really hammered the stock. We bought in August 1995, the day after Dell reported earnings that exceeded Wall Street's expectations. We were there wonderfully early.

When will you take your profits with Dell and move on?

We generally don't own companies where confidence about future growth is extremely high, because there's no edge for us. It's just pure risk. But we do buy companies that are going to surprise, and people continue to underestimate Dell. The company can probably sustain a 25% growth rate for the next three years, but the stock is selling at a P/E of only 16 [in June 1997] based on our estimate of next year's earnings of $6.50 a share. We have a price target of $135. If the P/E got ahead of 25, it would reflect everything we know about Dell, and we'd sell. I'll wave goodbye and have tears in my eyes—it's like sending your kids off to school. But it won't belong in our world anymore.

You say high-expectation stocks "just terrify" you. Which ones are you talking about?

They tend to be motherhood and apple pie—the large names in the S&P, like Coca-Cola. As the market has gone higher, people get more and more frightened and say, "If I keep my money in these stocks, I should be better off if we have a recession." They buy index funds. And what do index funds buy? Coca-Cola, GE, Microsoft, Intel, Wal-Mart, Home Depot. The top 20 stocks in the S&P 500 make up a third of the capitalization.

You don't sound as if you like index funds.

An index fund is ... let me think of a word ... it is without conscience. It doesn't think. That is how you get overvalued stocks. At this point, lots of money is going into just a few names. People think they're buying the whole market, but they're mostly buying 15 or 20 stocks, many of which, on a fundamental basis, appear to be overvalued.

That means that when the market moves down, active managers—those holding cash or holding diversified portfolios—are going to do much better than index funds. The reason index funds are beating everybody is that the market has been going straight up. When we are not in a straight-up market, everybody will beat them.

Why do you hate consumer stocks?
I just don't have the confidence that others do in the persistence of their growth rates. The consumer is not the same engine that he was. People of my generation—I'm the beginning of this huge wave of baby-boomers—overconsumed and overspent, and now they've decided that they need to save. The reflection of that is in the stock market—it's just another consumer product. People aren't buying McDonald's cheeseburgers. They're buying stocks.

WISING UP TO MUTUAL FUND FEES
BY MAGGIE TOPKIS

◆◆◆

If you don't care about mutual fund fees
because of great returns, get a load of
what you're leaving on the table.

◆◆◆

So, you've found the fund manager of the gods, a stock picker par excellence, who seemingly spins straw into golden returns. Congratulations. But experience teaches that no matter how deft, such a money manager is likely to blow hot and cold over the years ahead. By contrast, it is the fees that investors pay that remain constant over time. Put bluntly, in all but a few cases, fees are the keys to future returns.

Consider these theoretical scenarios. An investor who sank $10,000 into the Vanguard Index 500 fund ten years ago would have ended up, partly as a result of its dirt-cheap expense ratio—0.20% in 1995—with a tidy nest egg of $38,433. But take the expenses of the actively managed Lindner Growth fund, incredibly inexpensive at 0.63% in 1996, and apply them to the index fund's returns (basically the stock market's performance) over the same ten years: Your little bundle totes up to just $36,268, roughly $2,100 less. Last, extrapolate the fees of a pricey offering like Alger Growth fund, which sported a portly 2.07% expense ratio in 1996, and apply that to the index fund's returns. That leaves you just $30,112, some $8,300 poorer.

The situation isn't getting any better for investors. According to Morningstar Inc., the average shareholder in a U.S. stock fund is paying $88 a year for every $10,000 invested, up from $80 in 1986. Why? As Brian Murray of Alameda Consulting puts it, "It's sheer, unadulterated greed."

Call it greed or smart business, depending on your perspective. The real question to ask is whether you're getting your money's worth. Sometimes you are. Take the Kaufmann fund, which is 26% pricier than its aggressive-growth peers. As Kaufmann co-manager Larry Auriana says, "The only people complaining are the ones who didn't invest." Indeed, the fund has returned an average of 21.4% annually for the past five years, vs. 15.7% for its peers. That's worth paying up for. But be prepared for a reassessment come a market downturn. Says consultant Geoffrey Bobroff: "The bull market has blinded investors to the role that costs play in returns."

To get to the bottom of the fee issue, zero in on the expense ratio that's in the front of the prospectus. Expressed as a percentage of assets, it is the single best gauge of expenses you'll find. It takes into account the management fee, which is also broken out separately. But it often doesn't itemize other expenses, like subadvisory or administrative fees, which are included as well.

Your expense ratio also may include a 12b-1 fee, which by law must be disclosed separately. That's a number well worth looking for—it can take an annual bite of up to 1% of your investment. Named for a rule added to the Investment Company Act of 1940, the 12b-1 was originally supposed to be used only to offset marketing costs. But nowadays almost anything goes. A big part of 12b-1s, for example, often gets funneled back to brokers and financial planners as a "service fee" for as long as you hold the fund. Says Murray: "It's a bribe to the broker to keep your money where it is."

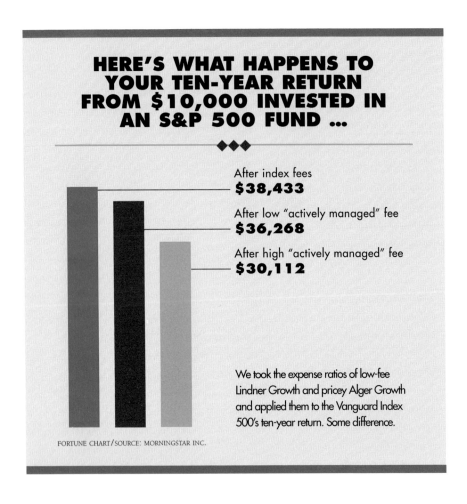

HERE'S WHAT HAPPENS TO YOUR TEN-YEAR RETURN FROM $10,000 INVESTED IN AN S&P 500 FUND ...

◆◆◆

After index fees
$38,433

After low "actively managed" fee
$36,268

After high "actively managed" fee
$30,112

We took the expense ratios of low-fee Lindner Growth and pricey Alger Growth and applied them to the Vanguard Index 500's ten-year return. Some difference.

FORTUNE CHART/SOURCE: MORNINGSTAR INC.

The 12b-1 gets abused in other ways. Some funds closed to new investors continue to charge it. Among them: Pimco Advisors Opportunity, State Street Research Small Cap Growth, Franklin Balance Sheet Investment, and AIM Aggressive Growth. Says Murray: "The reality is, companies don't want to let go of that revenue stream." Of course you needn't scratch every fund that charges a 12b-1 fee—or high expenses generally—from your list of possibilities. But if it charges a 12b-1 above 0.25%, treat that as a warning.

The flashing yellow light should also go on when you see that a mutual fund sponsor is "absorbing" a portion of one of its fund's expense ratios. This practice is common among new offerings, whose asset bases are as yet so small that socking the fund with the full expense charge would gut returns, scaring off shareholders. What's wrong with a company's absorbing costs? Nothing, except that companies will very likely phase in the true expenses later, when you may not be paying attention. If your fund is absorbing costs, bully for you. But check whether there's a date set when the generosity ends.

Some investors assume that a high-expense fund implies better research and snazzier stock picking. But it's more likely to signal lax budgeting or a willingness to charge what the market will bear. Vanguard Group—with its stable of el cheapo index and other funds—has been at the forefront of turning thrift into marketing prowess. It rewards employees for saving shareholder money, and CEO John Brennan is fond of telling reporters how cutting the size of a brochure by an eighth of an inch saved Vanguard $75,000 per mailing. In 1996 the company cut the subadvisory fees that it pays to some outside managers, including Wellington Management, which runs the multibillion-dollar Windsor fund.

Other outfits are serious about cost cutting. Twentieth Century Mutual Funds sports a "unified fee" of 1% on domestic stock funds. That's 42% below the average for aggressive-growth funds, Twentieth Century's specialty. The company claims the fee imposes fiscal discipline. Nicholas and Lindner funds save phone costs by restricting their toll-free number to shareholders. Since the fund's 1994 inception, Bridgeway Capital's aggressive-growth fund has a subsidized expense ratio that helped its investors achieve an annualized return of 27.4%. That's 33% higher than the fund's peers.

Manager John Montgomery offers a neatly typed and Xeroxed annual report. Says he: "We'll always be low rent." As is often the case at Vanguard, Montgomery's management fee is pegged to performance. Using a sliding scale, he earns a fat fee of 1.6% when he beats the S&P 500 by 15 percentage points. If returns trail the index by a like amount, he earns just 0.2%.

High turnover offers another go-slow signal. Brokerage costs that your fund incurs when it trades aren't part of the expense ratio but are deducted from assets before calculating returns. The $775 million Strong Total Return fund, with a turnover rate of 502%, racked up $6.4 million in such expenses in fiscal 1996.

By making use of electronic trading systems, outfits like Twentieth Century really do make an effort to keep brokerage costs under control. That's a good idea for Twentieth Century because of its funds' high turnover. Others may use "soft dollar" payments from brokerages that muddy the expense waters. In return for the fund's order flow, many brokerages reward fund companies with free research. That can be a good barter deal. But such swaps may also include conference trips and other perks, and the use of barter may keep a fund's expenses deceptively low. A recent ruling by the SEC requires funds to disclose average commissions and whether they get research in exchange for order flow.

CHAPTER FIVE

◆◆◆

HOW TO RETIRE WELL: A GUIDE TO PROSPERITY

UNRAVELING THE MYSTERIES OF YOUR PENSION PLAN

BY EVAN SIMONOFF

*Not all defined-benefit plans are equal.
If you're evaluating a job offer, the
terms of the pension plan are worth
asking about.*

Once upon a time in the world inhabited by our parents, people spent most of their adult lives working for one or two companies. In return for such loyalty, many employers provided lavish pensions, often amounting to 50% to 65% of preretirement salary. Modest personal savings and a big Social Security check made the transition to retirement oh, so smooth and financially painless.

Today, such lush retirement pensions seem as *au courant* as a Norman Rockwell magazine cover. The fact is, they just don't make pensions like that anymore, and the once popular image of a paternalistic world in which your employer took care of you has, for the most part, faded away. Sure, some people working in the public sector or at a handful of large companies like Motorola, Ford, and Exxon continue to receive hefty pension checks, but their ranks are slowly, surely shrinking. If you're like most Americans, the reality is that you will have to provide the preponderance of your own retirement income.

But while traditional pensions may no longer be the bulwark of the nation's retirement savings system, they are still footing an enormous chunk of its retirement bill. According to a 1994 report by the Pension and Welfare Benefits Administration, about 25 million private-sector workers were still covered by defined-benefit plans; 14 million of them also had 401(k)s. Big companies are the most likely to offer defined-benefit plans: A survey of 1,050 major employers by Hewitt Associates found that 79% did so.

If they are so prevalent, why are pensions such a convoluted mystery to the very people they are supposed to help: dusty, neglected weapons in their financial arsenals? There are several reasons. The vast majority of these plans don't have, as a 401(k) does, an easily accessible account value: Tracking down the worth of your pension is likely to result in a lengthy bout of phone tag with your human resources department. Then there's all the actuarial jargon these benefit formulas rely on. Once you get hold of your company's plan, you're likely to find yourself confused by its tortuous workings.

But once broken down to their core components, defined-benefit plans can be simple to get your arms around. Chances are your company pension, assuming it has one, is a **final-average-pay** or **highest-average-pay plan**, the most common variety. If so, count yourself lucky, because they are usually the most generous plans. These pensions provide a payout based upon either the average compensation of an employee's final three or five years at the company or—even better—the average of their highest-income years multiplied first by a benefit percentage and then by a "credited service factor," typically their length of service.

Here's an example of how it works: A standard plan would take a benefit percentage, say, 1.25%, and multiply that by the employee's years of service, say 30 years. The result of that simple multiplication is a larger percentage, in this case 37.5%, which is then applied to an average of the employee's five best years of pay. Thus, 37.5% of a final average salary of, say, $150,000 produces an annual pension of $56,250. If you spend less than 30 years at a company, you still get a pension, but a lesser one. Based on the example above, an employee retiring with only 15 years of service would get an annual pension of $28,125 (1.25% × 15 × $150,000).

The benefit percentage changes from company to company, but if you spend 30 years with one employer, expect a monthly check of between 30% to 45% of your final average pay. Some companies still offer a generous 1.5% or 2.0% per year of employment, but that practice is on the wane.

In fact, companies have grown increasingly chintzy with the terms of their plans. In recent years, for example, many plans have started maxing the benefit out at 50% of an employee's highest salary no matter how long he works. If your current plan is a generous one, don't feel too smug: It's perfectly legal for a company to reduce or even terminate a plan whenever it sees fit as long as it notifies participants and protects all the benefits that have accrued to date.

HOW THEY FIGURE YOUR PENSION

◆◆◆

Retirement can be easy or tough, depending on the plan.

Plan	Description	Typical formula
Final average pay or Highest average pay	Final average pay is typically based on your average annual earnings over the last three or five years of employment. Highest average pay can be better—using your highest earnings regardless of what you're making at retirement. Both are adjusted for years of service.	1.25% x Years of service x Final pay (5-year average)
Career average pay	Like the final- or highest-average-pay plan but based on earnings over your entire career, including those hand-to-mouth early years. That may well translate into a far smaller pension.	1.25% x Years of service x Career average pay
Cash balance	Takes a percentage of your earnings each year, say 5%, and invests that in a conservative investment vehicle, like a GIC, yielding 6% or so. Young employees make out well. But the pension is still likely to fall far short of a final- or highest-average-pay plan.	Annual earnings x 5% x Compounding annually at 6%

Although the lion's share of employers follow the basic formula, each plan has its own twists and turns. For example, different plans have their own vesting schedules, with full vesting after five years the most common. Whereas some companies once rewarded older workers for their loyalty and increased the benefit percentage after, say, 20 years, most now send a different message by reducing the benefit percentage after 25 or 30 years.

One constant: Age 55 is still the magic milestone for most plans. "That's when employees are entitled to certain early-retirement benefits," says managing director Sheldon Gamzon of Price Waterhouse. "It's not unusual to see the value of a pension increase between 50% and 100% for working one additional year." Why? Regardless of how generous its pension, a company is likely to apply a stiff penalty if you retire—that is, start receiving benefits—before age 65. However, once you turn 55, that unkind cut, usually 6% per year, gets greatly reduced, typically to just 3% per year.

The second most popular variety of defined-benefit plan is the so-called **career-average-pay plan**. It works just the way it sounds. Your employer simply takes your aggregate career earnings and divides by your length of service to determine your average annual salary. It does the same multiplications used in the earlier example, but now it's working with a lower salary because it uses your career average pay, not your final or highest pay.

How do career-average- and final-average-pay plans compare? FORTUNE asked consulting firms to run the numbers for two 35-year-old buddies: Chester signs on to a company with a career-average-pay plan; Freddie joins an outfit with a five-year-final-average plan. Each started out earning $30,000, received 5% annual raises, and retired after 30 years. The companies' benefit percentage in each case was a run-of-the-mill 1.25%, and they both ended up with final salaries of $123,484. Results: Chester, whose pension is calculated on career average pay of $66,438, winds up with a measly $24,914-a-year pension. Freddie, with the five-year-final-average-pay plan, ended up with a tidy annual pension of exactly $42,000. As that difference suggests, if you're ever in the position of evaluating a new job offer, the terms of the pension plan are worth asking about.

In recent years a new type of plan called the **cash-balance plan**, which defines the benefit as an account value, has gained popularity. A cash-balance plan with an annual contribution of, say, 5% is more akin to a company contribution to a 401(k) plan because it has an explicit account value that grows over time. Come your farewell lunch, you get your vested balance or a range of annuity options.

How does the cash balance stack up? Assume a friend of Freddie's and Chester's—Barney—joined a third company with a cash-balance plan the same year at the same salary, got identical raises, and retired the same year. The company contributed 5% of Barney's salary each year to the cash-balance plan, which earned a typical 6% return annually. Come retirement at age 65, Barney gets a cash balance of $219,536, which he opts to take as an annuity: It will provide him an income of just $25,956, slightly more than the career-average pension plan but still far less than the final-average-pay one.

A t retirement you, too, may face the same decision Barney does. More and more companies, an estimated 40% of them, are giving retirees the option of taking their pensions in a lump sum roughly equivalent to the present value of their projected lifetime payouts. There are no pat answers, whether from actuaries or from financial advisers, as to whether it is wise to do so. Part of the question revolves around what kind of cost-of-living adjustment, or COLA, is imbedded in your pension. Says Bob Winfield, a financial adviser with Legacy Wealth Management in Memphis: "Some plans are fairly generous, and if they include a COLA, it's hard to project with any confidence that you can earn more with a lump sum than you would with an inflation-adjusted pension."

Corporations are eager to have you take a lump sum, even if, by simple arithmetic, it costs them more. Why? They get to write pension liabilities off their books, says Paul Holzman, co-director of the National Center for Retirement Benefits in Northbrook, Illinois. He suggests resisting the temptation to grab "the biggest check most people will ever see in their lives." But individuals with lots of other money might want to take the lump sum just to increase their investment flexibility. For others the lump vs. no-lump decision is going to be a stab in the dark.

To know definitively whether a lump sum is better or worse than a lifetime of pension payments, you would really need to know how long you'll live. That's because the lump sum is figured on the value of annual payouts over a typical life expectancy once you hit age 65: That's 82 years for a male and 86 years for a female. What you do have working in your favor is knowledge of your own health and the longevity of parents and grandparents. Thus, if your parents are in their 80s or 90s, the law of probability says you should lean toward the lifetime payout. If they passed away in their 60s or 70s, tilt toward the lump sum.

If you opt for the lump sum, current interest rates will determine how much you get. What companies essentially are trying to do is give you enough money to buy an annuity that would replicate the income stream from a lifetime payout. The relationship is counterintuitive. When rates are low, the lump sum will be greater than when rates are high, since the cost of an annuity that will produce a fixed income of, say, $2,000 per month rises as rates fall. The amount of

WHAT YOUR 401(k) WILL BE WORTH

◆◆◆

With a 401(k), you, the employee, are master of your own destiny. Yes, some factors are beyond your control—a company's matching policy, for example. But you decide what percentage of salary to kick in. And the mix of stocks and bonds is largely up to you as well.

With this freedom comes responsibility, for you will reap the consequences of your actions. Say you're 40 with $100,000 in your plan, making a fat $90,000, and plunking 8% of that into your 401(k). You're getting regular raises, and the company matches 50% of your contributions, which you divvy—on a 60%–40% basis—between a zippy stock fund, returning 11.5% annually, and a bond fund returning 6%. Come retirement at age 65, you'll have $2.3 million. But cut back your investment to 6% of your salary, and by age 65 you'll be $350,000 poorer. Increase your contribution to 10%—assuming you're allowed to do so— and you'll end up with nearly $2.7 million.

Bearish? Cut your stock exposure to 30%, boost your bond portfolio proportionately, and you will likely end up with just $1.8 million. By contrast, raising your stock exposure to 90% and leaving the rest in bonds will increase your payout to $3.1 million.

You get the point: Each one of those little shifts has powerful implications for your future. If you should choose a conservative investment mix for a while, or cut back on your contributions because of a sudden expense, that's fine. Just don't forget to readjust the dials when the skies clear.

your lump sum is regulated by Uncle Sam and friends. As part of the General Agreement on Tariffs and Trade, or GATT, passed by Congress in late 1994, companies may now use either the rate on the 30-year Treasury bond or the old standard Pension Benefit Guaranty

THE COST OF JOB HOPPING

◆◆◆

Hewitt Associates tracked the effects on a pension of changing jobs over the course of a career. Both Peter and Freddie are hired at age 35 with a $30,000 salary and retire at age 65 with final salaries of $123,484. But check out the big differences in their final pensions.

Assume a benefit formula of 1.25% of final 5-year average pay, multiplied by total years of service.

$42,000

$42,000
30 years at
same job

$26,400

$14,000
Job 5: 10 years

PETER JOB-HOPPER'S PENSION

STEADY FREDDIE'S PENSION

$4,300
Job 4: 5 years

$3,400
Job 3: 5 years

$2,600
Job 2: 5 years

$2,100
Job 1: 5 years

WHY DOES FREDDIE GET MORE?
Freddie's entire pension is based on his final average salary. Peter's five pensions are based on his final average salary at each job.

Corp. rate, which had been the yardstick for calculating lump-sum payouts. Because the rate on the 30-year long bond is often as much as 2% higher, this will mean lower lump-sum payouts.

Your pension plan also probably offers you something called a contingent annuitant option. That means that in return for a reduced payout, your spouse will continue to receive half the pension's income should you die first. Like the lump vs. no-lump dilemma, decisions on whether to take it should factor in your age, health, and financial status as well as those of your spouse. A few plans reduce your pension income by a flat amount, regardless of your spouse's age. Here, obviously, robbing the cradle works in your favor. But most adjust the reduction to reflect your spouse's age. Assume Freddie's wife is three years his junior. That $42,000 pension he's taking home is likely to be cut to $35,300 if he wants his wife to continue to receive half of it in the event that he dies first.

Given all the nips and tucks in the defined-benefit payment, many employees prefer the more accessible 401(k) plan. Employers favor 401(k) plans because they avoid the liability of paying pension benefits at some point 30 years in the future. But that's one of the main reasons employees shouldn't be so quick to dismiss their defined-benefit plans. Consider: To achieve a $40,000 annual annuity that will run for 30 years, you'd have to start out with a lump sum of $365,600. That's what a full pension is worth in our example, and unlike 401(k)s, it's not market-sensitive, and you don't have to contribute a penny. But with 401(k) performance flying high lately, such bennies are hardly noticed.

Says Bruce J. Temkin, an actuary at Louis Kravitz & Associates in Encino, California: "It will take a prolonged down market for stocks before employees appreciate a defined-benefit plan again."

Of course, younger workers, weaned on downsizing and job-hopping, know they can take a 401(k) with them without penalty, and that's an advantage over defined-benefit plans. To find out how much, Hewitt Associates ran the numbers and compared defined-benefit plans for two 35-year-old employees: one, like Freddie in the example above, a career-long employee, and the other, Peter, a job-hopper. Each again earns $30,000 and, working for 30 years, receives 5% annual raises at companies with five-year vesting schedules. Peter puts in four separate five-year stints at different employers and retires after spending ten years at his fifth job. We remember that Freddie took home a retirement pension of $42,000, based on the traditional final five-year average-pay plan and a benefit percentage of 1.25%. Peter, the job-hopper, however, receives five separate pension checks totaling just $26,400 per year. Ouch!

By contrast, had Freddie and Peter worked for companies with 401(k) plans, even skimpy ones, contributing 6% of their annual salary and earning annual returns of 8%, they both would have likely ended up with an account, or accounts in the case of the job-hopper, with identical values of $344,400. If they were to convert this lump sum into an annuity based on the 1984 Unisex Mortality Table and 8% interest rate, each would get an annual income of $42,000. That is without the help of a company match, typically 50% or so. Sure, the 401(k) is the better way to go if you're on the move. But what a great deal if your company offers both a defined-benefit plan and a 401(k)!

If all this talk about the munificent machinations providing for your retirement sounds optimistic for you, your skepticism is healthy and warranted. There are plenty of cases, in fact, of employees' not getting their due. But if you are like most Americans, you have few other options, besides increasing your savings rate. No one seriously believes any major companies are likely to sweeten the traditional pensions they offer. Instead, they expect further cutbacks in defined-benefit plans and continued growth for 401(k) plans. Whichever plan you have, it's important to understand what it will mean to you later on.

HOW TO SAVE FOR OLD AGE AND THE KIDS' COLLEGE TUITION

BY ANNE FIELD

◆◆◆

*You may have to save fast for old age
and the kids' college. It won't be easy,
but you still have time to do both.
Here's how.*

◆◆◆

The numbers are so ludicrous, my husband and I have tried to ignore them for a few years now. At least $425,000 to send our 6-year-old and 7-month-old to a private four-year college. Perhaps

$2.9 million to support us after we stop working. And with retirement just 20 or so years away, the situation seems more impossible with each passing day.

How did this happen? Like a lot of baby-boomers, we put off having kids until well into our 30s. Now that decision is coming back to haunt us as we face the daunting double whammy afflicting many of our peers: saving for our old age and the kids' education when the specters of both aren't far away. With a decent six-figure income and a 401(k) plan offering a 6% company match, we're not starting from scratch. But $3 million? Help! If you're one of the 46 million baby-boomers age 40 and over, our nightmare may well be yours.

Let's look at more numbers. Say you have just 11 years to go before Junior graduates from high school. (The largest group of kids born to baby-boomers was hatched in 1990, so this may be a good example for many of you.) With private-college expenses typically running $20,000 a year and education inflation at 5% to 6% a year, you're faced with a four-year bill of $166,000. And figure you want to retire at the generally accepted rate of 70% of your current income. If you make $150,000, you'll need $3.8 million, assuming you and your spouse are 40 years old and plan to live till you're 90. To reach both goals, the experts suggest you put aside on the order of $500 a month for each child, plus as much as 20% of your gross income, depending on how much you've already saved.

Be assured, that's not going to happen in many families. They simply don't have that much to put aside. And it's unlikely you'll be able to save enough to fund all of your college and retirement goals at the same time. You'll probably wind up supplementing your retirement income with proceeds from the sale of a home or a part-time job at the 7-Eleven. But the good news is, there's still time to accumulate much of what you'll need—without eating Hamburger Helper every night.

While many experts figure that the inflation rate for tuition will remain high, others, like Melissa Levine, a financial planner in New York, think it may be lower—4% or so. Plus, you don't have to save for all of the college tuition. A more reasonable goal is 30% to 40% of the bill. You'll just have to cobble together the rest from an assortment of sources—summer jobs for the kids, for instance. And

DOUBLE WHAMMY

◆◆◆

If you're worried about tuition terror, here's some advice from Boston financial planner Jeff Levine on how to save for both college and retirement.

Years to retirement	Parents' ages	Income	Kids' ages	Years to college
15	50, 50	$150,000	12, 9	5, 8
15	50, 48	$175,000	10	7
17	48, 46	$200,000	4, 4	13
20	45, 44	$225,000	10, 7, 4	7, 10, 13
23	42	$90,000	5, 3	12, 14
25	40, 40	$150,000	7, 4	11, 13

FORTUNE CHART / SOURCE: ALKON & LEVINE

Advice*

No time to waste for this crew. I'd go with Treasury bonds for the oldest child, just to make sure the kid will have something for school. Only bet on stock if you've got five years or more. For the 9-year-old—and the parents' retirement outside the 401(k)—I'd go with growth and income funds, a safe bet.

Invest in a growth fund to make up for lost time. But do it in a deferred annuity. They'll be able to withdraw money without a penalty in nine years for college—if they need it. And they'll pay no current taxes on the income, a big consideration since they may be in a 36% tax bracket.

These folks are not spring chickens. That's why they should invest in growth funds for both college and retirement. Two things these parents have going for them: Their children are still very young, and they make a good living. Thus they should be able to sock away a good amount of money.

They have 20 years until retirement, they're in a 36% tax bracket, and the youngest is just 4. The upshot: Invest in a deferred annuity in growth funds—you can tell I like them—to fund both retirement and college for the youngest. For the older kids, add a growth and income fund to the mix.

This client should invest in growth funds for both retirement and college. She should also buy term life insurance. It's good advice for anyone, but especially in the case of a single parent with two young kids. If something happens to the mother, the policy will help pay for college tuition.

For college: Because the younger child has 13 years to go, I'd invest in growth funds. For the older one, with less time before school starts, try growth and income funds. Such funds tend to be a safer bet. For retirement: With a quarter of a century to save, go wild. Go for growth funds.

*These examples assume maximum investment in aggressive growth funds for 401(k) plans.

maybe you'll be earning more money, adjusted for inflation, a decade from now. "Even if you have to borrow, or saddle the kids with tons of debt, you'll do it," says Watertown, Massachusetts, financial planner and author Jonathan Pond.

The upshot: Worry more about retirement, and figure you'll somehow muddle through funding college. (To Ivy League–obsessed parents: You might also want to consider the real-world strategy of Steven Lee and Karen Platt-Lee of San Diego. "We'll keep the college costs down," says Steven, by sending his three daughters to cheaper state schools.)

There are some fairly simple ways to get you going. First, a reality check. No one source can provide information precisely tailored to your situation. That's where an accountant or personal financial planner fits in. You must also have attainable savings goals. Just about every financial planner acknowledges that in real life, you still need money for the mortgage, groceries, and tickets to *Rent*.

While these strategies differ in many respects, they all share the assumption that you'll try to maximize your 401(k) plan, especially if there's a company match. We're also assuming that you don't have parents who will help with the grandkids' tuition and that you're not a candidate for financial aid from colleges. (If you're lucky, you might get some aid if you have a couple of kids in private school at the same time.) We assume as well that you're a fairly conservative investor, content with annual returns of 8%. Finally, many experts suggest that you don't try to save on taxes by putting money in your child's name. There's no way to know whether today's 7-year-old will be, at 18, tomorrow's Lyle Menendez. Another disadvantage of those kiddie accounts is that financial aid officers include a good portion of your child's savings in determining how much you will have to pay. They don't if the same money is socked away in your retirement fund. Here are some other simple tips to balance college and retirement.

◆ *Home is where the cash is.* A good place to start is your mortgage. Planners don't broadcast this strategy—there are big fees when you can talk your client into buying inverse floaters—but for conservative investors, aggressively prepaying your mortgage can save a big hunk of change. Also, in some cases the equity in your home doesn't count when applying for financial aid. One caveat: Planners say you get the most out of this strategy the longer you stay in your home.

Here's how it goes: Say you have 15 years to go till college and a 30-year, $200,000 mortgage at an 8% rate. If you add an extra $500 a month, you'll pay off the mortgage in about 14 years. You will also save $193,000 in interest. And you'll have created a $200,000 line of credit to tap when you're through, which you can use for either goal. Can't afford the $500? Try $200. You'll pay the debt off in 20 years and save $125,000 in interest.

Once you're finished with monthly mortgage payments, you can use that money to pay tuition or invest it in order to get further savings for retirement, says Gary Halbert, president of Pro Futures Capital Management in Austin, Texas. Say your monthly payment was $2,000. Assuming a conservative 8% return, you can accumulate about $360,000 in ten years.

◆ *A sure thing.* Since your retirement is a long-term investment, it's hard to beat the stock market for maximum returns. But truth be told, many people like to know exactly what they'll have in hand when their kids graduate from high school—even if they might be leaving money on the table. If you fit that description, buying a bond can be one of the safest investments to make. There's an array of choices in bonds, ranging from Treasuries to corporate. Whatever the flavor, zero coupons are usually the bond of choice for tuition planning. You buy them at a deep discount and redeem them at face value. No messy questions about what they'll be worth. For $2,722, a 20-year zero will bring you $10,000 at maturity. Say your little one has 13 years before college. Buy a 13-year zero for $4,500 at a 6.4% yield; that will give you $10,000 in 2010. The next year, purchase a 12-year bond for $4,800; that, too, will grow to $10,000 at maturity.

As you get closer to graduation, each zero you buy will be a little more expensive; in the last year you'll pay $9,600. The final tally: $89,000 for a face amount of $130,000. For retirement you can use a similar approach. But you'll also have to invest in an equity growth fund if you want to build up enough savings. One final word: Great as zeros are, you'll have to pay taxes on the bonds' imputed interest, even though you don't collect it until maturity.

◆ **More bang with stocks.** Okay, you're not a wimp. Here's how to juice up a college portfolio with stocks. Even if your child is as old as 7, you still have time to take some chances. Put 80% of your total portfolio in stocks, tempered by 20% in bonds. (You'll gradually change the ratio until it's fifty-fifty a year or so from graduation.) The equity portion would look like this: 40% in large-cap funds investing in companies with market capitalizations between $5 billion and $25 billion, 15% in small companies of less than $1 billion in market value, and 25% in international funds with a well-diversified group of mostly established overseas companies.

The idea here, says Peter Wall, director of investment management for Chase Investment Services Corp., is to reduce risk by including asset classes that don't closely correlate. When one is up, the others tend to be down. That's particularly true for U.S. and overseas funds. One caveat is that when foreign markets are pricey, as they were in mid-1997, they might drop in sympathy with a decline in U.S. markets.

◆ **Behind the eight ball.** Finally, here's some advice if you've begun saving for retirement, as we have assumed, but haven't moved off the dime saving for college: Put all your college money into stocks.

Take a boomer couple—he's 42, she's 41—with two kids, ages 7 and 5, and an income of $150,000. They have $30,000 in her 401(k) and nothing saved for college. Assuming just an 8% rate of return, if they contribute a total of $15,000 to their 401(k) stock plans each year, they'll have about $1.4 million when they retire. For college, they'll put $318 a month into their portfolio and should wind up with $65,000 by the time their older child is ready to graduate from high school. Then they'll continue to grow that portfolio until they're finished with college. Result: enough to send both kids to school, although probably not very expensive ones.

And for the rest of us baby-boomers, it provides some hope. Who says you have to give up the golf vacation in Orlando?

SHOULD YOU BUILD AN IRA?

BY JEFFREY H. BIRNBAUM

◆◆◆

Conventional wisdom says retirement money
should go where the tax deferrals are—in
nondeductible IRAs, for example. Sometimes
conventional wisdom is wrong. Here's why.

◆◆◆

Investing for retirement has long been more a reflex than a thought process. Wherever Uncle Sam situated a tax break, that's where people put their money. The result has been a boom in vehicles like individual retirement accounts and 401(k)s. Gib Watson of KPMG Peat Marwick expresses this strategy succinctly: "Rule One is: Maximize your contributions into tax-deferred plans."

Not so fast. These days there are also Rules Two, Three, and even Four. True, IRAs and 401(k)s are usually the wisest investments for retirement. The tax deductions they can provide for contributions at the front end are almost too good to pass up.

But not always. An analysis of the alternatives done by Price Waterhouse for FORTUNE indicates that sometimes the conventional wisdom is just plain wrong. In particular, the type of IRA available to couples with taxable income over $40,000 ($50,000 beginning in 1998)—the one that doesn't provide a deduction for contributions up front—can actually lag behind or be a tossup compared with your basic, fully taxable account. Says Andrew B. Lyon, a principal consultant at Price Waterhouse: "The tax-preferred account isn't always the best investment for retirement."

How is that possible? The answer, ironically enough, has to do with the taxes you end up owing on a tax-deferred account. That's because distributions from IRAs and 401(k)s are taxed at ordinary income-tax rates, while long-term appreciation in taxable stock and mutual fund accounts is taxed at the capital gains rate. This means that the costs of withdrawing money from the two types of accounts can be quite different for those at higher income levels.

Price Waterhouse's case study quantified those cost differences. Its conclusion? Sometimes the lower withdrawal costs on a taxable

BEATING THE IRA

◆◆◆

Set aside $2,000 for your retirement, and what you end up with depends on where you put it, and for how long. If you focus solely on tax deferral—a popular strategy—you could lose out. The numbers in bold show where a taxable account beats out a nondeductible IRA, under the new tax law.

$2,000 GROWS TO...

Years until retirement	Nondeductible IRA	Taxable account (20% capital gains)
5	$2,679	$2,816
10	$3,773	$4,063
15	$5,535	$5,965
20	$8,373	$8,869
25	$12,943	$13,303

Assumes 10% annual appreciation on all accounts; 30% of taxable account gains are in the form of dividends and realized short- or long-term capital gains. Investor's marginal tax rate is 44.366%. All returns are after tax.

FORTUNE CHART / SOURCE: PRICE WATERHOUSE

account actually made up for the tax-free compounding benefits on a tax-deferred account.

The study began with a few assumptions. First, a 36% federal tax rate, which in mid-1997 applied to individuals with annual incomes between $124,650 and $271,050, or to couples with income between $151,750 and $271,050. Adding in the phaseout of personal exemptions, limits on itemized deductions, and the imposition of state income taxes (which were calculated at 9%, roughly California's level), the study ended up with a marginal tax rate of 44.366%. In other words, that fat gain on your IRA would get sliced nearly in half.

The case study then compared a basic, nondeductible IRA with various taxable accounts, all assumed to appreciate at 10% annually. In one scenario, the investment considered is a "growth and income" mutual fund that throws off 7% a year in dividends and short- and long-term capital gains. (The rest of the appreciation is unrealized capital gains.) The result: Investors who are within about five years of retirement would actually get more by holding the fund in a taxable account rather than an IRA. For periods longer than that, the compounding advantage of the IRA would win out.

But what if the two accounts were invested in a large-cap index fund that throws off only 3% a year in dividends and realized capital gains? In that scenario, a taxable account offers a greater after-tax return over as long a period as 15 years.

Another reason to think again about IRAs was provided by Congress in 1997 when it cut the tax on long-term capital gains to 20% from the top rate of 28%. That change created a differential of over 19% between the top ordinary tax rate, now 39.6%, and the top capital gains tax rate, which could make a big difference when it comes to deciding where to dump your retirement savings. [For a discussion on IRAs introduced in the new tax code, see Chapter Four, "Real-World Questions and Answers on the New Tax Law."]

In the Price Waterhouse study, the lower capital gains tax opens even more advantages for taxable plans. With a top federal tax rate of 20%, holding a large-cap index fund outside a tax-preferred account would actually work out better than putting it in a nondeductible IRA for investments held as long as 25 years. (The growth and income fund in the case study, with its higher level of currently taxable gains, would still be better than a nondeductible IRA over a ten-year investment horizon.)

That said, it's important to keep these findings in perspective. Investors normally can't go wrong if they put as much as they can into a 401(k) or other account that permits a deduction for the contribution: The Price Waterhouse analysis indicates that this is true even with the capital gains levy slash. "A tax-deductible retirement account dominates other forms of retirement savings," Lyon of Price Waterhouse says. And, yes, IRAs do work out better for those who can take the $2,000-a-year per person deduction—starting on 1998 returns, that's only for those who earn up to $30,000 a year ($50,000 for couples).

Those who make more, and who have pension plans through their employers, can't deduct their contributions. And it's precisely when an investor is forced to resort to accounts that aren't tax-subsidized at the front end that doubts should emerge.

WHAT TO EXPECT FROM TOMORROW'S TAXES

BY SHELLY BRANCH

◆◆◆

Thanks to Uncle Sam, retirement may be more expensive than you think.

◆◆◆

Sure, you know the new rules of retirement: no more fat pensions, no gold watch, no guarantees about Social Security. Less talked about, though, is another golden-years myth—the one about how Uncle Sam finally lays off a bit. "Most people have the expectation that they can drop to a lower tax bracket in retirement," says Steve Oaks, a financial planner with Price Waterhouse. "But today, that's just not reality."

In fact, Oaks estimates that some 85% of his clients will, at best, remain in their preretirement tax brackets. Other planners agree; Ron Rogé of Bohemia, New York, figures that roughly one of every three clients can expect marginal rates to take a hike.

How's that? A major culprit is the so-called back-end tax—the levy that is at long last due on withdrawals from your 401(k) and other tax-deferred accounts. "You'd be surprised how many people totally ignore the tax hit on this money" when planning the finances of their retirement, says Rogé.

What a mistake, since distributions from these plans are subject to ordinary tax rates, not the more favorable capital gains rate, which Congress newly topped out at 20% in July 1997. So as heartening as it may be to see your 401(k) plan soak up the stock gains of the decade—not to mention tax-free compounding and an

THE BRACKET SQUEEZE

◆◆◆

*Figure you won't have to worry as much about taxes when you retire? Consider this hypothetical couple, who saved enough ($1.5 million) to match their pre-retirement lifestyle. From one year before retirement (age 64) to six years later (age 70), their tax bracket actually rises.**

BEFORE RETIREMENT		DURING RETIREMENT	
Income	$115,000	Minimum retirement account distribution	$95,000
		Taxable Social Security benefits	$20,000
LESS:			
401(k) contributions	−$18,500	LESS:	
Deductions	−$15,000	Deductions (without mortgage interest)	−$ 8,000
Personal exemptions	−$ 5,100	Personal exemptions	−$ 5,100
Taxable income	$76,400	Taxable income	$101,900
TAX RATE: 28%		**TAX RATE: 31%**	

* Based on 1997 federal tax rates only.   FORTUNE CHART / SOURCE: GRANT THORNTON

employer's matching contributions—they may end up throwing off just enough income to land you in Bill Gates's bracket.

If you can't imagine you're headed for such a scenario, just consider the basics. Let's assume that you and your spouse have a combined income of (just to keep things simple) $100,000 and have been putting aside $15,000 or so a year into your 401(k) or other tax-deferred plans. Meanwhile, you've been lapping up tax deductions on your mortgage and writing off the kids too.

By age 70½, when retirees must begin making mandatory minimum plan withdrawals, you could easily have a million-dollar-plus stash. At the same time, you will probably have lost at least some of those cushy deductions you've gotten so used to counting on. Edward Miller, a senior tax manager at accounting firm Grant Thornton, points out, "The distributions you take will affect your overall bracket."

What's more, all of this assumes that you choose not to do any free-lance work after you retire—like consulting for your former employer. Do that—as many baby-boomer seniors are expected to—and you get socked by an additional tax burden: the 15.3% self-employment tax.

The obvious solution is to save even more for retirement, especially since many planners are also chucking the old notion that you'll need just 75% of your preretirement income to subsist on Golden Pond. With dependent parents, the doubling of the cost of living every 14 years, and so on, more planners agree that you will probably need to maintain your current income in retirement.

Is there any way to lighten the tax load? Putting retirement savings in taxable accounts can sometimes be preferable to opening a nondeductible IRA. Another loophole: If you own shares of your company's stock within a 401(k), keep them there. This is important, because if the stock is rolled over into a self-directed IRA, it will be taxed at income-tax rates when withdrawn. But if you keep those shares in your 401(k), then upon withdrawal they will still be taxed at the capital gains rate, which is lower. And who knows? Maybe by the time you retire—and have actually started drawing on that 401(k) money—Congress will have hacked those rates down even further.

WILL SOCIAL SECURITY BE THERE FOR YOU?

BY JEFFREY H. BIRNBAUM

◆◆◆

Don't panic. Social Security isn't broken
yet and won't be for years. But that
doesn't mean the system won't change.

◆◆◆

Washington has a new growth industry: fixing Social Security. Almost every think tank and interest group in town has a Social Security project under way. The Cato Institute has budgeted

$3 million to promote privatization. The Concord Coalition is developing a parlor game that will enable taxpayers to role-play ways to save the system. And a new organization called Economic Security 2000 is training activists across the country to lobby for reform. So much is happening that an umbrella group called the Social Security Reform Coalition publishes a special calendar just to keep track of it all.

The only problem is, Social Security isn't broken yet and won't be for a long time. According to government estimates, the Social Security trust fund will be perfectly solvent for the next 32 years. After that it will still be able to pay benefits at a respectable 75% of current levels. Baby-boomers may fret. Gen Xers may despair. We'll all hear plenty of scare stories between now and 2029, since fear mongering is a way of life in Washington. But truth be told, there isn't much reason to panic.

Social Security will undergo some revision—perhaps within the next decade—and its outline can already be discerned. The system of the future will cost a bit more in taxes, delay retirement by a couple of years, distribute fewer benefits to upper-income retirees, and possibly permit the private investment of a small portion of the money that now goes into the trust fund. Most of these changes are what Carolyn Weaver of the American Enterprise Institute calls "shin kickers"—momentarily painful but relatively minor. For all the Chicken Little–ism, they are probably all that will be needed to cope with the biggest challenge in the system's 60-year history: providing for the retirement of the boomers, who will begin turning 65 in 14 years. Not by coincidence, the trust fund will start paying out more than it collects the very next year, 2012.

This isn't a mere policy debate. What we're talking about here is how big a check you will receive from the government's most important pension fund. That depends upon a number of variables, including how long you worked, how much you earned, and your retirement age. For example, a 35-year-old who started working at 22 and earns $40,000 in 1997 can expect to receive an annual Social Security benefit of $14,748—in 1997 dollars—if she retires at 65. A person with a relatively higher income will receive somewhat smaller benefits. Here is a closer look at the leading options to keep your payout as close as possible to full strength.

◆ *The rich will pay more and get less.* Social Security already dispenses its largesse in a highly progressive manner. Retirees who had low incomes during their working lives get a higher percentage of that income back than do individuals who were top earners prior to retiring. Experts agree that any "fix" will skew those figures even more against upper-income earners. Rich folks will probably get whacked with higher payroll taxes too. At the moment, only wages up to $65,400 are hit by the 6.2% FICA tax, which finances Social Security. When the system is repaired, watch that ceiling rise.

◆ *Everyone will have to work longer.* One of the main problems with Social Security is that people are living too long—or at least longer than they used to. When the program started, the average life expectancy was under 65, the age at which full retirement benefits were then paid. Now life expectancy is over 75. As a result, more people are collecting Social Security for a greater number of years. To stop the inevitable drain on the trust fund, policymakers are likely to peg retirement more closely to life expectancy. A leading plan would gradually raise the retirement age to 69 from the current 67 (for people born after 1959) and also increase the number of work years counted in the benefit calculation, to 40 from 35.

◆ *The taxman cometh.* Nobody likes a tax increase, but to keep Social Security up to par, a boost in the payroll tax is always a possibility. But there are other, slyer alternatives. The most inviting is a kick to the shins of the rich. Retirees with incomes over $34,000 ($44,000 for couples) already pay taxes on up to 85% of their benefits. Lawmakers will be tempted to make changes in that same direction by taxing more, and perhaps all, of Social Security payments received by the affluent. Slyer still is the old cost-of-living ploy. Under it, the government's annual inflation adjustment would be pared, which would slow the rise in Social Security benefits for everyone. It would also push people—especially big earners—into higher tax brackets sooner, inflicting yet another bruise on the well-off.

◆ *Gambling (with the future) may be legalized.* Wall Street is salivating at the prospect of investing even a fraction of the half-trillion-dollar Social Security trust fund. Critics say that would only make it

ESTIMATED SOCIAL SECURITY BENEFITS

◆◆◆

The annual benefits shown below—in 1997 dollars—are for employees who begin working at age 22 and retire at age 65.[1]

Your age in 1997	Your earnings in 1996		
	$40,000	$50,000	$62,700+[2]
35	$14,748	$16,248	$18,528
45	$14,748	$16,248	$18,228
55	$14,712	$15,924	$17,220
65	$14,460	$15,264	$15,912

[1] Age at which full benefits are paid will rise from 65 to 67 between 2003 and 2027.
[2] Earnings above this amount ($65,400 in 1997) are not taxed for, or applied to, Social Security.

For a more precise calculation of your Social Security benefits, call 800-772-1213 or go online to http://www.ssa.gov/

FORTUNE CHART / SOURCE: SOCIAL SECURITY ADMINISTRATION

harder to erase Social Security's pending shortfall: Why, after all, divert money from a fund that's already in deficit? And how safe is the stock market? But don't count out some form of privatization. Most people think they are smarter investors than Uncle Sam. One compromise would allow people who are still working to keep and invest part of the money they now lose to the payroll tax. In exchange, these folks would receive lower Social Security benefits when they retire. Another option would permit the government to invest part of the trust fund in private securities rather than in low-yielding Treasury bills. Theoretically this would improve the return of the entire system.

Social Security never was supposed to provide retirement benefits to satisfy everyone. It was designed as a safety net for low-wage workers. Even today, its average monthly check, $745 per worker

($1,256 per couple), isn't much. Instead of worrying about the size of your Social Security paycheck, you should save, save, save as much of your own paycheck as you can. At the same time, don't believe all the hype about the system disappearing. A little fiddling here and there will almost certainly guarantee its survival. Isn't that a kick?

WHAT TO KNOW ABOUT WHOLE LIFE INSURANCE

BY MARCIA VICKERS

◆◆◆

When you hit your 40s, expect that someone will try to sell you a whole life insurance policy. Here's what you should know before you sign up.

◆◆◆

A bloated fly buzzes around your head as the wall clock interminably ticks away the minutes. On the couch sits the insurance salesman—a hint of Binaca on his breath—who drones on about many meaningless things, until it comes time for the Pitch. "As you get ooolder," he says, leaning across the coffee table, "the cost of term insurance skyrockets, so we should really talk about switching you into a whole life policy." He has some dramatic charts to bolster his point, even a laptop that maps out the crisscrossing trajectories of the different premium payments. You've never trusted this guy, even if he is an old college chum, but you have to admit that what he says seems to make a lot of sense.

His line goes something like this: The term life you bought years ago has a premium that's been rising steadily. Now that you're 45, you still need insurance, but because you're older that premium is set to ratchet up again. By contrast, the whole life he's trying to sell you sports premiums that will stay fixed until you die. After you express some shock at how sky high those premiums are, he releases part two of that pitch: They're high because whole life policies have built-in savings accounts that let you build "cash value" on a tax-deferred basis. You can borrow against it or even pocket it—it's a wonderful little nest egg. The kicker: You can convert your term policy into whole life without a physical. Now you're truly befuddled: Does a switch make sense?

The answer: probably not. Says James Hunt, life insurance actuary at the Consumer Federation of America in Washington, D.C.: "Insurance salesmen will always go for the easy sale and try to push you into full-commission whole life. But there are many products and strategies out there." Weigh each and every one before you make a move.

Your first, most obvious option may be your wisest: Stand pat with term life. Term rates can be so cheap these days, it might pay to stick with them, even into your 60s, long past the age most salesmen will tell you it's time to switch to whole life. Can't stomach a premium hike when it's time to renew? Check out the 1-800 number and Internet quote services offering free price comparisons on term policies tailored for you (two are www.quotesmith.com and www.quickquote.com). But be aware that such services earn commissions. They also offer cash-value policies that are, as Hunt puts it, "often schlock."

Your salesman will point out that no term policy can match the tax-deferred status of the cash-value portion of a whole life. He's right, but it's time for a reality check. According to the Consumer Federation of America, the estimated average annual return for a whole life policy held 20 years is just 6%. By contrast, U.S. diversified equity mutual funds have returned 15.1% annually on average over the past 20 years, according to the Chicago research firm Morningstar Inc. Stocks may not match that strong return going forward, but it still makes sense to buy dirt-cheap term and sock away money in a fund that will beat the pants off any whole life policy. And if you crave that tax deferral, put the fund in an IRA.

Does all this mean you should stick with term under any circumstances? No. Your insurance-salesman friend is right when he says that term can get mighty pricey. A 40-year-old nonsmoking male, for example, might pay a first-year premium of $502 for $400,000 of annual, renewable term insurance. (Whole life would cost him $5,741 annually.) But by the time he is 67 years old, the term premium may have just topped $5,576 a year. At age 79, if he were to stick with the same term policy, his premium would have risen to an incredible $27,154 a year. Says professor Travis Pritchett of the University of South Carolina: "Term generally becomes prohibitively expensive for most people in their 60s and 70s." If you plan to keep insurance into those years, you'll want to sign on to some sort of cash value policy in your 40s.

It pays to shop around and find one of the low-load variety. These can shave 10% to 15% off the cost of your death benefit over time. The first type of policy you're likely to come across is universal, which builds cash value much like whole life: You'll still get subpar returns on the cash value, but you can vary the premium amount and even adjust the face amount of the policy from year to year. Low-load variable universal offers the same kind of premium flexibility, but the holder can invest the cash-value portion in mutual funds offered by the insurer. These can goose returns. One overlooked course of action: By your 60s, with the kids grown and the mortgage paid, you might not need life insurance anymore, so let your policy lapse. This tactic has an added benefit. Say that to your insurance salesman loudly and clearly, and he's sure to grab his hat but quick.

ESTATE PLANNING: MISTAKES TO AVOID

BY LAWRENCE A. ARMOUR

◆◆◆

Even sophisticated people make mistakes when planning their estates— and it costs them millions.

◆◆◆

Estate plainning isn't only for the rich and famous anymore. The booming stock market and its impact on 401(k) plans have created a lot of "average Joe and Jane" millionares. To help you get serious about your estate, FORTUNE asked four experts to discuss critical issues in the changing world of estates. The panel included

S. Stacy Eastland, a partner in Houston's Baker & Botts; **Elizabeth L. Mathieu**, president and CEO of Neuberger & Berman Trust Co.; **Carlyn S. McCaffrey**, a partner in Weil Gotshal & Manges; and **Arthur D. Sederbaum**, a partner in Patterson Belknap Webb & Tyler.

What's the biggest estate planning mistake people are making these days?

Sederbaum: Forgetting that assets in a retirement plan like a 401(k) were never taxed. When they are finally distributed, the beneficiary has to pay an income tax. In addition, an estate tax will be imposed on whatever remains in the retirement plan at death, and a third tax—which is generally called the success tax—could take another 15% bite out of the excess retirement accumulation.

Mathieu: People also forget they have to make decisions before they turn 70$^{1}/_{2}$ about how they are going to take distributions from their retirement plans, and who has rights to those assets after their death. If they don't, the bill for income, estate, and success taxes could reach 85%. The total tax bill can actually go to 125%, but Uncle Sam is only authorized to take 100% of your assets. The government wants us to save for retirement, but not too much.

McCaffrey: The purpose of retirement plans wasn't to enable us to accumulate money that we'd leave to our children. They were established so we'd be able to take care of ourselves when we retire, and Uncle Sam feels he's done his bit if he takes it all back after we die.

Can't creative estate planning get around the problem?

McCaffrey: You can delay and defer taxes on assets that have accumulated in a retirement plan, but you can't completely escape them. On the other hand, there are some things you can do to ease the pain. For example, if you need money when you're in retirement and have the option of selling Microsoft stock you own outright or taking cash out of your IRA, the smart thing would be to dip into the IRA. At your death, your Microsoft and your IRA will be subject to the same estate tax, but there will be a step up in the cost basis of the stock. That is, your estate won't pay income tax on the appreciation in the stock, but it will have to pay income tax on the IRA.

The boom in the stock market and its impact on 401(k) plans have created a lot of new millionaires. If someone wanted to get serious about estate planning, what's the first step?

Mathieu: Deciding whether your priority is retirement income or estate planning, and what you want to accomplish in each.

Sederbaum: Then you'd need a balance sheet. You don't have to get into the nitty-gritty of how many shares of XYZ you own, but you need to separate assets into broad categories—real estate, marketable securities, cash, life insurance, retirement plans—and divide them into classes that show whether they're owned by husband or wife, or jointly. Then you would figure out what the income and cash-flow situation would be if one of the two were to die. And then you'd want to focus on the individual or institutional executors, trustees, and guardians you'd want to include in your estate planning process.

Eastland: In thinking about the fiduciary appointments, it's important to recognize that the person you'd want as a guardian for your minor children would almost certainly be different from the person you would want as an executor or a trustee. And then the key question is, How would you distribute your property if you didn't have taxes to worry about?

Are you suggesting that the goal is not to avoid taxes?

Eastland: That would be the tail wagging the dog. Once you figure out where you want the properties to go, then you go to work and try to save taxes.

Sederbaum: A plan is worth nothing if it saves gobs of estate tax dollars and yet doesn't do what you want it to accomplish.

Who should be part of the estate planning team?

McCaffrey: This may not be a popular thing to say, but if we're talking about someone who has a house, some insurance, a salary, and an uncomplicated tax return, you don't need to bring in layers of professionals. A lawyer can prepare all the estate planning documents.

Mathieu: I'd disagree. Most people have mutual funds, an IRA, and stocks they own outright. Even with the greatest legal documents and the best planning in the world, you can end up with a mess if the money is poorly managed or the investment manager has no clue how to respond to the retirement income and estate planning that's been done.

McCaffrey: To the extent the person has investments that need to be managed, I agree. But I draw a distinction between the things we do as estate planners and the things others do as financial planners. Investment planning is important, but it's not necessarily part of the estate planning process, which involves wills and trusts and that sort of thing.

Let's get back to goals. I want to make sure my wife has enough to live comfortably and my grandchildren go to college. Where should I begin?

Eastland: Right at the start. The most important document is your will, which would deal, among other things, with the guardianship of your children. You should also probably have a health care power of attorney, a financial power of attorney, and other documents that deal with your care while you're alive.

McCaffrey: You'd need a durable power of attorney, which means it lasts after incompetency. A health care proxy gives another person the right to make medical decisions for you, and you might want a living will, which is an ancillary document that describes the care you would or would not want if you couldn't speak for yourself.

Mathieu: We're seeing increasing use of the standby living trust, which tells a trustee what to do in case of incompetency or illness. It is fully revocable and amendable by the client. It requires a trustee to act as you wish, whereas a power of attorney only authorizes a person to act as they wish.

To what extent is it necessary to establish trusts if we're not talking about a megamillion-dollar estate?

McCaffrey: A revocable trust is for a person who's alive, and there's debate about its value. But once an individual dies and we're dealing with the way property passes to members of the family, most people with an estate in excess of $600,000 or with small children need at least one form of trust. Someone with minor children certainly needs a trust, or the money would go to the child outright and be managed by a guardian subject to the supervision of a surrogate's court. You would want it to be managed by a trustee you would appoint, and you would want to have control over the age at which the children get the money. In the absence of a trust, a child in New York would get the money at age 18, which is not what most people feel is appropriate.

The next issue is whether you need trusts for your spouse. When the marriage is a happy one, most wills leave the bulk of the estate to the surviving spouse, which enables you to defer estate taxes until the death of the surviving spouse. But you can accomplish this either with outright bequests or through a trust, so why pick a trust? You might if you didn't think your spouse were capable of managing money. Or if you were worried that your spouse would remarry and leave all the money you earned to the new spouse. Or if you wanted to make sure your property goes to your children when your spouse dies.

Eastland: Also, using a trust doesn't mean that you have to deny a spouse decision-making authority. You can design a trust under which the spouse has control over who gets the assets after he or she passes away. Many people want their spouse to have this kind of leverage over the children and grandchildren. If that's the case, you can build the power of appointment—one of my clients calls it the power of disappointment—into the trust.

Mathieu: That's another reason to have a trust. It enables you to get an impartial arbiter into the act. Think about it. Do you really want to give your brother the problem of dealing with your five kids who can't stand one another?

McCaffrey: A fourth reason for a trust might be to protect your spouse from creditors. An individual generally can't protect assets from creditors, but if my husband were in an automobile accident and got sued for millions, I could have made sure there was always something there for him by leaving at least part of what I left him in trust.

Eastland: W.C. Fields was a pretty good estate planner, because he always said he didn't want to be a millionaire, he just wanted to live like one. That's what a trust does: takes assets off your books. There are lots of advantages to that, including creditor, divorce, and tax protection.

Sederbaum: Let's not forget the generation-skipping trust, which is in addition to all the others we've discussed. The GST allows a grandparent, say, to create a trust that passes up to $1 million through the child's generation to a grandchild's generation without having transfer taxes imposed. Some states—South Dakota, Delaware, Wisconsin, Idaho, and Alaska—allow these trusts to exist in perpetuity. But any trust that skips a generation is by definition a lengthy one, and the other 45 states allow trusts to exist for 90 years or more.

Mathieu: This is an important concept for all transfer taxes—gift, estate, and GST—because assets are distributed when a trust ends. When the person who receives them dies, an estate tax has to be paid. If the trust never ends, the assets never in effect get transfer-taxed.

Eastland: This is something for people in their 40s or 50s to think about whose parents are alive. They should at least plant the seed that the best way parents can leave assets to them may be in a trust. The money won't be taxed in the child's estate if the trust is properly drawn up to the $1 million exemption. And it's always better to receive an asset in trust. The children can be named as trustees if the parents think they are responsible, but no creditor or divorce court can take away property that a child receives in trust.

Any other advice for older parents?

McCaffrey: They might think about paying tuition for their grandchildren. So long as it's paid directly to the educational institution, there's no gift tax, and it doesn't use up the annual exclusion. Grandparents can also write checks for orthodontist bills and their grandchildren's other medical expenses. It's a way to deplete an estate to reduce estate taxes.

Eastland: One thing I've tried to emphasize with grandparents is that gift taxes are cheaper than estate taxes, even though they're the same rate. The way the IRS calculates the estate tax, you pay a tax on the tax of whatever's left to your beneficiaries, which can add up to 122%. The gift tax, by contrast, is 55%.

Are there any other trusts to look at?

McCaffrey: Most people should think about a trust to save estate taxes on life insurance. Let's say a husband has $500,000 of life insurance. He should put the policy into an irrevocable trust that says the funds are available for his wife's care if she survives him. She could have a lot of control over the trust, even the right to fire the trustee if the trustee isn't sensitive to her needs. On her death the remaining money would go to the children, free of estate tax, in trust until whatever age the client thinks is appropriate.

What other tips have you got on insurance and trusts?

Sederbaum: Here's something to think about. The process of diminishing one's estate for tax purposes is often a difficult pill to swallow because you have to give something away or, as the tax code puts it, "part with the dominion and control" over an asset. It can be hard for someone to give away 100 shares of Microsoft, because he gets benefits from the stock. Life insurance is easy—or let's say it's a lot easier—to give away because it matures after the insured dies. In other words, telling someone it's better to assign ownership rights in a life insurance policy to a trust is a lot easier than counseling him to give away other assets.

Mathieu: Trusts by nature are customized to whatever needs you're trying to meet. The other thing to remember is that you have to make assumptions about how long you're going to live and how much you think you'll be spending on retirement living, health care, and so on before you set up the trust. And then you have to review it on a regular basis. It's a dynamic process. You don't just create a trust and file it away in a drawer.

CHAPTER SIX

◆◆◆

HOT STUFF
IN THE DIGITAL WORLD

WHERE TO FIND MEDICAL ADVICE ON THE INTERNET

BY ERYN BROWN

When illness strikes, the Internet can be a great place to go for help and information.

Two years ago, graphic designer Sheri Wood found out that she had thyroid cancer. Isolated from big-city medical resources—she lives in rural Versailles, Kentucky—she turned to the Web to learn more about her illness. Today, post-treatment and healthy, she's still logging on as a frequent visitor to Mediconsult.com's Cancer Emotional Support Group (www. mediconsult.com), which is monitored by a doctor and lets her share her experiences with other far-flung patients. "The Internet has been really wonderful for this," she says. "I got addicted."

The Internet has long been a rich source of medical information—information you're likely to ignore until you or a loved one gets sick. When that time comes, you'll find the Web can be a great place to go for help. Online bulletin boards are a natural medium for patient-support groups, especially for people in hard-to-reach places, like Sheri Wood. What's more, the Internet is searchable. Why hike to the medical library to dig through cumbersome volumes of the *New England Journal of Medicine* when you can stay at home, type "heart disease," and get much of what you need in a flash?

Using the Web can also help you deal with health care workers. Your doctor might be too tight-lipped, protective, or busy to explain things as fully as you'd like. But armed with information from the Internet, you can ask intelligent questions and draw him out. The way he reacts can help you assess his competence as well.

Finding the site that suits you best may require a bit of rooting around. In fact, the biggest obstacle you're likely to face online is information overload. Commercial services like CompuServe, with their scores of active support groups, can focus your search. But most of the action these days is on the Web; indeed, everyone in health care from the government to your HMO seems to be there, offering support groups, medical research, and advice.

A good way to find precisely the help you need is to start with a visit to a search engine, which will generate a list of sites tailored to any topic. Old standbys like Yahoo (www.yahoo.com) serve well, or you can try medical-specific search sites like HealthAtoZ (www.healthatoz.com) and Achoo (www.achoo.com).

If you have serious questions about a disease, national health organizations' Websites are highly dependable. The American Medical Association (www.ama-assn.org) lists local physicians, while the Centers for Disease Control (www.cdc.gov) and the National Cancer Institute (wwwicic.nci.nih.gov) have excellent databases. Standout academic sites include Emory University's MedWeb (www.gen.emory.edu/MEDWEB), with amazing links for research, and the University of Pennsylvania's Oncolink (www.oncolink.upenn.edu), perhaps the Web authority on cancer.

One of the most approachable sites is the Mayo Clinic Health O@sis (www.mayo.ivi.com). It has easy-to-use sections on cardiac health and cancer, and lets you search for more esoteric topics. The information is hardly sugar-coated. One page deals with tongue maladies such as furred tongue and black hairy tongue, complete with blurbs and photos. This is pretty unsettling stuff, though the Health O@sis reassures the user that both disorders are treatable with a toothbrush. At the bottom of the page is a link that lets you ask, "Is it cancer?" (It's not.)

You can find pop medical advice too. A Web fave is Ask Dr. Weil (www.drweil.com), which features Q&A with Dr. Andrew Weil, the popular natural medicine specialist. A typical question might ask about alternative remedies for depression. The depression Q&A sends the user not only to the predictably New Age BuddhaNet Meditation Workshop but also to the Mental Health Net Depression Guide and to PharmInfoNet, both with comprehensive link lists.

Wherever you roam, beware. The Internet is also an open forum for all kinds of quacks. If you use common sense, you should be okay: Information from the American Cancer Society's page will be more dependable than a note in a chat group. Some sites try to do the weeding for you. Mediconsult.com President Ian Sutcliffe says his editors have screened out dubious advice, including one participant's suggestion that cancer patients drink a bit of their own urine each morning. But you can't rely on gatekeepers. And never let cybermedicine replace your real-life physician.

FINANCIAL PLANNING ON THE WEB

BY SHELLY BRANCH

Even the numerically challenged can find help from the interactive worksheets and other aids on the Internet.

Pardon us for prying, but how's your safety net? You know, that elaborate system of investments, savings, and insurance known as a financial plan? If yours is outdated, or even nonexistent, don't worry. These days you can spin your own safety net with the help of, well, the Internet.

Not long ago only math wonks would've dispensed with professionals to wrestle personally with the intricacies of financial planning. Today, though, anyone with an Internet connection can reach into the Web's 90 million pages and pull out richly detailed information about asset allocation, mutual funds, and interest rates—even wedding insurance. To help the numerically challenged, many sites provide cheat sheets: interactive worksheets, or "calculators," into which you enter your data to make your planning more effective and fun. Says John Markese, president of the American Association of Individual Investors (AAII): "There's always been a demand for financial data, but the trend now is about more robust, educational information. And that's reflected on the Internet."

Does this Web data windfall mean you can do without a financial planner altogether? Probably not. But many services on the Internet can help you economize on a planner's services (typical rates: $125 to $200 an hour) by making you a better-informed client.

Don't be intimidated by the 600 or more Websites that pop up if you search using the keyword "investing." You can get a solid start at the AAII's own site (www.aaii.org). Its pages are packed with information on portfolio management and investment terminology, plus useful tips on coping with "data overload"—something you'll surely encounter on your planning journey. What's more, the pages are advertising-free.

Next explore the sites of the two mutual fund giants Fidelity (www.fidelity.com) and Strong (www.strong-funds.com). The sales pitches you'll encounter on these sites may be annoyingly zealous, but you'll also find useful tools for 401(k) asset allocation and calculators to help forecast your savings needs. Fidelity offers the Web's best retirement tool: an interactive worksheet that gauges your total nest-egg needs based on age, assets, and other information you provide.

In building a financial plan, most investors prefer the instant diversification of mutual funds to the task of assembling a portfolio of individual stocks. The Web is rich in up-to-date fund industry data, much of it free. Get the big picture from Marla Brill, a personal-finance columnist for the *Boston Globe*. She stuffs content into every pixel of her Mutual Funds Interactive site (www. fundsinteractive.com). You won't find interactive bells and whistles here; the site's forte is original analysis and commentary—the sort of wisdom you need to hone your portfolio for the long term.

The website's mix includes basics on fund strategies, a news group section where you can trade tips and ideas with other fundophiles, and unpretentious articles in the Expert's Corner. Investing gurus who have weighed in include Thurman Smith of the *Equity Fund Outlook* newsletter and Ron Rogé, a fee-only financial planner from Centereach, New York.

For more detailed data and impressive screening tools, click on NETworth (www.networth.galt.com). Software innovator Intuit

BUILDING YOUR WEALTH ON THE WEB

◆◆◆

Want to pick funds like a seasoned pro? Put your retirement savings on the fast track? These sites, all with free access, can help boost your knowledge and your assets.

INVESTING BASICS/MUTUAL FUND STRATEGY	
American Association of Individual Investors	www.aaii.org
Fidelity	www.fidelity.com
Strong	www.strong-funds.com
Mutual Funds Interactive	www.fundsinteractive.com
NETworth	www.networth.galt.com

DEBT MANAGEMENT	
Financenter	www.financenter.com
Bank Rate Monitor	www.bankrate.com
HSH Associates	www.hsh.com

INSURANCE	
Insurance Resource Center	www.insureinfo.com
LifeNet	www.lifenet.com
Quotesmith	www.quotesmith.com
Insurance News Network	www.insure.com

PLANNERS	
National Association of Personal Financial Advisors	www.napfa.org
International Association for Financial Planning	www.iafp.org

operates this site, which lets you schuss through mountains of data supplied by Morningstar. Whether you're thinking micro (what's the hottest tech fund?) or macro (how have equity funds fared this year?), you'll find plenty to keep you busy. You may get addicted to NETworth's powerful screening device, which narrows down 7,000 fund possibilities to those that suit your needs. You pick the criteria: up to 13 variables, such as ten-year performance history and 12b-1 fees.

Rescuing clients from debt overload is one of the trickiest tasks financial planners face, but unless your debt is totally out of hand, the Web can help you assess and manage what you owe.

Take credit cards. If you're like the typical American, you owe a balance of $1,900 per card. How big a drag on your finances does that represent? For the sobering truth, tap into the credit card pages at Financenter (www.financenter.com), where a nifty payment calculator lets you confront your personal horror in seconds. Got $5,000 packed on at 18%? If you make just the minimum payment of $100 monthly, the program informs you, you'll need 101 months and about $10,100 out of your pocket to repay the loan.

For those not ready to slice up the old Visa, another way to avoid plastic hell is to carry a low-rate card. You can get free access to the nation's best credit card deals at Bank Rate Monitor's Infobank (www. bankrate.com). The site posts a weekly 70-city survey of the best rates, depending on your payment habits, and even lets you apply online for some cards. You'll find other banking rates and news here too, including information on auto, personal, and home-equity loans.

What about your mortgage, surely the biggest debt of your life? Whether you're shopping for a new loan or looking to refinance, it pays to know your rates. How much do you stand to save with a 15-year vs. a 30-year loan? Are you better off with a fixed-rate or adjustable-rate product? When does refinancing make sense?

For answers to such borrowing conundrums, check out the calculators at Financenter. You can estimate your monthly payments for a hypothetical mortgage; reckon the amount you can afford to borrow now; and weigh a loan with more points against one with a lower rate. To work with these calculators, you'll need to have your financial facts on hand—they ask for particulars such as origination fees and property taxes. But the quality of the answers is high.

To size up fixed-rate financing, Hugh Chou's mortgage calculators are a powerful aid. You'll find them at the HSH Associates site (www.hsh.com). For the truly motivated, Chou even offers a worksheet that shows how to do mortgage amortizations by hand. Both

HSH and the Bank Rate Monitor Infobank are useful for sorting out different types of mortgage products, and both offer updates on interest rate trends.

A good planner wouldn't dare cut you loose without making sure that your home, other assets, and income are properly insured. Although you can't yet purchase a policy on the Web (a hard signature is required), you can use the Web to boost your insurance IQ and reduce the risk of getting ripped off. There's plenty of unbiased information at the Insurance Resource Center (www. insureinfo.com). The site has helpful checklists and answers to frequently asked questions on life, auto, and homeowner's policies.

If you suspect that you've got too little life insurance—a common shortfall for couples with dependents—you can do a quick needs analysis at LifeNet (www.lifenet.com). You might be suspicious that its calculator would overstate your insurance requirements; in fact, FORTUNE found that its output matched an independent planner's recommendation almost dollar for dollar.

Should you decide you need another 50 grand of coverage, you can get instant quotes on term policies, the purest form of life insurance, with a quick hit at Quotesmith (www.quotesmith.com). By typing in your birth date, coverage level, and health information, you'll prompt the best rates from over 100 companies.

Your coverage, though, is only as good as the company that underwrites it. So don't forget to check your insurer's financial strength at the Insurance News Network (www.insure.com). You'll find free information on your carrier's claims-paying history from the two top ratings firms, Standard & Poor's and Duff & Phelps.

If all this financial empowerment proves too darned much, it's easy to click on relief. Both the National Association of Personal Financial Advisors (NAPFA) and the International Association for Financial Planning (IAFP) have Websites that offer planner referrals. You'll find them at www.napfa.org and www.iafp.org. Hiring a planner could free you up to start another self-improvement project: becoming your own shrink.

TRAVEL ARRANGING IN CYBERSPACE

BY MARC GUNTHER

◆ ◆ ◆

*You can rent cars, buy plane tickets,
and book hotel rooms online. But don't
dump your travel agent just yet.*

◆ ◆ ◆

Long before packing his bags for a three-week summer vacation to Europe, Dave Hatunen traveled to the World Wide Web. He downloaded city maps and railway schedules, made plans for the theater in London, checked into the Stockholm–Helsinki ferry, and, most important, bought three round-trip plane tickets from San Francisco to London for $2,317 from an online travel agency called Travelocity. "I was able to hunt down the cheapest fare available, short of charters," says Hatunen, an engineering technician from Palo Alto. "I felt I was in control of my destiny, rather than crossing my fingers and hoping some travel agent was going to do his best."

Hatunen is just one of thousands of travelers who bypass conventional travel agents to buy airline tickets, book hotels, and reserve rental cars online. So it's no surprise that airlines, hotel chains, and yes, worried travel agents are setting up shop online to serve do-it-yourself, computer-savvy travelers. These new sites offer direct access to databases previously available only to travel agents, easy-to-use software, online guidebooks, and occasionally honest-to-goodness bargains available only on the Internet. Their goal: to capture a slice of the estimated $200 billion worldwide market for leisure travel.

Unlike most Internet ventures, travel companies are already racking up serious online sales. In 1995, AMR Corp.'s consumer-oriented reservation system sold 1.6 million tickets online. Airlines have been using the Net to promote dirt-cheap, last-minute weekend airfares. The 150,000 people who have signed up for NetSAAvers at the American Airlines Website, for example, are alerted to specials once a week via E-mail, helping fill seats that would otherwise have gone empty. Preview Travel, a San Francisco–based cyberagency backed by America Online, Landmark Communications, and US

WHERE TO GO ONLINE TO PLAN YOUR NEXT TRIP

◆◆◆

Here's a list of hot links to sites for airline reservations, hotel bookings, car rentals, and vacation packages. All you need is a browser, an Internet connection, and plenty of time.

◆ TRAVELOCITY
(www.travelocity.com)
Airline tickets, destination information
Biggest all-purpose travel site

◆ PREVIEW TRAVEL
(www.vacations.com and on America Online)
Airline tickets, destination information
Easy to use, lots of pictures and video

◆ INTERNET TRAVEL NETWORK
(www.itn.net)
Plane, hotel, car bookings; destination information
Big site backed by travel agents

◆ FLIFO
(www.flifo.com)
Airline tickets
Easy-to-use, discount-driven site

West, says it sells $50,000 to $100,000 of airline tickets a day on AOL and the Web.

Why buy travel services online? For now, the key reasons are convenience and control. Virtual travel agents are open all night and on weekends, and travelers can spend as much time as they want sizing up potential destinations and fiddling with itineraries. No one would think of keeping a human travel agent on the phone for an hour to book a single flight or fantasize over a long list of hotels in Bermuda—but there's no hurry on the Web. "When you think about what you need to plan a trip, it's all about information," says

- **AMERICAN AIRLINES**
  (www.americanair.com)
  NetSAAver fares, tickets, frequent-flier info
  Weekly E-mailings offer last-minute bargains

- **TRAVELWEB**
  (www.travelweb.com)
  Airline tickets, hotel bookings
  Best listing of hotels around the world

- **ROSENBLUTH VACATIONS**
  (www.rosenbluth.com)
  Airline tickets, vacation packages
  Lots of packages, fun cruise database

- **MOUNTAIN TRAVEL SOBEK**
  (www.mtsobek.com)
  Adventure travel
  Offbeat trips, quality travel writing

- **EXPEDIA**
  (www.expedia.com)
  Airline tickets, hotel bookings
  Destination information, rental cars

Greg Slyngstad, manager of travel products for Microsoft. "It's about organizing all that information, conveniently, in one place."

That may be easier said than done, but Slyngstad's got the right goal. Yes, you can click here to book a plane ticket to Chicago, click there to rent a condo in Florida, and click over there to take a dogsled across the Yukon—but all that clicking takes some time. Here are some guideposts to help.

◆ *Airline tickets.* Dozens of companies, including many airlines, sell tickets online, so it pays to shop around. While no site stands out as Bargain Central, some offer good deals. Flifo, headquartered in Houston, has a nifty "fare beater" feature that seeks out low fares. Cathay Pacific holds online auctions of off-peak tickets to Hong Kong. Most sellers take credit cards by E-mail or over the phone and send out tickets by overnight mail at no extra charge.

You're entitled to a price break; after all, you're taking on work that would otherwise be done by a travel or an airline-reservations agent. The airlines like the Web because selling directly to customers cuts the $6.4 billion a year they now spend on travel agent commissions—which is just $1.8 billion less than they spent on fuel in 1995.

◆ *Hotels and rental cars.* In theory, online agencies should allow you to search through databases of thousands of hotels till you find the perfect spot. In practice, there are glitches. Visiting TravelWeb, a popular site that promises access to 9,000 hotels, we asked for a health club–equipped Seattle hotel with cable TV and a modem line in a room that cost no more than $150 a night. The responses we got were inconsistent and sometimes incomplete. Less ambitious sites can be more user-friendly. Bed & Breakfast Cape Cod, for instance, offers a list of 100 places to stay on the Cape and nearby islands. As for rental cars, check out the Internet Travel Network, which lets you compare rates and availability—but only after you plug in an airline itinerary.

◆ *Vacation packages.* You'll find them all over the place—but make sure you know whom you're dealing with. Travelocity offers more than 200,000 pages of travel-related content. Nevertheless, the only packages it sells are assembled by American Airlines, whose parent company is a partner in the site.

By contrast, Rosenbluth Vacations' cruise database lists more than 500 cruises from many operators. Travelers with special interests are especially well served: Mountain Travel Sobek, an adventure-travel specialist, has a site with good writing, great pictures, and exotic-sounding trips like a sea-kayaking expedition to northeastern Greenland.

A word of caution: By the time you get your PC booted up, log on to an Internet provider, sign up for a Website, figure out how to use the search engine, and sort out the airport codes, you may need a lengthy vacation. Unless you're a do-it-yourself type who enjoys playing around online, you'll probably want to rely on a travel agent to hammer out the details—provided yours is knowledgeable. Frequent traveler John Levine, author of *Internet for Dummies*, says, "Doing your booking on the Net is not as good as talking to a really good agent, but it's a lot better than talking to an inept agent, and unfortunately, a lot of agents are pretty bad."

In the not-too-distant future, though, online agents may gain the edge by enabling travelers to shop for vacation opportunities with a simple click. Imagine watching videos of beach resorts you're considering for a vacation and getting a look at the room you want to book. Or receiving a single weekly bulletin alerting you to last-minute bargains at airlines and hotels that are trying to shed unsold inventory.

That, in theory, is the beauty of the Web. Online commerce should bring out the best in capitalism, efficiently matching buyers and sellers, eliminating middlemen, and lowering distribution costs and prices. With travel services that's already happening, albeit on a small scale. If such practices spread, cyberspace will become the first stop on a savvy traveler's itinerary.

COLLEGE APPLICATIONS 1-2-3

BY MICHAEL J. HIMOWITZ

◆◆◆

A new CD-ROM—called Apply '98—almost makes applying for college a breeze. It won't, however, write the essays—or pay the fees.

◆◆◆

If there's a high school senior in your house, you know that filling out applications may be the hardest thing about getting into college. These paper and pencil–age relics, which you have to get perfect, are complex, confusing, and unforgiving. Completing one by hand or typewriter—if you can even find a typewriter—is an ordeal. Filling out eight or ten applications is cruel and unusual punishment.

But help is finally at hand. Apply '98 is a CD-ROM with digitized applications to over 600 popular colleges, including top-rated schools like Princeton, Harvard, and Duke; smaller private colleges like Middlebury, Bard, and Kenyon; and a handful of state colleges, including Illinois and Massachusetts. All your student has to do is pick a school, fill in the blanks onscreen, and hit the print button. Out comes a completed application with all the proper fonts and graphics, ready for mailing.

The software, produced by Apply Technology of Burlington, Massachusetts, works like a dream if you've got a PC with lots of horsepower. Best of all, the program is free. That's because companies like the Website BOLT, Burton Snowboards, Discover Card, Federal Express, Jam TV, Microsoft, and Point Cast have all paid big bucks for some unobtrusive advertising onscreen.

Apply '98 is actually two programs in one. Students can fill in an onscreen interview that matches their academic record and personal preferences with a database of 1,500 colleges and universities. Anyone who has used the Princeton Review's College Advisor software will be on familiar ground—Apply Technology licensed the Advisor's clever interface.

You can skip this process and go directly to the applications. These look like the real thing, thanks to Adobe Acrobat Exchange, an electronic publishing program that comes on the CD. Apply Technology guarantees that the admissions offices of the colleges included have agreed to accept applications created with Apply '98 (provided, of course, that they come with a check attached). Small wonder—applications created on a PC tend to be much neater than handwritten efforts. Unlike struggling with paper applications, if you make a mistake here, you just go back and press delete—forget the Wite-Out. And while Apply '98 won't write your student's application essay, it does allow her to paste a word-processor document directly onto the form.

Apply '98 has one invaluable timesaving feature. It remembers what was typed into the first application. When your student starts a new one, the program fills in the corresponding blanks. Type in those addresses and phone and Social Security numbers once, and you're done for good.

Of course, none of this is perfect. Apply '98 has the rough edges one might expect of a CD-ROM cobbled together to meet fall application deadlines. You won't want to send off multiple applications without first proofreading them—while the program is good about replicating basic items such as names and addresses, it isn't consistent with other items. And even though the publisher says Apply '98 will run on a 486 machine with eight megabytes of memory, in reality it crawls on anything less than a Pentium PC with 16 megabytes. Even on a Pentium, an application of a couple of dozen pages can take a few minutes to load. You may want even more memory so you can run a Web browser simultaneously—Advisor comes with links to many college home pages.

Despite such glitches, Apply '98 sure beats wading through a stack of paper applications. The CD includes versions for Windows 3.1, Windows 95, and Mac. Apply '98 is not available in stores. You can get your free copy by calling 203-740-3504, or you can order online by visiting Apply's Website (www.weapply.com). And for those of you who haven't entered the digital age, the CD can be ordered by writing to Apply '98, P.O. Box 8406, New Milford, Connecticut 06776-9848.

E-MAIL GETS RICH

BY J. WILLIAM GURLEY

◆◆◆

Get ready for messages with hyperlinks,
interactive forms, and, of course, advertising.

◆◆◆

Like it or not, in the past couple of years you've probably come to accept E-mail as a regular part of your working life. Those pings from your PC alerting you to incoming messages are as much a part of your office environment as the warble of the telephone. For many people in big corporations, E-mail has become the office phone's digital equivalent: ubiquitous and annoying.

Well, all that's about to change. It's about to get a whole lot worse—and a whole lot better. After all, E-mail does have a few benefits: It's affordable, with the cost of a single message well below a penny; it's convenient, giving you the freedom to read and respond at your leisure; and finally, it's an incredibly efficient way to communicate with many people simultaneously. (Which would you rather do, go through the rigmarole of setting up a conference call, or click on one button in your E-mail program and get the word out to 15 people at once?)

Combine that kind of efficiency with the continued growth of the Internet, and you get a product poised to take off. Over the next two years, as the percentage of home-PC owners who go online rises and Internet connectivity becomes more popular around the world, the number of active electronic mailboxes could double, from an estimated 75 million now to somewhere over 150 million.

An early example of the potential of rich E-mail is a Netscape program called InBox Direct, which you can sign up for by logging onto Netscape's Website (www.netscape.com). With InBox Direct, you can have online editions of the *New York Times*, the *Financial Times*, and *PC Week* delivered to your E-mail address. Depending on the service, you get complete or abridged versions of stories appearing in the regular paper editions. But unlike text delivered via traditional E-mail, the stories come embedded with hyperlinks, photos, and advertising—as if a page of the publisher's Website had been delivered directly to your electronic mailbox.

In effect, InBox Direct creates another distribution channel for publications. But E-mail that carries video, interactive forms, and hyperlinks will affect everyone, not just content providers. Here are changes it will help bring about.

Inside corporations: Rich E-mail will have a significant impact on how we conduct everyday business. Take all those forms that your human-resources department distributes. You fill out the paper form and return it in an interoffice envelope, and some unlucky HR employee types your info into the database.

With rich E-mail, by contrast, HR will send you the form electronically. You'll fill it out onscreen; if you have a question, you'll click on hyperlinks that take you to pages of helpful information. When you're done, you'll click on the "submit" button; not only will your form get returned to the HR exec who sent it, but it will also get routed to the database, which will update your information. If you've made a mistake in the form, you'll get back an automated message inviting you to correct the problem.

Between businesses and customers: Electronic bills will likely be standard fare by the end of 1997. Sometime very soon, one of those MBAs at your local utility will realize how much money his company can save by sending bills electronically to customers with PCs. Sign up for E-mail billing, and all you'll have to do is type in a credit card number on the interactive bill the company sends you.

As soon as one industry starts doing this, others will quickly follow suit. This could have a serious impact on mail-order marketers like music and book clubs, which take advantage of people's laziness in responding to paper-based offers to help sell the CD of the month. Tomorrow, a "no" response will be as simple as clicking a button.

Among friends: Skeptics claim E-mail has destroyed the art of correspondence—whatever was left of it in the age of the telephone. In fact, lots of people now use E-mail to stay in touch with friends and may even prefer it to the phone because it's cheaper. With rich E-mail, personal communications will take on a whole new meaning.

Consider the combination of digital cameras and rich E-mail. It's Christmas 1998, your parents are vacationing in Fresno, and you and the kids are stuck in Duluth. A phone call is fine, but now you'll be able to dump digital photos of the kids opening their presents into an E-mail and zip it to Grandma over the Net.

Several factors could slow the spread of rich E-mail. If consumers are to send, as well as receive, rich E-mail, they'll need others to have applications capable of viewing it. So as with many applications, the full impact of rich E-mail will be felt only after it becomes a mass market.

Second, some analysts worry that rich E-mail will further tax an already overloaded Internet. But the problem of Net traffic may be resolved via new pricing mechanisms that allow people to pay for priority service. Third, junk E-mail will become a real nuisance. Internet junk-mail, called spam, is already a problem. Think how excited junk-mailers will get when it becomes easier to incorporate video, links, and photos into E-mail solicitations! E-junk may drive consumers to use two mailboxes, one public and one private, just as some consumers use two phone numbers.

In spite of the hassle, the benefits of rich E-mail will eventually make it a personal computing mainstay. Upcoming products from Netscape and Microsoft will blur the boundaries between your rich E-mail and your favorite word-processing, spreadsheet, and browser applications. Soon you may feel as if you're spending almost all your time doing E-mail—whether you like it or not.

IS CYBERCHAT GETTING SERIOUS?

BY ALISON L. SPROUT

◆◆◆

"Chat rooms," computerized conversations where users swap messages on chosen topics, are finding their way into business.

◆◆◆

Prime-time television is finished for the night; the dinner dishes have been cleared away. And at thousands of computer terminals in dens and living rooms across America, strangers are exchanging messages like these:

Naked Foxy RedHead: "Lick!! Lick!! Lick!! Lick!! Lick!!"
Ggotcha: "thanks foxy, jeez, what did I walk into?"
Naked Foxy RedHead: "U Lick Me I Lick U. cosmic orgasm."
Bondage Bitch Barbi: "Lick! Lick! Lick! Lick!"
Gr8 in Bed: "RUB me WITH Jello & LICK!"

To many, this is what is meant by chat, the computerized mode of conversation that is a mainstay of online services like America Online and CompuServe. In a chat room, each participant types a message in a small window at the bottom of his or her screen, hits the return key, and then watches as the words join a scroll of messages from other people. Such chat areas, whether they be filled with hormonally pumped teenagers or adults who want to talk about how to pick stocks, generate a hefty chunk of online service revenues—by some estimates as much as 30%.

But chat is changing as it moves to the Web. Corporations have begun to provide chat rooms on their Websites, giving the conversations a new spin and often attracting a different type of audience. Unlike online services, most companies aren't likely to make a lot of money directly from chat. What they will get is a greater number of Website visitors, allowing them to charge more for advertising space on their sites. And scheduled chat "events" hosted by a celebrity or a corporate spokesperson can focus conversation on specific products or services.

Still, chat entails risks, and companies should think twice before opening a chat room and inviting the hordes. Web surfers in general, and chatters in particular, are likely to be young, and the conversations that take place in a completely unstructured chat area could well resemble the one above, having little or nothing to do with the company footing the bill.

Athletic-shoe maker K-Swiss added chat to its Website to promote its status as official footwear maker for the 1996 U.S. Open tennis tournament. For K-Swiss, the demographics of chat were a plus: Consumers ages 18 to 25 account for the bulk of the company's sales. So K-Swiss hired WebGenesis to set up and maintain a U.S. Open chat room. To keep the conversation focused on tennis and shoes, K-Swiss created a character named Ace who filed daily reports from the Open and visited the chat room frequently. After the Open, the company renamed the room Club K-Swiss, tying it to a promotion that awards free music CDs. Since K-Swiss opened the chat room, traffic on its Website has quadrupled.

For most companies, deciding whether to add chat and how it should function is not so simple. Like K-Swiss, California winery Kendall-Jackson wants to attract young consumers. But Kendall-Jackson also has an image to maintain as a maker of premium wines purchased mainly by people 35 and over. Its solution is to invite the public to moderated discussions—regularly scheduled chat events where people ask questions about wine.

The first session, a virtual winetasting with Kendall-Jackson winemaker Steve Reeder, took place in June 1996. Sitting in the vintner's Santa Rosa, California, offices, freelance wine writer Richard Paul Hinkle interviewed Reeder online about different Kendall-Jackson vintages, then invited wine lovers to join in. About 30 people asked questions ranging from "What is your favorite wine and why?" to "What are the taste characteristics of the Syrah grape?" At least 60 more tried to log on but couldn't because of a glitch.

NationsBank of Charlotte, North Carolina, is using chat to reach a select group of customers: corporate treasurers and cash managers. In September 1995, NationsBank and consulting firm Treasury Strategies joined to create a Website called Treasury Connection. Its 1,100 members post questions about cash management and receive a weekly E-mail digest with answers from other participants.

The site's chat component, Treasury Connection Live, allows subscribers to log on for a monthly chat with independent cash management experts on such topics as how to manage investment risk and how banks can profit from the Internet. As in Kendall-Jackson's wine events, a moderator screens and selects questions. The level of participation in each session helps NationsBank figure out which services are most important to customers. A spirited chat on electronic data interchange persuaded NationsBank to speed product development in that area.

Besides adding chat to their public Websites, companies are also beginning to build chat into their internal web networks, or intranets. Microsoft is trying out scheduled chat events to replace the executive Q&A session at its annual employee meeting. Microsoft has more than 20,000 staffers worldwide, so the Q&A was growing unwieldy: Employees submitted questions via the company newspaper and then waited months to hear the carefully scripted answers. Naturally, the software behemoth will use its own intranet chat product, Microsoft Internet Chat.

As chat becomes as useful to buttoned-up bank executives as it is to libidinous online-service subscribers, it could shed its off-color reputation and become just another tool, like word processors or spreadsheets. With time, it may even become associated with something new: serious adult conversation.

THE 1997
FORTUNE 500 DIRECTORY

◆◆◆

Confounding expectations, America's largest companies tallied up a stunning 23.3% increase in profits in 1996—an extraordinary performance in the sixth year of a recovery. Not only did earnings sprint ahead in 1996; they also grew faster than revenues, which increased 8.3%. By 1996, this uncommon—and ultimately unsustainable—phenomenon had been occurring for four straight years. That means corporate America, hell-bent on controlling costs, was finding new ways to squeeze more profit from each dollar of sales. Helped by an almost magically favorable economic climate—with low interest rates and benign labor costs—the companies of the FORTUNE 500 restructured, reengineered, refinanced, downsized, laid off, split up, and merged their way to prosperity.

An awesome performance, to be sure. But how long can companies raise profits at a double-digit pace without also expanding revenues at a similar rate? Joel Friedman, a managing partner of Andersen Consulting, says: "Reengineering got rid of the bloat. That's fine as far as it goes, but now it's done. What do you do for an encore?" How will FORTUNE 500 companies better serve their markets, reshape business, and outsmart rivals? In short, how will they find new ways to keep earnings growing? So begins the next phase of competition.

RONALD HENKOFF

RANK 1996	COMPANY	REVENUES $ millions	PROFITS $ millions	Rank	ASSETS $ millions	Rank
1	**GENERAL MOTORS** Detroit	168,369.0	4,963.0	7	222,142.0	7
2	**FORD MOTOR** Dearborn, Mich.	146,991.0	4,446.0	8	262,867.0	5
3	**EXXON** Irving, Texas	119,434.0[E]	7,510.0	1	95,527.0	28
4	**WAL-MART STORES** Bentonville, Ark.[1]	106,147.0	3,056.0	14	39,501.0	72
5	**GENERAL ELECTRIC** Fairfield, Conn.	79,179.0	7,280.0	2	272,402.0	4
6	**INTL. BUSINESS MACHINES** Armonk, N.Y.	75,947.0	5,429.0	5	81,132.0	34
7	**AT&T** New York	74,525.0[¶]	5,908.0	4	55,552.0	51
8	**MOBIL** Fairfax, Va.	72,267.0[E]	2,964.0	16	46,408.0	61
9	**CHRYSLER** Auburn Hills, Mich.	61,397.0	3,529.0	12	56,184.0	49
10	**PHILIP MORRIS** New York	54,553.0[E]	6,303.0	3	54,871.0	52
11	**TEXACO** White Plains, N.Y.	44,561.0[E]	2,018.0	37	26,963.0	99
12	**STATE FARM INSURANCE COS.** Bloomington, Ill.	42,781.2	2,567.9	28	93,245.1	29
13	**PRUDENTIAL INS. CO. OF AMERICA** Newark, N.J.	40,175.0	1,006.0	87	219,072.0	9
14	**E.I. DU PONT DE NEMOURS** Wilmington, Del·	39,689.0[E]	3,636.0	11	37,987.0	74
15	**CHEVRON** San Francisco	38,691.0[E]	2,607.0	26	34,854.0	80
16	**HEWLETT-PACKARD** Palo Alto[2]	38,420.0	2,586.0	27	27,699.0	96
17	**SEARS ROEBUCK** Hoffman Estates, Ill.	38,236.0	1,271.0	62	36,167.0	78
18	**PROCTER & GAMBLE** Cincinnati[3]	35,284.0	3,046.0	15	27,730.0	95
19	**AMOCO** Chicago	32,726.0[E]	2,834.0	23	32,100.0	84
20	**CITICORP** New York	32,605.0	3,788.0	10	281,018.0	3
21	**PEPSICO** Purchase, N.Y·	31,645.0	1,149.0	74	24,512.0	109
22	**KMART** Troy, Mich.[1]	31,437.0	(220.0)	487	14,286.0	166
23	**AMERICAN INTERNATIONAL GROUP** New York	28,205.3	2,897.3	17	148,431.0	17
24	**MOTOROLA** Schaumburg, Ill.	27,973.0	1,154.0	72	24,076.0	111
25	**CHASE MANHATTAN CORP.** New York[4]	27,421.0	2,461.0	30	336,099.0	2

STOCKHOLDERS' EQUITY		MARKET VALUE 3/14/97		EARNINGS PER SHARE				TOTAL RETURN TO INVESTORS			
				1996 $	% change from 1995	1986–96 annual growth rate %	Rank	1996 %	Rank	1986–96 annual rate %	Rank
$ millions	Rank	$ millions	Rank								
23,418.0	6	49,538.6	21	6.06	(16.0)	4.0	238	8.7	321	10.1	282
26,762.0	4	38,164.5	36	3.72	3.9	1.9	261	16.7	263	13.9	199
43,542.0	1	125,597.3	3	6.02	16.2	5.0	222	26.3	188	16.0	136
17,143.0	14	65,948.3	11	1.33	11.8	20.9	30	3.1	353	15.2	155
31,125.0	2	169,387.8	1	4.40	12.8	12.4	96	40.4	102	19.9	75
21,628.0	8	74,332.5	10	10.24	41.6	2.7	255	67.6	31	5.8	335
20,295.0	12	57,836.9	16	3.66	3,966.7	53.6	5	(7.4)	401	12.4	234
19,072.0	13	51,412.3	19	7.38	25.7	7.9	176	13.2	289	16.9	118
11,571.0	33	21,428.7	65	4.77	80.0	4.2	235	25.1	198	14.8	167
14,218.0	19	104,591.3	7	7.68	18.5	17.4	53	31.0	154	25.0	28
10,372.0	41	26,776.6	56	7.52	258.1	9.6	148	29.7	164	17.6	106
30,078.4	3	N.A.		N.A.	—	—		—		—	
9,788.0	44	N.A.		N.A.	—	—		—		—	
10,709.0	39	63,294.1	12	6.47	15.3	11.8	106	38.3	113	17.0	117
15,623.0	18	44,002.3	27	3.99	179.0	14.3	71	28.5	168	16.1	132
13,438.0	23	56,322.2	17	2.46	6.3	17.2	54	21.2	227	18.1	99
4,945.0	111	21,484.7	64	3.12	(30.7)	(1.5)	296	20.4	233	12.7	228
11,722.0	32	85,442.7	8	4.29	15.6	15.1	65	32.1	147	21.9	47
16,408.0	16	43,511.6	30	5.69	51.3	14.6	70	16.9	262	14.0	193
20,722.0	10	53,675.3	18	7.50	4.0	7.7	179	56.4	47	18.8	89
6,623.0	75	48,354.2	22	0.72	(28.0)	9.5	150	6.2	337	23.0	36
5,072.0	107	5,994.0	225	(0.45)	—	—		45.6	72	0.5	367
22,044.2	7	58,632.8	15	6.15	16.0	13.4	82	17.5	257	18.0	101
11,795.0	31	32,785.4	43	1.90	(35.2)	17.4	52	8.4	322	22.5	40
20,994.0	9	43,242.6	31	5.02	(25.4)	(4.0)	312	56.8	46	14.5	176

RANK 1996	COMPANY	REVENUES $ millions	PROFITS $ millions	Rank	ASSETS $ millions	Rank
26	**LOCKHEED MARTIN** Bethesda, Md.	**26,875.0**	**1,347.0**	58	**29,257.0**	90
27	**DAYTON HUDSON** Minneapolis[1]	**25,371.0**	**463.0**	178	**13,389.0**	174
28	**KROGER** Cincinnati	**25,170.9**	**349.9**	218	**5,825.4**	270
29	**FANNIE MAE** Washington, D.C.[5]	**25,054.0**	**2,725.0**	25	**351,041.0**	1
30	**MERRILL LYNCH** New York	**25,011.0**	**1,619.0**	45	**213,016.0**	10
31	**CONAGRA** Omaha[6]	**24,821.6**	**188.9**	315	**11,196.6**	195
32	**ALLSTATE** Northbrook, Ill.	**24,299.0**	**2,075.0**	36	**74,508.0**	37
33	**J.C. PENNEY** Plano, Texas[1,7]	**23,649.0**	**565.0**	150	**22,088.0**	119
34	**UNITED TECHNOLOGIES** Hartford	**23,512.0**	**906.0**	98	**16,745.0**	145
35	**METROPOLITAN LIFE INSURANCE** New York[8,9,10]	**23,000.0**	**800.0**[12]	106	**190,000.0**	13
36	**BOEING** Seattle	**22,681.0**	**1,095.0**	79	**27,254.0**	98
37	**UNITED PARCEL SERVICE** Atlanta	**22,368.0**	**1,146.0**	75	**14,954.0**	155
38	**BANKAMERICA CORP.** San Francisco	**22,071.0**	**2,873.0**	19	**250,753.0**	6
39	**JOHNSON & JOHNSON** New Brunswick, N.J.	**21,620.0**	**2,887.0**	18	**20,010.0**	125
40	**TRAVELERS GROUP** New York	**21,345.4**	**2,331.0**	32	**151,067.0**	16
41	**GTE** Stamford, Conn.	**21,339.2**	**2,798.3**	24	**38,422.0**	73
42	**USX** Pittsburgh	**21,076.0**[E]	**943.0**	92	**16,980.0**	140
43	**INTEL** Santa Clara, Calif.	**20,847.0**	**5,157.0**	6	**23,735.0**	112
44	**INTERNATIONAL PAPER** Purchase, N.Y.	**20,143.0**	**303.0**	241	**28,252.0**	93
45	**DOW CHEMICAL** Midland, Mich	**20,053.0**	**1,907.0**	39	**24,673.0**	107
46	**LOEWS** New York	**19,964.8**[E]	**1,383.9**	56	**67,683.0**	41
47	**COLUMBIA/HCA HEALTHCARE** Nashville	**19,909.0**	**1,505.0**	50	**21,272.0**	121
48	**MERCK** Whitehouse Station, N.J.	**19,828.7**	**3,881.3**	9	**24,393.1**	110
49	**COSTCO** Issaquah, Wash.[13,14]	**19,566.5**	**248.8**	276	**4,911.9**	305
50	**HOME DEPOT** Atlanta[1]	**19,535.5**	**937.7**	93	**9,341.7**	220

STOCKHOLDERS' EQUITY		MARKET VALUE 3/14/97		EARNINGS PER SHARE				TOTAL RETURN TO INVESTORS			
				1996 $	% change from 1995	1986–96 annual growth rate %	Rank	1996 %	Rank	1986–96 annual rate %	Rank
$ millions	Rank	$ millions	Rank								
6,856.0	71	16,283.2	86	6.80	107.3	6.0	212	18.0	251	15.6	147
3,790.0	154	9,463.2	154	2.02	50.4	6.6	204	59.9	38	13.2	218
(1,181.7)	496	7,392.0	188	2.66	5.6	17.1	56	24.4	203	15.3	154
12,773.0	27	40,981.1	32	2.48	15.3	28.2	22	—		—	
6,892.0	70	15,384.4	90	8.20	50.7	14.3	72	62.6	36	19.4	80
2,255.5	236	13,206.4	105	0.79	(61.7)	1.5	266	23.3	210	17.1	112
13,452.0	22	28,619.5	50	4.63	9.2	—		42.6	96	—	
5,952.0	91	12,655.6	109	2.29	(34.2)	3.7	241	6.5	335	14.8	166
4,306.0	136	18,086.1	83	3.45	21.1	38.3	9	42.3	97	14.8	168
12,000.0	29	N.A.		N.A.		—		—		—	
10,941.0	36	37,135.3	38	3.19	177.4	5.3	218	37.6	117	19.3	82
5,901.0	92	N.A.		2.01	9.8	7.3	185	—		—	
20,713.0	11	40,234.0	34	7.31	12.6	—		58.2	42	24.2	30
10,836.0	38	77,073.2	9	2.17	16.7	34.1	15	18.2	249	31.0	17
13,085.0	25	34,023.4	40	3.50	27.0	28.2	21	46.6	67	26.4	24
7,335.7	62	43,941.3	29	2.89	—	9.4	152	8.0	325	14.9	163
5,022.0	108	10,370.9	140	N.A.		—		—		—	
16,872.0	15	113,195.4	5	5.81	44.2	—		131.2	9	43.8	6
9,344.0	46	13,019.3	106	1.04	(76.9)	(3.3)	307	9.6	311	10.9	261
7,954.0	57	20,074.8	74	7.71	(0.1)	11.7	108	15.9	270	11.6	248
8,731.2	50	11,916.9	119	11.91	(20.5)	13.5	80	21.7	221	13.7	204
8,609.0	53	29,126.3	48	2.22	14.8	—		20.7	230	—	
11,970.5	30	106,633.5	6	3.20	18.5	19.5	39	24.0	207	22.1	45
1,777.8	275	6,165.0	221	1.24	79.7	(0.1)	284	64.8	35	(2.3)	373
5,955.2	90	27,715.0	54	1.94	26.0	36.1	12	5.4	339	40.2	10

RANK 1996	COMPANY	REVENUES $ millions	PROFITS $ millions	Rank	ASSETS $ millions	Rank
51	**XEROX** Stamford, Conn.	19,521.0	1,206.0	67	26,818.0	100
52	**ATLANTIC RICHFIELD** Los Angeles	19,168.5ᴱ	1,663.0	44	25,715.0	103
53	**BELLSOUTH** Atlanta	19,040.0	2,863.0	20	32,568.0	83
54	**CIGNA** Philadelphia	18,950.0	1,056.0	81	98,932.0	27
55	**WALT DISNEY** Burbank, Calif.[15]	18,739.0	1,214.0	65	37,306.0	76
56	**AMERICAN STORES** Salt Lake City[1]	18,678.1	287.2	250	7,881.4	237
57	**SARA LEE** Chicago[3]	18,624.0	916.0	95	12,602.0	181
58	**COCA-COLA** Atlanta	18,546.0	3,492.0	13	16,161.0	148
59	**MCI COMMUNICATIONS** Washington, D.C.	18,494.0	1,202.0	68	22,978.0	117
60	**COMPAQ COMPUTER** Houston	18,109.0	1,312.9	59	10,525.8	204
61	**AMR** Fort Worth	17,753.0	1,016.0	86	20,497.0	124
62	**NATIONSBANK CORP.** Charlotte, N.C.[16]	17,509.0	2,452.0	31	185,794.0	14
63	**NEW YORK LIFE INSURANCE** New York	17,347.0	579.4	148	78,809.3	36
64	**AMERICAN EXPRESS** New York	17,280.0	1,901.0	40	108,512.0	23
65	**SAFEWAY** Oakland	17,269.0	460.6	181	5,545.2	274
66	**RJR NABISCO HOLDINGS** New York	17,063.0ᴱ	611.0	139	31,289.0	86
67	**AETNA** Hartford[17]	16,900.2	651.0	129	92,912.9	30
68	**CATERPILLAR** Peoria, Ill.	16,522.0	1,361.0	57	18,728.0	133
69	**FLEMING** Oklahoma City	16,486.7	26.7	447	4,055.2	328
70	**SUPERVALU** Eden Prairie, Minn.[18]	16,486.3	166.4	329	4,183.5	324
71	**UAL** Elk Grove Township, Ill.	16,362.0	533.0	156	12,677.0	180
72	**EASTMAN KODAK** Rochester, N.Y.	15,968.0	1,288.0	61	14,438.0	162
73	**J.P. MORGAN & CO.** New York	15,866.0	1,574.0	46	222,026.0	8
74	**PHILLIPS PETROLEUM** Bartlesville, Okla.	15,807.0ᴱ	1,303.0	60	13,548.0	171
75	**FEDERATED DEPARTMENT STORES** Cincinnati[1]	15,229.0	265.9	265	14,264.1	167

STOCKHOLDERS' EQUITY		MARKET VALUE 3/14/97		EARNINGS PER SHARE				TOTAL RETURN TO INVESTORS			
				1996 $	% change from 1995	1986–96 annual growth rate %	Rank	1996 %	Rank	1986–96 annual rate %	Rank
$ millions	Rank	$ millions	Rank								
5,088.0	106	20,151.8	72	3.49	—	9.4	154	17.9	252	14.9	162
7,801.0	58	20,417.1	71	10.18	20.9	11.7	109	25.2	197	13.5	208
13,249.0	24	43,984.8	28	2.88	—	5.5	217	(3.6)	387	13.1	220
7,208.0	64	11,747.0	120	13.85	384.3	3.4	246	36.1	128	15.2	156
16,086.0	17	50,461.3	20	1.96	(24.6)	15.7	62	19.3	241	21.2	58
2,535.4	215	6,586.6	205	1.97	(8.8)	15.3	63	55.6	48	21.8	49
4,320.0	135	18,820.4	80	1.83	13.0	13.7	77	19.1	242	19.0	85
6,156.0	81	147,619.1	2	1.40	18.1	16.6	57	43.3	89	29.8	18
10,661.0	40	20,103.6	73	1.73	116.3	—		25.3	192	26.7	23
6,144.0	83	20,793.6	68	4.72	63.9	34.0	16	54.9	50	36.9	11
5,668.0	96	7,800.8	183	11.63	451.2	9.6	145	18.7	246	5.1	343
13,709.0	21	45,385.7	24	8.26	15.8	12.6	94	44.4	76	20.6	66
4,007.5	149	N.A.		N.A.	—	—		—		—	
8,528.0	54	30,499.4	45	3.90	25.4	3.5	244	39.2	109	11.9	244
1,186.8	354	10,955.0	134	1.93	43.0	—		66.0	33	3.4	353
10,148.0	42	9,152.9	162	1.74	13.7	—		17.2	259	—	
10,889.7	37	13,714.9	103	4.74	114.5	(6.3)	318	18.4	248	9.1	300
4,116.0	144	15,442.2	89	7.07	23.6	33.8	17	30.8	158	16.0	138
1,076.0	368	656.6	445	0.71	(36.6)	(8.9)	321	(14.8)	423	(3.5)	376
1,216.2	351	2,049.4	387	2.44	300.0	7.1	195	(6.9)	398	4.1	351
995.0	378	4,094.6	292	5.16	3.1	55.5	3	40.1	106	21.0	60
4,734.0	122	29,326.5	47	3.82	4.1	13.2	86	22.4	216	12.0	241
11,432.0	35	19,717.4	75	7.63	18.8	4.9	225	26.6	184	13.5	209
4,251.0	139	10,630.8	136	4.96	177.1	18.7	43	33.7	137	18.7	90
4,669.2	123	7,496.0	187	1.28	228.2	—		25.2	195	—	

RANK 1996	COMPANY	REVENUES $ millions	PROFITS $ millions	Rank	ASSETS $ millions	Rank
76	**BRISTOL-MYERS SQUIBB** New York	15,065.0	2,850.0	22	14,685.0	157
77	**AMERITECH** Chicago	14,917.0	2,134.0	34	23,707.0	113
78	**DIGITAL EQUIPMENT** Maynard, Mass.[3]	14,562.8	(111.8)	477	10,075.4	210
79	**ROCKWELL INTERNATIONAL** Seal Beach, Calif.[15]	14,343.0[¶]	726.0	120	10,065.0	211
80	**LEHMAN BROTHERS HOLDINGS** New York[19]	14,260.0	416.0	196	128,596.0	19
81	**MINNESOTA MINING & MFG.** St. Paul	14,236.0	1,526.0	48	13,364.0	175
82	**SPRINT** Westwood, Kansas	14,234.9	1,183.8	70	16,953.0	142
83	**AMERICAN HOME PRODUCTS** Madison, N.J.	14,088.3	1,883.4	41	20,785.3	122
84	**ALLIEDSIGNAL** Morristown, N.J.	13,971.0	1,020.0	84	12,829.0	178
85	**SBC COMMUNICATIONS** San Antonio	13,898.2	2,101.0	35	23,499.0	115
86	**COLLEGE RETIREMENT EQUITIES FUND** New York	13,864.6	N.A.		98,974.9	26
87	**MCDONNELL DOUGLAS** Berkeley, Mo.	13,834.0	788.0	107	11,631.0	191
88	**TEACHERS INSURANCE & ANNUITY ASSN.** New York	13,828.1	934.5	94	86,357.5	32
89	**ALBERTSON'S** Boise[1]	13,776.7	493.8	167	4,714.6	311
90	**MCKESSON** San Francisco[20]	13,718.8	135.4	356	3,503.9	353
91	**NYNEX** New York	13,453.8	1,477.0	52	27,659.1	97
92	**SYSCO** Houston[3]	13,395.1	276.9	258	3,325.4	363
93	**ARCHER DANIELS MIDLAND** Decatur, Ill.[3]	13,314.0	695.9	122	10,449.9	207
94	**ENRON** Houston	13,289.0	584.0	145	16,137.0	149
95	**KIMBERLY-CLARK** Irving, Texas	13,149.1	1,403.8	55	11,845.7	189
96	**MORGAN STANLEY GROUP** New York[19]	13,144.0	1,029.0	82	196,446.0	11
97	**ALCOA** Pittsburgh	13,128.4	514.9	161	13,449.9	173
98	**GOODYEAR TIRE & RUBBER** Akron	13,112.8	101.7	383	9,671.8	214
99	**BELL ATLANTIC** Philadelphia	13,081.4	1,881.5	43	24,856.2	106
100	**GEORGIA-PACIFIC** Atlanta	13,024.0	156.0	337	12,818.0	179

STOCKHOLDERS' EQUITY		MARKET VALUE 3/14/97		EARNINGS PER SHARE				TOTAL RETURN TO INVESTORS			
				1996 $	% change from 1995	1986–96 annual growth rate %	Rank	1996 %	Rank	1986–96 annual rate %	Rank
$ millions	Rank	$ millions	Rank								
6,570.0	76	62,348.9	13	2.84	58.7	10.6	127	31.2	152	14.6	174
7,687.0	59	34,164.5	39	3.87	6.6	7.0	197	6.8	333	16.2	131
3,606.2	164	4,641.0	274	(0.97)	(264.4)	—		(43.5)	451	(10.1)	380
4,256.0	137	14,830.7	96	3.34	(2.3)	5.0	224	25.3	193	14.5	180
3,874.0	151	3,151.0	332	3.24	84.1	—		48.9	58	—	
6,284.0	79	37,411.0	37	3.65	57.3	7.9	175	28.5	170	14.7	170
8,519.9	55	18,494.3	82	2.78	148.2	11.9	104	22.1	219	18.3	94
6,962.1	67	40,313.2	33	2.96	9.2	8.6	166	24.3	204	16.4	128
4,180.0	141	20,680.8	69	3.61	16.8	8.3	174	43.2	90	16.7	120
6,835.0	72	33,578.6	41	3.46	—	7.3	187	(6.3)	394	16.0	137
N.A.		N.A.		N.A.	—	—		—		—	
3,038.0	185	13,545.4	104	3.64	—	12.3	98	44.0	78	22.1	46
4,750.7	121	N.A.		N.A.	—	—		—		—	
2,247.0	238	9,166.0	161	1.96	6.5	18.0	47	10.0	310	22.7	38
1,064.6	370	2,824.3	353	N.A.	—	—		12.7	292	—	
7,059.3	65	21,344.9	66	3.38	—	1.2	274	(6.4)	396	10.2	280
1,474.7	321	6,134.9	222	1.52	10.1	16.3	58	2.0	358	17.1	115
6,144.8	82	9,921.6	145	1.27	(9.3)	13.1	87	29.7	165	16.5	125
3,723.0	158	10,368.7	141	2.31	11.6	46.0	7	15.6	273	20.4	69
4,483.1	131	29,841.5	46	4.98	4,050.0	13.0	90	17.8	253	20.9	61
6,538.0	77	9,850.7	147	4.18	0.4	11.5	110	43.8	82	20.1	73
4,462.4	133	12,940.2	108	2.94	(33.6)	7.1	193	20.6	232	17.1	114
3,279.1	174	8,407.2	174	0.66	(83.6)	1.3	272	15.6	271	12.3	236
7,422.8	60	28,181.4	52	4.28	101.9	11.3	117	102.5	15	20.3	70
3,521.0	167	7,072.1	197	1.72	(84.8)	(4.4)	315	7.9	326	10.0	286

RANK 1996	COMPANY	REVENUES $ millions	PROFITS $ millions	Rank	ASSETS $ millions	Rank
101	**WINN-DIXIE STORES** Jacksonville[3]	**12,955.5**	**255.6**	271	**2,648.6**	403
102	**US WEST** Englewood, Colo.	**12,911.0**	**1,178.0**	71	**40,855.0**	69
103	**MAY DEPARTMENT STORES** St. Louis[1]	**12,601.0¶**	**755.0**	113	**10,059.0**	212
104	**IBP** Dakota City, Neb.	**12,538.8**	**198.7**	308	**2,174.5**	428
105	**ITT HARTFORD GROUP** Hartford	**12,473.0**	**(99.0)**	474	**108,840.0**	22
106	**DELTA AIR LINES** Atlanta[3]	**12,455.0**	**156.0**	337	**12,226.0**	185
107	**NATIONWIDE INS. ENTERPRISE** Columbus, Ohio[8]	**12,358.3**	**412.9**	198	**74,145.2**	38
108	**RAYTHEON** Lexington, Mass.	**12,330.5**	**761.2**	112	**11,136.3**	198
109	**ASHLAND** Russell, Ky.[15]	**12,300.7ᴱ**	**211.1**	296	**7,269.5**	248
110	**FEDERAL HOME LOAN MORTGAGE** McLean, Va.	**12,116.0**	**1,243.0**	64	**173,866.0**	15
111	**NORTHWESTERN MUTUAL LIFE INS.** Milwaukee	**12,110.0**	**620.2**	135	**62,680.5**	44
112	**VIACOM** New York	**12,084.2**	**1,247.9**	63	**28,800.0**	92
113	**INGRAM MICRO** Santa Ana, Calif.	**12,023.5**	**110.7**	373	**3,366.9**	360
114	**FIRST UNION CORP.** Charlotte, N.C.	**11,985.0**	**1,499.0**	51	**140,127.0**	18
115	**COASTAL** Houston	**11,920.2ᴱ**	**402.6***	202	**11,613.1**	192
116	**WALGREEN** Deerfield, Ill.[13]	**11,778.4**	**371.7**	209	**3,633.6**	344
117	**TEXAS INSTRUMENTS** Dallas	**11,713.0¶**	**63.0**	423	**9,360.0**	219
118	**PFIZER** New York	**11,306.0**	**1,929.0**	38	**14,667.0**	158
119	**DEERE** Moline, Ill.[2]	**11,229.4**	**817.3**	104	**14,652.7**	159
120	**EMERSON ELECTRIC** St. Louis[15]	**11,149.9**	**1,018.5**	85	**10,481.0**	205
121	**IKON OFFICE SOLUTIONS** Wayne, Pa.[15,21]	**11,122.6¶**	**210.7**	297	**5,384.6**	279
122	**WEYERHAEUSER** Federal Way, Wash.	**11,114.0**	**463.0**	178	**13,596.0**	170
123	**FLUOR** Irvine, Calif.[2]	**11,015.2**	**268.1**	262	**3,951.7**	331
124	**ABBOTT LABORATORIES** Abbott Park, Ill.	**11,013.5**	**1,882.0**	42	**11,125.6**	199
125	**TENNECO** Greenwich, Conn.	**10,982.0¶**	**410.0***	199	**7,587.0**	242

STOCKHOLDERS' EQUITY		MARKET VALUE 3/14/97		EARNINGS PER SHARE				TOTAL RETURN TO INVESTORS			
				1996 $	% change from 1995	1986–96 annual growth rate %	Rank	1996 %	Rank	1986–96 annual rate %	Rank
$ millions	Rank	$ millions	Rank								
1,342.3	336	4,954.1	263	1.69	8.7	9.1	158	(11.9)	416	14.2	189
11,549.0	34	28,482.8	51	N.A.	—	—		—		—	
3,650.0	163	12,043.9	117	2.84	4.0	8.8	163	24.3	205	14.6	171
1,203.7	352	2,211.9	380	2.06	(22.8)	—		(3.6)	386	—	
4,520.0	129	8,922.9	167	(0.84)	—	—		42.6	95	—	
2,540.0	214	6,274.9	215	1.42	(77.5)	1.9	262	(3.5)	385	5.4	340
7,016.5	66	N.A.		N.A.	—	—		—		—	
4,598.0	126	11,157.8	128	3.30	1.5	10.0	141	3.5	349	14.0	194
1,814.5	274	2,631.6	360	2.97	3,612.5	(0.3)	288	28.5	171	7.8	323
6,731.0	73	21,276.0	67	1.65	16.0	18.2	46	34.2	135	—	
3,514.7	168	N.A.		N.A.	—	—		—		—	
12,600.0	28	12,942.6	107	3.23	651.2	—		(26.4)	437	—	
825.2	395	N.A.		0.88	—	—		—		—	
10,008.0	43	25,143.0	57	5.35	6.2	7.8	178	37.6	116	16.5	126
3,036.5	186	5,051.8	256	3.62	50.8	20.5	31	33.4	141	13.6	207
2,043.1	257	10,614.8	138	1.50	15.4	13.6	78	36.5	127	19.3	84
4,097.0	146	16,338.0	85	0.33	(94.1)	10.8	124	25.5	190	14.3	186
6,954.0	68	58,741.7	14	2.99	19.6	11.9	105	34.0	136	21.7	50
3,557.2	166	11,644.4	122	3.14	15.9	—		17.3	258	21.4	57
5,353.4	100	22,071.9	61	4.55	12.1	9.3	155	21.2	225	16.6	124
2,255.5	235	5,032.8	259	1.48	(11.4)	6.2	210	36.7	124	22.1	44
4,604.0	125	9,470.6	153	2.34	(40.5)	6.3	209	13.5	288	10.6	269
1,669.7	294	4,845.5	269	3.17	14.0	—		(3.9)	389	19.5	78
4,820.2	120	44,821.2	26	2.41	13.7	15.3	64	24.4	202	18.6	91
2,646.0	202	6,734.0	202	2.33	(44.0)	—		(5.9)	393	6.6	328

RANK 1996	COMPANY	REVENUES $ millions	PROFITS $ millions	Rank	ASSETS $ millions	Rank
126	LIBERTY MUTUAL INSURANCE GROUP Boston	10,967.0	511.0	164	39,926.0	71
127	ANHEUSER-BUSCH St. Louis	10,883.7[E]	1,189.9	69	10,463.6	206
128	MCDONALD'S Oak Brook, Ill.	10,686.5	1,572.6	47	17,386.0	138
129	OCCIDENTAL PETROLEUM Los Angeles	10,557.0[E]	668.0	125	17,634.0	137
130	CSX Richmond	10,536.0	855.0	103	16,965.0	141
131	PUBLIX SUPER MARKETS Lakeland, Fla.	10,526.0	265.2	266	2,921.1	381
132	BERKSHIRE HATHAWAY Omaha	10,500.3	2,488.6	29	43,409.5	64
133	SOUTHERN Atlanta	10,358.0	1,127.0	78	30,292.0	87
134	WMX TECHNOLOGIES Oak Brook, Ill.	10,321.6[1]	192.1	311	18,366.6	134
135	TRW Cleveland	10,310.1	480.0	171	5,899.0	269
136	FEDERAL EXPRESS Memphis[6]	10,273.6	307.8	238	6,699.0	253
137	BANC ONE CORP. Columbus, Ohio	10,272.4	1,426.5	54	101,848.1	25
138	MARRIOTT INTERNATIONAL Bethesda, Md.	10,172.0	306.0	239	5,075.0	296
139	FIRST CHICAGO NBD CORP. Chicago	10,117.0	1,436.0	53	104,619.0	24
140	UNITED HEALTHCARE Minnetonka, Minn.	10,073.8	355.6	216	6,851.1	251
141	TIME WARNER New York[22]	10,064.0	(191.0)*	485	35,064.0	79
142	UNION PACIFIC Bethlehem, Pa.[23]	10,051.0[1]	904.0	99	27,914.0	94
143	JOHNSON CONTROLS Milwaukee[15]	10,009.4	234.7	284	5,122.6	293
144	BERGEN BRUNSWIG Orange, Calif.[15]	9,942.7	73.5	413	2,489.8	416
145	TOYS "R" US Rochelle Park, N.J.[1]	9,932.4	427.4	191	8,023.0	234
146	TOSCO Stamford, Conn.[24]	9,922.6	146.3	346	3,554.8	346
147	NORTHWEST AIRLINES St. Paul	9,880.5	536.1	155	8,511.7	229
148	SUN Philadelphia	9,875.0[E]	(115.0)	478	5,025.0	299
149	CPC INTERNATIONAL Englewood Cliffs, N.J.	9,844.3	580.0	146	7,874.4	238
150	APPLE COMPUTER Cupertino, Calif.[15]	9,833.0	(816.0)	494	5,364.0	280

STOCKHOLDERS' EQUITY		MARKET VALUE 3/14/97		EARNINGS PER SHARE				TOTAL RETURN TO INVESTORS			
					% change from	1986–96 annual growth rate				1986–96 annual rate	
$ millions	Rank	$ millions	Rank	1996 $	1995	%	Rank	1996 %	Rank	%	Rank
5,620.0	98	N.A.		N.A.	—	—		—		—	
4,029.1	148	21,574.7	63	2.28	83.1	10.4	131	22.7	214	14.5	181
8,718.2	51	30,786.7	44	2.21	12.2	13.5	81	1.2	362	17.2	110
5,140.0	104	8,181.6	177	1.77	35.1	9.4	151	14.2	282	5.3	341
4,995.0	109	10,979.8	133	4.00	36.1	11.4	116	(5.4)	392	14.7	169
1,751.2	278	N.A.		1.20	12.1	13.3	83	—		—	
23,426.3	5	39,196.7	35	2,065.00	238.0	23.7	25	6.2	336	28.3	20
9,216.0	47	14,146.7	99	1.68	1.2	0.6	279	(2.9)	383	13.9	196
4,876.3	117	15,342.0	91	0.39	(68.5)	0.7	277	11.4	301	10.4	277
2,189.0	245	6,998.6	198	3.64	8.8	7.2	189	30.9	157	12.6	231
2,576.1	211	6,174.3	220	5.39	2.3	7.4	184	140.9	8	10.9	258
8,647.0	52	19,125.0	77	3.23	11.0	11.0	122	30.4	160	18.2	96
1,260.0	346	6,480.8	207	2.24	19.8	—		45.4	73	—	
9,007.0	48	18,851.3	79	4.39	27.2	9.8	142	40.8	100	19.6	77
3,839.6	152	10,035.6	144	1.76	12.1	31.1	18	(31.1)	443	36.0	12
9,502.0	45	24,306.1	58	(1.04)	—	—		(0.1)	370	9.3	296
8,225.0	56	14,779.6	97	4.14	(10.0)	—		23.8	208	13.1	221
1,507.8	314	3,495.7	311	5.39	19.0	8.6	165	23.3	209	14.9	164
579.0	437	1,277.9	425	1.83	13.7	10.3	135	17.7	256	14.1	191
4,191.0	140	8,131.8	179	1.54	190.6	11.5	112	37.4	119	8.9	305
1,070.3	369	3,600.3	308	3.49	69.4	2.8	253	110.4	13	25.1	27
92.9	483	3,812.4	300	5.67	36.0	—		(23.3)	434	—	
1,438.0	326	1,989.0	389	(2.17)	(268.2)	—		(7.5)	402	1.2	365
2,083.5	254	12,184.2	115	3.93	14.6	13.1	88	15.4	274	17.7	104
2,058.0	256	2,064.8	385	(6.59)	(291.0)	—		(34.5)	444	1.2	364

RANK 1996	COMPANY	REVENUES $ millions	PROFITS $ millions	Rank	ASSETS $ millions	Rank
151	FARMLAND INDUSTRIES Kansas City[13,25]	9,788.6	N.A.		2,568.4	409
152	GILLETTE Boston[26]	9,697.7	948.7	90	10,435.3	208
153	PG&E CORP. San Francisco[27]	9,610.0	775.2	110	26,129.9	102
154	PACIFIC TELESIS GROUP San Francisco	9,588.0	1,142.0	76	16,608.0	147
155	BANKERS TRUST NEW YORK CORP. New York	9,565.0	612.0	137	120,235.0	20
156	WESTINGHOUSE ELECTRIC Pittsburgh	9,401.0[¶]	30.0	445	19,889.0	128
157	PRINCIPAL FINANCIAL Des Moines[8]	9,387.0	526.0	158	59,142.0	46
158	TEXTRON Providence	9,274.0	253.0	272	18,235.0	135
159	MONSANTO St. Louis	9,262.0	385.0	206	11,191.0	196
160	MASS. MUTUAL LIFE INS. Springfield, Mass.	9,230.0	287.9	249	56,904.5	48
161	H.J. HEINZ Pittsburgh[28]	9,112.3	659.3	128	8,623.7	225
162	DEAN WITTER DISCOVER New York	9,028.6	951.4	89	42,413.6	67
163	SALOMON New York	9,002.0	907.0	97	195,000.0	12
164	AMERADA HESS New York	8,929.7[E]	660.1	127	7,784.5	239
165	NORWEST CORP. Minneapolis	8,882.9	1,153.9	73	80,175.4	35
166	CARDINAL HEALTH Dublin, Ohio[3]	8,862.4	111.9	372	2,681.1	401
167	COLGATE-PALMOLIVE New York	8,749.0	635.0	134	7,901.5	236
168	JOHN HANCOCK MUTUAL LIFE INS . Boston	8,743.5	313.8	233	58,361.0	47
169	WELLS FARGO & CO. San Francisco[29]	8,723.0	1,071.0	80	108,888.0	21
170	ITT INDUSTRIES White Plains, N.Y.	8,718.1	222.6	290	5,491.2	276
171	WHIRLPOOL Benton Harbor, Mich.	8,696.0	156.0	337	8,015.0	235
172	MICROSOFT Redmond, Wash.[3]	8,671.0	2,195.0	33	10,093.0	209
173	LIMITED Columbus, Ohio[1]	8,664.8	434.2	190	4,120.0	326
174	LOWE'S North Wilkesboro, N.C.[1]	8,600.2	292.2	247	4,435.0	319
175	SEAGATE TECHNOLOGY Scotts Valley, Calif.[3,30]	8,588.4	213.3	293	5,239.6	287

STOCKHOLDERS' EQUITY		MARKET VALUE 3/14/97		EARNINGS PER SHARE				TOTAL RETURN TO INVESTORS			
				1996 $	% change from 1995	1986–96 annual growth rate %	Rank	1996 %	Rank	1986–96 annual rate %	Rank
$ millions	Rank	$ millions	Rank								
755.3	415	N.A.		N.A.	—	—		—		—	
4,490.9	130	45,243.8	25	1.71	(7.6)	49.2	6	50.8	53	31.6	15
8,765.4	49	9,684.3	152	1.75	(41.5)	(3.9)	311	(19.7)	431	6.0	334
2,773.0	195	17,132.8	84	2.67	—	0.6	278	15.6	272	12.9	225
5,234.0	101	7,388.1	189	6.78	234.0	1.2	273	37.2	120	12.3	237
5,742.0	95	11,628.3	123	0.07	—	(29.2)	330	22.7	212	(0.2)	368
4,654.0	124	N.A.		N.A.	—	—		—		—	
3,183.0	176	8,413.3	173	2.94	(46.6)	0.2	283	42.7	93	15.1	160
3,690.0	161	24,108.8	59	0.64	(49.7)	1.4	268	61.5	37	21.5	55
2,638.6	203	N.A.		N.A.	—	—		—		—	
2,706.8	201	15,332.9	92	1.75	10.3	9.1	157	11.6	300	13.6	206
5,164.4	103	12,458.7	113	2.79	(42.8)	—		43.1	91	—	
4,857.0	118	5,901.2	230	7.88	116.5	8.6	167	35.3	132	4.2	350
3,383.6	171	5,014.3	260	7.09	—	—		10.4	307	10.8	264
6,064.2	86	18,573.4	81	3.07	11.2	17.6	50	35.4	130	26.0	26
930.7	382	6,190.0	219	1.73	29.1	18.9	42	59.9	39	31.5	16
2,034.1	258	16,033.9	87	4.19	302.9	12.8	92	34.3	134	19.4	79
2,856.1	190	N.A.		N.A.	—	—		—		—	
14,112.0	20	28,059.8	53	12.21	(40.1)	9.3	156	27.4	174	22.5	41
799.2	405	2,872.1	351	1.85	—	—		3.9	347	—	
1,926.0	264	3,782.0	303	2.08	(25.7)	4.4	231	(10.1)	409	6.5	330
6,908.0	69	119,112.4	4	3.43	47.8	44.5	8	88.3	16	51.0	3
1,922.6	267	5,421.2	243	1.54	(42.5)	9.8	144	9.5	312	2.9	354
2,217.5	241	6,748.2	201	1.74	23.4	17.9	49	7.0	332	20.2	71
2,466.1	220	11,001.1	132	2.06	(41.5)	11.1	121	66.3	32	15.2	157

RANK 1996	COMPANY	REVENUES $ millions	PROFITS $ millions	Rank	ASSETS $ millions	Rank
176	**UNOCAL** El Segundo, Calif.	**8,587.5**[E,¶]	36.4	442	**9,123.0**	222
177	**EDISON INTERNATIONAL** Rosemead, Calif.	**8,545.0**	717.0	121	**24,559.0**	108
178	**CVS** Woonsocket, R.I.[31]	**8,345.9**[¶]	75.4	409	**2,831.8**	387
179	**CROWN CORK & SEAL** Philadelphia	**8,331.9**	284.0	252	**12,590.2**	182
180	**GENERAL RE** Stamford, Conn.	**8,295.7**	893.5	100	**40,161.0**	70
181	**ULTRAMAR DIAMOND SHAMROCK** San Antonio[32]	**8,208.4**[E]	(35.9)	463	**4,420.0**	320
182	**BURLINGTON NORTHERN SANTA FE** Fort Worth	**8,187.0**	889.0	101	**19,846.0**	130
183	**US AIRWAYS GROUP** Arlington, Va.[33]	**8,142.4**	263.4	267	**7,531.4**	245
184	**WOOLWORTH** New York[1]	**8,092.4**	168.7	328	**3,476.4**	354
185	**NORTHROP GRUMMAN** Los Angeles	**8,071.0**	234.0	285	**9,422.0**	217
186	**FLEET FINANCIAL GROUP** Boston	**8,043.0**	1,139.0	77	**85,518.0**	33
187	**TELE-COMMUNICATIONS** Englewood, Colo.	**8,022.0**	278.0	257	**30,249.0**	88
188	**COCA-COLA ENTERPRISES** Atlanta	**7,921.0**	114.0	368	**11,234.0**	194
189	**DANA** Toledo	**7,890.7**	306.0	239	**6,160.0**	263
190	**DELL COMPUTER** Round Rock, Texas[1]	**7,759.0**	518.0	159	**2,993.0**	380
191	**CAMPBELL SOUP** Camden, N.J.[34]	**7,678.0**	802.0	105	**6,632.0**	255
192	**PANENERGY** Houston	**7,536.8**	344.4	220	**8,567.8**	227
193	**HALLIBURTON** Dallas	**7,385.1**	300.4	242	**4,436.6**	318
194	**ELI LILLY** Indianapolis	**7,346.6**	1,523.5	49	**14,307.2**	165
195	**HONEYWELL** Minneapolis	**7,311.6**	402.7	201	**5,493.3**	275
196	**PHARMACIA & UPJOHN** Kalamazoo, Mich.	**7,286.0**	562.0	152	**11,173.0**	197
197	**NGC** Houston	**7,260.2**	113.3	369	**4,193.6**	323
198	**WARNER-LAMBERT** Morris Plains, N.J.	**7,231.4**	786.5	108	**7,197.3**	249
199	**PPG INDUSTRIES** Pittsburgh	**7,218.1**	744.0	115	**6,441.4**	259
200	**BEST BUY** Eden Prairie, Minn.[18]	**7,217.4**	48.0	433	**1,890.8**	445

STOCKHOLDERS' EQUITY		MARKET VALUE 3/14/97		EARNINGS PER SHARE				TOTAL RETURN TO INVESTORS			
				1996 $	% change from 1995	1986–96 annual growth rate %	Rank	1996 %	Rank	1986–96 annual rate %	Rank
$ millions	Rank	$ millions	Rank								
2,275.0	233	9,838.8	148	0.07	(92.3)	(21.2)	329	43.3	87	14.8	165
6,397.0	78	9,231.4	159	1.64	(1.2)	(0.3)	286	19.5	239	8.6	310
1,245.1	347	4,889.4	268	0.57	—	(12.6)	323	54.5	51	9.0	301
3,563.3	165	6,928.0	200	2.16	160.2	10.1	139	32.9	144	17.1	113
7,326.0	63	13,825.3	102	11.00	10.9	13.1	89	3.2	352	13.0	223
1,240.9	348	2,436.0	368	(0.54)	(131.2)	—		27.4	175	—	
5,981.0	88	12,522.9	112	5.70	750.7	—		12.4	294	14.2	188
(584.4)	495	1,628.6	404	2.69	389.1	(2.1)	302	76.4	23	(4.2)	378
1,334.6	337	3,076.7	337	1.26	—	(2.5)	304	69.2	29	4.5	348
2,128.0	248	4,315.7	282	4.33	(15.3)	17.1	55	32.3	146	12.4	233
7,415.0	61	15,903.8	88	3.97	152.9	4.4	232	27.4	177	12.6	230
4,253.0	138	14,328.9	98	N.A.	—	—		(28.7)	441	8.7	309
1,550.0	312	7,871.0	182	0.85	37.1	9.0	161	80.9	20	13.4	213
1,428.7	327	3,296.8	325	3.01	6.0	13.6	79	15.0	279	10.6	268
806.0	402	12,277.8	114	2.70	102.2	—		206.9	2	—	
2,742.0	198	21,627.3	62	3.22	15.0	14.1	74	36.5	126	21.6	54
2,452.5	221	6,590.3	204	2.28	12.3	—		66.0	34	10.9	262
2,159.2	247	8,699.6	169	2.38	61.9	—		26.7	181	13.1	222
6,100.1	85	46,091.6	23	2.78	(31.0)	10.7	126	32.5	145	18.1	97
2,204.9	244	9,237.3	158	3.18	21.4	—		37.7	115	19.7	76
6,241.0	80	19,434.7	76	1.07	(25.2)	(2.3)	303	2.3	355	5.5	338
552.4	442	3,183.3	331	0.83	1.2	—		163.2	5	—	
2,581.0	210	23,899.5	60	2.90	5.8	10.7	125	58.1	43	21.1	59
2,482.6	219	10,339.6	142	3.96	4.2	19.5	37	25.7	189	15.4	152
431.6	457	432.7	449	1.10	(17.3)	27.5	23	(34.6)	445	7.2	325

RANK 1996	COMPANY	REVENUES $ millions	PROFITS $ millions	Rank	ASSETS $ millions	Rank
201	ENTERGY New Orleans	7,163.5	420.0	192	22,966.3	118
202	AFLAC Columbus, Ga.	7,100.2	394.4	203	25,022.8	105
203	SUN MICROSYSTEMS Mountain View, Calif.[3]	7,094.8	476.4	174	3,800.9	337
204	CIRCUIT CITY GROUP Richmond[18]	7,029.1	179.4	320	2,526.0	411
205	REYNOLDS METALS Richmond	7,016.0	89.0	393	7,516.0	246
206	AMERICAN GENERAL Houston	6,979.0	577.0	149	66,254.0	43
207	EATON Cleveland	6,961.0	349.0	219	5,307.0	284
208	CONSOLIDATED EDISON OF NEW YORK New York	6,959.7	694.1	123	14,057.2	168
209	UNICOM Chicago	6,937.0	666.1	126	23,388.0	116
210	GUARDIAN LIFE INS. CO. OF AMERICA New York	6,904.1	173.2	326	18,195.7	136
211	LINCOLN NATIONAL Fort Wayne	6,882.8	513.6	162	71,713.4	40
212	UNITED SERVICES AUTOMOBILE ASSN. San Antonio	6,831.1	855.3	102	23,622.1	114
213	HUMANA Louisville	6,788.0	12.0	455	3,153.0	373
214	INGERSOLL-RAND Woodcliff Lake, N.J.	6,702.9	358.0	215	5,621.6	272
215	TJX Framingham, Mass.[1]	6,689.4	363.1*	211	2,561.2	410
216	KELLOGG Battle Creek, Mich.	6,676.6	531.0	157	5,050.0	298
217	R.R. DONNELLEY & SONS Chicago	6,599.0	(157.6)	481	4,849.0	306
218	ITT New York	6,597.0	249.0	275	9,275.0	221
219	DRESSER INDUSTRIES Dallas[2]	6,561.5	257.5	269	5,150.2	291
220	TEXAS UTILITIES Dallas	6,550.9	753.6	114	21,375.7	120
221	ARROW ELECTRONICS Melville, N.Y.	6,534.6	202.7	303	2,710.4	394
222	CHUBB Warren, N.J.	6,497.4¶	512.7	163	19,938.9	126
223	NIKE Beaverton, Ore.[6]	6,470.6	553.2	153	3,951.6	332
224	TYSON FOODS Springdale, Ark.[15]	6,453.8	86.9	394	4,544.1	315
225	DILLARD DEPARTMENT STORES Little Rock[1]	6,412.1	238.6	282	5,059.7	297

STOCKHOLDERS' EQUITY		MARKET VALUE 3/14/97		EARNINGS PER SHARE				TOTAL RETURN TO INVESTORS			
				1996 $	% change from 1995	1986–96 annual growth rate %	Rank	1996 %	Rank	1986–96 annual rate %	Rank
$ millions	Rank	$ millions	Rank								
6,640.9	74	5,917.4	229	1.83	(19.7)	(1.9)	299	1.0	363	12.8	226
2,125.6	249	5,634.8	238	2.73	17.2	15.1	66	49.1	57	21.8	48
2,251.5	237	11,088.5	130	2.42	168.1	—		12.6	293	24.0	31
1,063.9	371	5,072.3	254	1.82	5.8	22.1	29	9.5	313	15.1	159
2,634.0	205	4,681.3	272	0.82	(84.7)	(14.8)	325	1.7	360	13.7	201
5,621.0	97	8,606.0	171	2.75	4.2	2.8	254	21.3	224	13.1	219
2,160.0	246	5,669.6	237	4.50	(12.3)	12.1	100	33.6	139	14.4	183
5,965.7	89	7,255.3	192	2.93	0.0	3.2	247	(1.5)	377	9.4	294
6,104.4	84	4,609.6	275	3.09	3.7	(4.1)	313	(12.2)	417	5.6	337
1,178.1	355	N.A.		N.A.	—	—		—		—	
4,470.0	132	6,375.0	211	4.91	6.7	4.8	226	1.5	361	13.7	205
5,877.8	93	N.A.		N.A.	—	—		—		—	
1,292.0	342	3,721.3	305	0.07	(94.0)	(15.4)	326	(30.6)	442	11.8	246
2,090.8	253	5,253.8	249	3.33	30.6	14.0	75	29.0	166	17.6	105
1,127.2	363	3,575.4	309	4.01	1,643.5	10.4	133	153.2	6	13.4	211
1,282.4	343	14,020.2	100	2.50	11.6	6.8	200	(13.1)	419	12.4	235
1,631.3	302	4,658.7	273	(1.04)	(153.3)	—		(18.6)	429	9.7	291
3,074.0	182	6,981.0	199	2.11	—	—		(18.2)	427	—	
1,582.2	307	5,406.4	245	1.44	33.3	37.4	10	30.1	161	16.1	133
6,032.9	87	8,141.8	178	3.35	—	(2.8)	305	4.3	343	11.4	251
1,358.5	333	2,919.5	346	3.95	(6.2)	—		24.4	201	24.2	29
5,462.9	99	10,382.4	139	2.90	(26.1)	5.1	221	13.6	287	16.7	121
2,431.4	223	18,924.0	78	3.77	38.6	25.5	24	73.5	25	46.9	5
1,541.7	313	2,431.5	369	0.60	(60.3)	4.3	233	31.7	150	14.5	179
2,717.2	199	3,478.5	315	2.09	41.2	10.3	136	8.8	319	9.7	290

RANK 1996	COMPANY	REVENUES $ millions	PROFITS $ millions	Rank	ASSETS $ millions	Rank
226	**UNISYS** Blue Bell, Pa.	6,370.5	49.7*	431	6,967.1	250
227	**CONTINENTAL AIRLINES** Houston	6,360.0	319.0	227	5,206.0	288
228	**PNC BANK CORP.** Pittsburgh	6,333.8	992.2	88	73,260.0	39
229	**TANDY** Fort Worth	6,285.5	(91.6)	473	2,583.4	408
230	**TRANSAMERICA** San Francisco	6,277.6	456.3	183	49,874.9	58
231	**ANTHEM INSURANCE** Indianapolis[35]	6,269.6	64.2	422	4,968.0	303
232	**LEAR** Southfield, Mich.[36]	6,249.1	151.9	340	3,816.8	336
233	**BANK OF BOSTON CORP.** Boston[37]	6,237.0	650.0	130	62,306.0	45
234	**PUBLIC SERVICE ENTERPRISE GROUP** Newark, N.J.	6,169.6	611.6	138	16,915.3	144
235	**ARAMARK** Philadelphia[15]	6,122.5	109.5	375	2,830.8	388
236	**RALSTON PURINA** St. Louis[15]	6,114.3	359.6	214	4,785.1	309
237	**UNION CARBIDE** Danbury, Conn.	6,106.0	593.0	143	6,546.0	256
238	**ST. PAUL COS.** St. Paul	6,095.2	450.1	186	20,681.0	123
239	**MANPOWER** Milwaukee	6,079.9	162.3	331	1,752.3	455
240	**OFFICE DEPOT** Delray Beach, Fla.	6,068.6	129.0	359	2,740.3	393
241	**KEYCORP** Cleveland	6,038.0	783.0	109	67,621.0	42
242	**FPL GROUP** Juno Beach, Fla.	6,036.8	579.5	147	12,219.3	186
243	**CHAMPION INTERNATIONAL** Stamford, Conn.	5,880.4	141.3	351	9,820.0	213
244	**AMERICAN ELECTRIC POWER** Columbus, Ohio	5,849.2	587.4	144	15,885.5	150
245	**AMERICAN STANDARD** Piscataway, N.J.	5,804.6	(46.7)	466	3,519.6	351
246	**BROWNING-FERRIS INDUSTRIES** Houston[15]	5,779.3	(101.3)*	475	7,600.9	240
247	**AMERICAN BRANDS** Old Greenwich, Conn.	5,776.3ᴱ	486.5	169	9,504.2	216
248	**BORDEN** Columbus, Ohio	5,765.1	81.9	401	3,306.0	364
249	**NAVISTAR INTERNATIONAL** Chicago[2]	5,754.0	65.0	421	5,326.0	283
250	**GENUINE PARTS** Atlanta	5,720.5	330.1	225	2,521.6	414

STOCKHOLDERS' EQUITY		MARKET VALUE 3/14/97		EARNINGS PER SHARE				TOTAL RETURN TO INVESTORS			
				1996 $	% change from 1995	1986–96 annual growth rate %	Rank	1996 %	Rank	1986–96 annual rate %	Rank
$ millions	Rank	$ millions	Rank								
1,606.0	305	1,158.3	430	(0.41)	—	—		22.7	213	(11.4)	381
581.0	436	1,835.1	396	N.A.	—	—		29.9	163	—	
5,869.0	94	13,977.6	101	2.90	143.7	2.7	256	22.1	218	11.5	249
1,264.8	345	3,045.0	343	(1.64)	(152.6)	—		8.0	324	2.3	359
4,140.6	143	6,003.6	224	6.59	0.2	6.3	208	11.4	302	14.6	172
1,347.4	335	N.A.		N.A.	—	—		—		—	
1,018.7	375	2,409.9	371	2.38	36.8	—		17.7	255	—	
4,934.0	112	11,415.2	126	3.99	(12.3)	5.0	223	43.3	88	13.4	214
5,213.0	102	6,318.7	213	2.52	(7.0)	2.9	251	(3.7)	388	8.1	316
296.2	468	N.A.		2.31	22.9	—		—		—	
689.0	421	8,551.2	172	3.39	24.6	—		19.8	235	—	
2,114.0	250	6,192.0	218	4.28	(33.5)	(1.1)	293	10.9	305	15.8	142
4,003.8	150	5,767.1	234	4.93	(17.7)	7.6	180	8.7	320	15.5	150
600.7	434	3,222.6	330	1.95	18.2	—		16.0	268	—	
1,155.9	361	3,417.1	317	0.81	(4.7)	—		(8.9)	407	—	
4,881.0	115	12,171.9	116	3.37	(2.3)	7.0	198	44.4	75	18.3	95
4,592.1	127	8,120.5	180	3.33	5.4	1.4	270	3.4	351	10.6	267
3,775.7	155	4,216.4	284	1.48	(81.5)	(3.3)	308	3.4	350	5.2	342
4,545.3	128	7,576.5	186	3.14	10.2	1.8	263	7.7	329	12.7	227
(379.9)	493	3,671.2	307	(0.60)	(140.0)	—		36.6	125	—	
2,510.3	216	6,391.7	210	(0.50)	(125.9)	—		(8.5)	404	3.9	352
3,684.2	162	9,104.7	164	2.80	(3.1)	5.8	215	16.6	264	13.9	197
495.4	451	N.A.		N.A.	—	—		—		—	
916.0	385	709.4	444	0.49	(73.2)	—		(14.1)	421	(15.2)	382
1,732.1	280	5,748.9	236	2.73	8.3	10.4	132	11.8	298	12.2	238

RANK 1996	COMPANY	REVENUES $ millions	PROFITS $ millions	Rank	ASSETS $ millions	Rank
251	**BANK OF NEW YORK CO.** New York	5,713.0	1,020.0	83	55,891.0	50
252	**PAINE WEBBER GROUP** New York	5,706.0	364.4	210	52,513.5	53
253	**JAMES RIVER CORP. OF VA.** Richmond	5,690.5	157.3	336	6,541.5	257
254	**SCHERING-PLOUGH** Madison, N.J.	5,655.8	1,212.8	66	5,398.1	278
255	**TENET HEALTHCARE** Santa Barbara[6,38]	5,559.0	350.0	217	8,332.0	232
256	**AMERISOURCE HEALTH** Malvern, Pa.[15]	5,551.7	35.4*	443	1,188.0	478
257	**MERISEL** El Segundo, Calif.	5,522.8	(140.4)	480	N.A.	
258	**RYDER SYSTEM** Miami	5,519.4	(41.3)	464	5,645.4	271
259	**CENTRAL & SOUTH WEST** Dallas	5,517.0	447.0	187	13,332.0	176
260	**AVATEX** Dallas[20,39]	5,502.3	(63.7)	471	1,577.1	459
261	**AMP** Harrisburg, Pa.	5,468.0	287.0	251	4,685.7	314
262	**RITE AID** Camp Hill, Pa.[18,40]	5,446.0	158.9	334	2,842.0	386
263	**BAXTER INTERNATIONAL** Deerfield, Ill.	5,438.0[41]	669.0	124	7,596.0	241
264	**GENERAL MILLS** Minneapolis[6]	5,416.0[42]	476.4	173	3,294.7	368
265	**CASE** Racine, Wis.	5,409.0	316.0	230	6,059.0	265
266	**VONS** Arcadia, Calif.	5,407.4	104.7	379	2,185.4	427
267	**FOOD 4 LESS** Compton, Calif.[43]	5,342.7	(204.6)	486	3,146.9	375
268	**BINDLEY WESTERN** Indianapolis	5,318.9	18.0	451	941.2	485
269	**GAP** San Francisco[1]	5,284.4	452.9	185	2,626.9	404
270	**COOPER INDUSTRIES** Houston	5,283.7	315.4	231	5,950.4	268
271	**W.R. GRACE** Boca Raton, Fla.	5,262.4¶	2,857.7	21	4,945.8	304
272	**CUMMINS ENGINE** Columbus, Ind.	5,257.0	160.0	333	3,369.0	359
273	**AVNET** Great Neck, N.Y.[3]	5,207.8	188.3	316	2,521.7	413
274	**QUAKER OATS** Chicago	5,199.0	247.9	278	4,394.4	321
275	**STONE CONTAINER** Chicago	5,141.8	(126.2)	479	6,353.8	260

STOCKHOLDERS' EQUITY		MARKET VALUE 3/14/97		EARNINGS PER SHARE				TOTAL RETURN TO INVESTORS			
					% change	1986–96 annual growth rate		1996		1986–96 annual rate	
$ millions	Rank	$ millions	Rank	1996 $	from 1995	%	Rank	%	Rank	%	Rank
5,127.0	105	15,295.4	93	2.47	8.1	7.1	192	42.9	92	18.6	92
1,730.4	281	3,092.0	335	3.59	564.8	12.4	97	43.7	83	10.0	287
2,306.4	231	2,894.1	349	1.15	42.0	(4.2)	314	40.3	104	2.8	355
2,059.9	255	28,635.6	49	3.30	37.5	19.8	34	20.8	229	23.8	32
2,636.0	204	8,690.3	170	1.67	79.6	12.0	103	6.1	338	9.6	293
(36.8)	487	1,231.0	426	1.54	175.0	—		46.2	69	—	
N.A.		63.9	462	(4.68)	—	—		(62.1)	455	—	
1,106.0	364	2,436.3	367	(0.51)	(127.4)	—		16.0	269	2.0	361
4,094.0	147	4,903.1	267	2.07	(1.4)	1.0	275	(2.0)	379	11.2	253
202.5	477	17.3	464	(4.95)	(425.7)	—		—		—	
2,789.9	194	8,398.7	175	1.31	(33.2)	5.6	216	2.9	354	10.5	274
1,103.6	365	5,407.8	244	1.90	13.8	9.6	146	18.9	244	13.2	216
2,504.0	217	12,648.0	110	2.46	4.7	3.8	239	8.3	323	12.7	229
307.7	467	9,721.9	150	3.00	28.8	11.3	118	14.1	283	16.8	119
1,904.0	268	3,925.9	298	4.17	(9.3)	—		19.6	238	—	
738.4	417	3,011.4	345	2.34	51.0	—		111.9	12	23.7	33
(278.5)	490	N.A.		N.A.	—	—		—		—	
222.1	475	214.6	455	1.52	7.0	8.5	169	14.5	280	4.9	345
1,654.5	295	9,703.9	151	1.60	160.2	29.5	19	44.8	74	22.6	39
1,890.2	269	5,035.5	258	2.93	248.8	6.8	202	18.5	247	10.8	263
632.4	429	4,503.1	276	31.06	—	—		30.9	156	16.4	127
1,312.0	340	2,103.0	384	4.01	(27.4)	—		27.3	178	5.8	336
1,505.2	315	2,678.7	357	4.31	29.8	20.5	32	31.9	148	10.5	272
1,229.9	349	5,060.9	255	1.80	(69.8)	4.8	227	14.3	281	10.4	279
795.2	408	1,278.5	424	(1.35)	(151.3)	—		7.7	328	(0.4)	370

RANK 1996	COMPANY	REVENUES $ millions	PROFITS $ millions	Rank	ASSETS $ millions	Rank
276	**VF** Wyomissing, Pa.	**5,137.2**	**299.5**	243	**3,449.5**	355
277	**BOISE CASCADE** Boise	**5,122.7**	**9.1**	456	**4,710.7**	312
278	**FMC** Chicago	**5,121.9**	**210.7**	298	**4,989.8**	301
279	**TYCO INTERNATIONAL** Exeter, N.H.[3]	**5,089.8**	**310.1**	236	**3,953.9**	330
280	**REVCO D.S.** Twinsburg, Ohio[6]	**5,087.7**	**76.2**	408	**2,133.5**	431
281	**LYONDELL PETROCHEMICAL** Houston	**5,082.0**	**126.0**	360	**3,276.0**	369
282	**HOUSEHOLD INTERNATIONAL** Prospect Heights, Ill.	**5,058.8**	**538.6**	154	**29,594.5**	89
283	**MILLENNIUM CHEMICALS** Iselin, N.J.	**5,057.0¶**	**(2,701.0)**	496	**5,601.0**	273
284	**GATEWAY 2000** North Sioux City, S.Dak.	**5,035.2**	**250.7**	273	**1,673.4**	457
285	**ECKERD** Largo, Fla.[44]	**4,997.1**	**93.5**	390	**1,490.7**	461
286	**ILLINOIS TOOL WORKS** Glenview, Ill.	**4,996.7**	**486.3**	170	**4,806.2**	308
287	**VALERO ENERGY** San Antonio	**4,990.7**	**72.7**	415	**3,149.6**	374
288	**BEAR STEARNS** New York[3]	**4,963.9**	**490.6**	168	**92,085.2**	31
289	**FIRST DATA** Hackensack, N.J.	**4,938.1**	**636.5**	133	**14,340.1**	164
290	**NATIONAL CITY CORP.** Cleveland[45]	**4,928.4**	**736.6**	117	**50,855.8**	56
291	**BLACK & DECKER** Towson, Md.	**4,914.4**	**229.6**	287	**5,153.5**	290
292	**DOMINION RESOURCES** Richmond	**4,842.3**	**472.1**	176	**14,905.6**	156
293	**AVON PRODUCTS** New York	**4,814.2**	**317.9**	228	**2,222.4**	426
294	**MEDPARTNERS** Birmingham, Ala.[46]	**4,813.5**	**(158.5)**	482	**2,266.0**	425
295	**THRIFTY PAYLESS HOLDINGS** Wilsonville, Ore.[15,47]	**4,798.9**	**(35.2)***	462	**2,067.9**	437
296	**NORAM ENERGY** Houston	**4,788.5ᴱ**	**90.9**	391	**4,017.5**	329
297	**EASTMAN CHEMICAL** Kingsport, Tenn.	**4,782.0**	**380.0**	207	**5,266.0**	286
298	**NORFOLK SOUTHERN** Norfolk, Va.	**4,770.0**	**770.4**	111	**11,416.1**	193
299	**MELLON BANK CORP.** Pittsburgh	**4,762.0**	**733.0**	118	**42,596.0**	66
300	**DUKE POWER** Charlotte, N.C.	**4,758.0**	**730.0**	119	**13,469.7**	172

STOCKHOLDERS' EQUITY		MARKET VALUE 3/14/97		EARNINGS PER SHARE				TOTAL RETURN TO INVESTORS			
				1996 $	% change from 1995	1986–96 annual growth rate %	Rank	1996 %	Rank	1986–96 annual rate %	Rank
$ millions	Rank	$ millions	Rank								
1,973.7	261	4,377.7	280	4.64	92.5	8.5	171	31.1	153	11.2	255
1,680.5	290	1,599.7	406	(0.63)	(110.6)	—		(6.4)	395	1.9	362
855.8	391	2,465.7	366	5.54	(3.1)	12.9	91	3.7	348	10.5	273
1,938.4	263	9,438.6	155	2.03	43.5	14.1	73	49.2	56	18.8	88
868.6	388	2,802.4	354	1.14	25.3	—		31.0	155	—	
431.0	458	1,890.0	394	1.58	(67.5)	—		0.3	365	—	
3,146.2	177	9,359.0	157	5.31	23.2	9.0	159	58.3	41	20.9	62
1,318.0	339	1,411.2	417	(35.33)	—	—		—		—	
815.5	398	4,107.3	291	3.21	46.6	—		118.6	11	—	
54.7	485	N.A.		—	—	—		43.4	86	—	
2,396.0	225	11,078.1	131	3.93	19.5	17.6	51	36.8	123	21.5	56
1,085.4	367	1,450.0	414	1.40	27.3	—		19.3	240	17.0	116
2,745.4	197	3,439.7	316	3.43	101.8	19.6	35	43.7	84	16.3	129
3,709.8	159	15,273.3	94	1.37	—	—		(27.2)	439	22.2	43
4,432.1	134	11,550.5	124	3.29	8.6	11.1	120	41.0	99	16.6	122
1,632.4	301	3,263.4	326	2.41	(0.4)	36.2	11	(13.4)	420	8.5	311
4,924.4	113	7,125.8	193	2.65	8.2	(0.3)	287	(0.2)	372	9.9	288
241.7	471	7,704.9	184	2.38	26.6	7.9	177	55.4	49	20.7	63
739.5	416	3,762.6	304	(1.02)	—	—		(37.1)	448	—	
378.8	464	N.A.		N.A.	—	—		—		—	
800.5	404	2,059.4	386	0.67	42.6	(5.7)	316	78.9	21	2.6	357
1,639.0	299	4,321.3	281	4.80	(29.2)	—		(9.0)	408	—	
4,977.6	110	11,477.7	125	6.09	11.9	8.3	173	13.8	285	15.8	140
3,746.0	157	10,627.4	137	5.17	14.9	2.3	259	37.6	118	11.8	245
4,888.7	114	8,895.2	168	3.37	3.7	5.3	220	2.0	359	13.3	215

RANK 1996	COMPANY	REVENUES $ millions	PROFITS $ millions	Rank	ASSETS $ millions	Rank
301	**MEAD** Dayton	4,706.5	195.3	309	4,985.9	302
302	**BETHLEHEM STEEL** Bethlehem, Pa.	4,679.0	(308.8)	490	5,109.9	294
303	**GANNETT** Arlington, Va.	4,665.1	943.1	91	6,349.6	261
304	**PACIFICARE HEALTH SYSTEMS** Cypress, Calif.[15]	4,637.3	72.0	417	1,299.5	472
305	**TECH DATA** Clearwater, Fla.[1]	4,598.9	57.0	427	1,545.3	460
306	**PACCAR** Bellevue, Wash.	4,584.7	201.0	306	5,298.8	285
307	**INLAND STEEL INDUSTRIES** Chicago	4,584.1	45.7	435	3,541.6	348
308	**SCI SYSTEMS** Huntsville, Ala.[3]	4,544.8	81.0	402	1,283.2	474
309	**WORLDCOM** Jackson, Miss.	4,485.1	(2,213.4)	495	19,862.0	129
310	**NORDSTROM** Seattle[1]	4,453.1	147.5	345	2,702.5	396
311	**PRAXAIR** Danbury, Conn.	4,449.0	282.0	254	7,538.0	244
312	**QUANTUM** Milpitas, Calif.[20]	4,422.7	(90.5)	472	1,975.4	442
313	**ALLEGIANCE** McGaw Park, Ill.	4,387.2	(477.7)	493	2,799.2	390
314	**WABAN** Natick, Mass.[1]	4,375.5	76.7	407	1,376.0	468
315	**CMS ENERGY** Dearborn, Mich.	4,333.0	240.0	280	8,615.0	226
316	**UTILICORP UNITED** Kansas City	4,332.3	105.8	378	4,704.9	313
317	**PACIFICORP** Portland, Ore.	4,293.8	504.9	165	14,634.5	160
318	**PECO ENERGY** Philadelphia	4,283.7	517.2	160	15,260.6	153
319	**COMPUTER SCIENCES** El Segundo, Calif.[20]	4,242.4	141.7	350	2,595.8	407
320	**ORACLE** Redwood Shores, Calif.[6]	4,223.3	603.3	140	3,357.2	361
321	**CORNING** Corning, N.Y.	4,199.5[¶]	175.6	325	4,321.3	322
322	**MUTUAL OF OMAHA INSURANCE** Omaha	4,199.1	65.6	420	11,749.8	190
323	**CORESTATES FINANCIAL CORP.** Philadelphia[48]	4,197.3	649.1	131	45,494.2	62
324	**AON** Chicago	4,191.2	335.2	222	13,722.7	169
325	**FHP INTERNATIONAL** Santa Ana, Calif.[3]	4,179.3	44.2	437	2,013.9	440

STOCKHOLDERS' EQUITY		MARKET VALUE 3/14/97		EARNINGS PER SHARE				TOTAL RETURN TO INVESTORS			
				1996 $	% change from 1995	1986–96 annual growth rate %	Rank	1996 %	Rank	1986–96 annual rate %	Rank
$ millions	Rank	$ millions	Rank								
2,246.4	239	3,054.4	341	3.67	(42.0)	20.3	33	13.6	286	10.4	278
966.0	379	950.6	439	(3.15)	(354.0)	—		(36.0)	446	4.2	349
2,930.8	188	11,963.7	118	6.69	96.2	22.8	26	24.6	200	10.5	276
823.2	396	3,485.7	313	2.27	(37.3)	34.2	14	(6.6)	397	41.3	8
438.4	456	1,108.0	432	1.35	141.1	28.7	20	82.5	18	32.3	14
1,358.0	334	2,759.9	356	5.17	(20.5)	14.7	69	75.6	24	18.0	102
789.0	409	978.2	437	0.75	(72.1)	6.5	206	(19.6)	430	1.8	363
472.3	453	1,471.1	413	2.69	65.0	15.0	67	44.0	79	14.3	185
12,960.0	26	20,666.7	70	(5.56)	(955.4)	—		47.9	61	53.0	2
1,473.2	322	3,074.4	340	1.82	(9.9)	7.2	190	(11.5)	415	6.4	331
1,924.0	266	7,969.3	181	1.77	(2.7)	—		38.4	112	—	
544.8	445	2,477.4	365	(1.74)	(201.2)	—		77.5	22	20.0	74
827.7	394	1,381.9	419	(8.70)	—	—		—		—	
631.9	430	943.6	440	2.31	5.0	—		39.6	107	—	
1,702.0	287	3,080.3	336	2.45	7.9	12.7	93	16.3	266	10.1	283
1,173.0	357	1,405.5	418	2.20	27.9	2.7	258	(2.1)	380	10.0	285
4,167.8	142	6,050.4	223	1.62	(1.2)	(0.6)	291	2.2	357	8.2	315
4,845.3	119	4,700.3	271	2.24	(15.2)	(1.5)	297	(10.2)	411	8.9	303
1,305.7	341	5,175.1	251	2.48	18.7	16.0	59	16.9	261	19.3	83
1,870.4	271	27,713.9	55	0.90	35.0	54.1	4	47.8	62	53.5	1
961.0	380	10,234.3	143	0.76	—	(2.8)	306	47.2	63	15.5	148
1,281.8	344	N.A.		N.A.	—	—		—		—	
3,695.7	160	11,682.2	121	2.97	(7.8)	7.3	188	42.7	94	16.1	135
2,832.9	192	7,118.8	194	2.87	(17.5)	1.5	267	27.9	172	17.9	103
1,167.6	358	1,540.3	408	0.43	48.3	(0.1)	285	—		—	

RANK 1996	COMPANY	REVENUES $ millions	PROFITS $ millions	Rank	ASSETS $ millions	Rank
326	**WELLPOINT HEALTH NETWORKS** Woodland Hills, Calif.	**4,169.8**	**202.0**	304	**3,405.5**	358
327	**MARSH & MCLENNAN** New York	**4,149.0**	**459.3**	182	**4,542.2**	316
328	**APPLIED MATERIALS** Santa Clara, Calif.[2]	**4,144.8**	**599.6**	141	**3,638.0**	343
329	**LTV** Cleveland	**4,134.5**	**109.2**	376	**5,410.5**	277
330	**SHERWIN-WILLIAMS** Cleveland	**4,132.9**	**229.2**	288	**2,994.6**	378
331	**AMERICAN FINANCIAL GROUP** Cincinnati	**4,115.4**	**233.3**	286	**15,051.1**	154
332	**CISCO SYSTEMS** San Jose[34]	**4,096.0**	**913.3**	96	**3,630.2**	345
333	**HOUSTON INDUSTRIES** Houston	**4,095.3**	**404.9**	200	**12,287.9**	184
334	**DOVER** New York	**4,076.3**	**390.2**	205	**2,993.4**	379
335	**SUPERMARKETS GENL. HOLDINGS** Woodbridge, N.J.[43]	**4,065.9**	**36.8**	441	**1,015.8**	482
336	**SUNTRUST BANKS** Atlanta	**4,064.0**	**616.6**	136	**52,468.2**	54
337	**UNUM** Portland, Me.	**4,042.7**	**238.0**	283	**15,467.5**	151
338	**FOSTER WHEELER** Clinton, N.J.	**4,040.6**	**82.2**	399	**3,510.3**	352
339	**COMCAST** Philadelphia	**4,038.4**	**(53.5)**	469	**12,088.6**	188
340	**AIR PRODUCTS & CHEMICALS** Allentown, Pa.[15]	**4,033.0**	**416.0**	196	**6,522.0**	258
341	**WACHOVIA CORP.** Winston-Salem, N.C.	**4,015.0**	**644.6**	132	**46,904.5**	60
342	**UNION CAMP** Wayne, N.J.	**4,013.2**	**85.3**	395	**5,096.3**	295
343	**NIAGARA MOHAWK POWER** Syracuse, N.Y.	**3,990.7**	**110.4***	374	**9,402.0**	218
344	**HERSHEY FOODS** Hershey, Pa.	**3,989.3**	**273.2**	260	**3,184.8**	371
345	**ROHM & HAAS** Philadelphia	**3,982.0**	**363.0**	212	**3,933.0**	333
346	**SAFECO** Seattle	**3,977.3**	**439.0**	188	**19,917.7**	127
347	**OWENS-ILLINOIS** Toledo	**3,976.2**	**191.1**	312	**6,105.3**	264
348	**STAPLES** Westborough, Mass.[1]	**3,967.7**	**106.4**	377	**1,151.3**	480
349	**SERVICE MERCHANDISE** Brentwood, Tenn.	**3,955.0**	**39.3**	438	**2,042.8**	438
350	**HILTON HOTELS** Beverly Hills[49]	**3,940.0**	**82.0***	400	**7,577.0**	243

STOCKHOLDERS' EQUITY		MARKET VALUE 3/14/97		EARNINGS PER SHARE				TOTAL RETURN TO INVESTORS			
				1996	% change from	1986–96 annual growth rate		1996		1986–96 annual rate	
$ millions	Rank	$ millions	Rank	$	1995	%	Rank	%	Rank	%	Rank
870.5	387	3,025.0	344	3.04	12.0	—		(8.6)	405	—	
1,888.6	270	9,192.7	160	6.34	14.6	6.7	203	21.2	226	9.3	297
2,370.4	227	9,430.3	156	3.27	27.7	76.3	1	(8.7)	406	40.6	9
1,710.7	285	1,358.3	420	1.01	(40.9)	—		(13.0)	418	—	
1,401.2	328	4,775.5	270	1.33	13.7	8.7	164	39.5	108	17.2	111
1,554.4	310	2,274.9	377	3.84	(0.8)	7.1	191	27.2	179	8.0	318
2,819.6	193	33,240.6	42	1.37	80.3	—		70.5	28	—	
3,828.0	153	5,010.5	261	1.66	(63.4)	(1.4)	295	(0.2)	371	11.2	257
1,489.7	319	5,992.2	226	3.45	40.8	19.0	41	38.8	110	18.8	87
(1,248.7)	497	N.A.		N.A.	—	—		—		—	
4,880.0	116	11,299.0	127	2.76	11.7	11.5	111	46.8	64	20.7	64
2,263.1	234	5,586.4	239	3.26	(15.8)	—		33.7	138	20.4	68
689.0	422	1,559.6	407	2.03	157.0	11.2	119	(11.0)	414	13.4	210
551.6	443	5,898.3	231	(0.21)	—	—		(1.5)	378	14.4	182
2,574.0	212	8,194.8	176	3.73	13.4	57.4	2	33.5	140	17.3	109
3,761.8	156	9,912.6	146	3.81	8.9	9.8	143	27.4	176	18.1	98
2,093.6	252	3,374.3	321	1.23	(80.9)	(3.6)	310	3.9	346	7.1	327
3,025.6	187	1,227.1	427	0.50	(65.3)	(15.5)	327	3.9	345	(0.3)	369
1,161.0	359	7,647.1	185	1.77	4.1	9.6	149	37.2	121	16.3	130
1,728.0	282	5,765.6	235	5.45	29.1	10.5	130	30.0	162	12.0	242
4,115.3	145	5,050.1	257	3.48	9.8	7.4	182	18.0	250	15.4	153
729.7	418	3,099.7	334	1.58	12.9	—		56.9	45	—	
761.7	414	3,516.8	310	0.64	37.1	—		11.2	304	—	
427.1	459	374.1	450	0.39	(22.0)	—		(15.4)	424	8.4	312
3,211.0	175	6,331.4	212	0.41	(53.9)	(1.8)	298	72.7	27	14.5	177

RANK 1996	COMPANY	REVENUES $ millions	PROFITS $ millions	Rank	ASSETS $ millions	Rank
351	GPU Parsippany, N.J.[50]	3,918.1	313.9	232	10,941.2	201
352	GIANT FOOD Landover, Md.[18]	3,860.6	102.2	382	1,447.1	464
353	PITNEY BOWES Stamford, Conn.	3,858.6	469.3	177	8,155.7	233
354	DOLE FOOD Westlake Village, Calif.	3,840.3	89.0	392	2,485.7	417
355	FIRST BANK SYSTEM Minneapolis	3,839.6	739.8	116	36,489.0	77
356	OWENS-CORNING Toledo	3,832.0	(284.0)	488	3,913.0	334
357	COMPUSA Dallas[3]	3,829.8	59.7	424	909.3	487
358	BARNETT BANKS Jacksonville	3,816.3	564.5	151	41,231.4	68
359	ALLEGHENY TELEDYNE Pittsburgh[51]	3,815.6	213.0	294	2,606.4	406
360	CONSOLIDATED NATURAL GAS Pittsburgh	3,794.3	298.3	244	6,000.6	267
361	NORTHEAST UTILITIES Berlin, Conn.	3,792.1	1.8	457	10,747.7	202
362	PHELPS DODGE Phoenix	3,786.6	461.8	180	4,816.4	307
363	MATTEL El Segundo, Calif.	3,786.0	377.6	208	2,893.5	383
364	H.F. AHMANSON Irwindale, Calif.	3,766.6	145.3	347	49,902.0	57
365	FRED MEYER Portland, Ore.[1]	3,724.8	58.5	426	1,693.4	456
366	CONRAIL Philadelphia[52]	3,714.0	342.0	221	8,402.0	230
367	MORTON INTERNATIONAL Chicago[3]	3,686.2	334.2	224	2,771.5	392
368	CNF TRANSPORTATION Palo Alto[53]	3,662.2[54]	27.5	446	2,081.9	435
369	HARRIS Melbourne, Fla.[3]	3,659.3	178.4	321	3,206.7	370
370	MICRON TECHNOLOGY Boise[13]	3,653.8	593.5	142	3,751.5	339
371	NUCOR Charlotte, N.C.	3,647.0	248.2	277	2,619.5	405
372	DTE ENERGY Detroit	3,645.4	309.3	237	11,014.9	200
373	PROVIDIAN Louisville	3,622.2	434.7	189	28,993.4	91
374	LITTON INDUSTRIES Woodland Hills, Calif.[34]	3,611.5	150.9	341	3,431.4	357
375	GENERAL DYNAMICS Falls Church, Va.	3,609.0	270.0	261	3,299.0	365

STOCKHOLDERS' EQUITY		MARKET VALUE 3/14/97		EARNINGS PER SHARE					TOTAL RETURN TO INVESTORS			
					% change	1986–96 annual growth rate			1996		1986–96 annual rate	
$ millions	Rank	$ millions	Rank	1996 $	from 1995	%	Rank		%	Rank	%	Rank
3,114.1	178	4,174.6	287	2.47	(34.8)	4.2	234		4.8	341	17.5	107
822.8	397	1,960.7	391	1.72	8.2	6.1	211		12.0	295	13.4	212
2,239.0	240	9,100.8	165	3.12	(18.5)	11.4	114		19.7	237	14.3	184
549.6	444	2,311.1	373	1.47	276.9	1.4	269		(2.2)	381	8.1	317
3,053.0	184	10,722.2	135	5.34	27.4	4.6	229		41.2	98	15.8	141
(484.0)	494	2,214.7	379	(5.50)	(218.5)	—			(4.9)	391	12.0	240
325.9	466	1,703.1	402	1.31	116.5	—			166.7	4	—	
3,370.3	172	9,151.5	163	2.89	9.1	7.1	194		43.9	80	14.1	190
871.5	386	4,989.9	262	1.20	(25.9)	—			27.9	173	—	
2,205.2	243	5,109.2	253	3.16	1,273.9	4.1	237		26.5	186	10.0	284
2,277.1	232	1,169.8	429	0.01	(99.6)	(43.0)	331		(40.6)	449	2.4	358
2,755.9	196	4,926.1	264	6.97	(34.6)	22.8	27		11.7	299	26.1	25
1,447.8	324	7,078.1	196	1.36	7.9	—			13.8	284	29.2	19
2,433.0	222	4,246.2	283	0.91	(35.0)	(11.9)	322		26.8	180	9.1	299
567.3	440	1,054.8	436	2.09	95.3	6.8	201		57.8	44	10.5	275
3,107.0	179	9,032.7	166	4.25	33.2	2.7	257		45.7	71	—	
1,672.8	293	6,289.4	214	2.24	14.3	—			15.2	276	—	
508.3	448	1,056.5	435	0.42	(61.8)	(15.7)	328		(14.6)	422	(1.4)	371
1,372.9	331	3,047.1	342	4.58	15.9	12.0	102		28.5	169	12.1	239
2,502.0	218	9,728.8	149	2.76	(30.1)	—			(26.3)	436	41.8	7
1,609.3	304	4,199.5	285	2.83	(9.9)	18.0	48		(10.2)	410	21.7	51
3,443.9	169	4,135.9	288	2.13	(23.9)	(1.9)	300		0.2	367	15.4	151
3,089.7	180	5,426.8	242	4.64	28.9	5.9	214		28.9	167	15.6	145
917.3	384	1,910.6	393	3.15	10.9	9.6	146		7.0	331	7.2	326
1,714.0	284	4,186.6	286	4.27	(16.3)	—			22.6	215	15.8	143

RANK 1996	COMPANY	REVENUES $ millions	PROFITS $ millions	Rank	ASSETS $ millions	Rank
376	STUDENT LOAN MARKETING ASSN. Washington, D.C.	3,590.1	419.4	193	47,629.9	59
377	LG&E ENERGY Louisville	3,589.5	104.0	381	3,011.9	376
378	PARKER HANNIFIN Cleveland[3]	3,586.4	239.7	281	2,887.1	385
379	UNIVERSAL Richmond[3]	3,570.2	72.2	416	1,889.5	446
380	AUTOMATIC DATA PROCESSING Roseland, N.J.[3]	3,566.6	454.7	184	3,839.9	335
381	GREAT WESTERN FINANCIAL CORP. Chatsworth, Calif.	3,565.8	115.8	363	42,874.6	65
382	FOUNDATION HEALTH Rancho Cordova, Calif.[3]	3,561.4	148.3	343	2,337.7	422
383	TRANS WORLD AIRLINES St. Louis	3,554.4	(284.8)	489	2,681.9	400
384	INTELLIGENT ELECTRONICS Exton, Pa.[43]	3,547.8	(103.8)	476	746.0	494
385	W.W. GRAINGER Lincolnshire, Ill.	3,537.2	208.5	299	2,117.2	433
386	WILLIAMS Tulsa	3,531.2	362.3	213	12,418.8	183
387	MICROAGE Tempe, Ariz.[2]	3,516.4	13.3	453	689.5	495
388	COMPUTER ASSOCIATES INTL. Islandia, N.Y.[20]	3,504.6	(56.4)	470	5,016.0	300
389	USF&G Baltimore	3,497.4	261.0	268	14,407.3	163
390	REEBOK INTERNATIONAL Stoughton, Mass.	3,482.9	139.0	353	1,786.2	453
391	PROGRESSIVE Mayfield Village, Ohio	3,478.4	313.7	234	6,183.9	262
392	MAPCO Tulsa	3,474.0[E]	97.5	387	2,170.7	429
393	TEMPLE-INLAND Diboll, Texas	3,460.0	133.0	357	12,947.0	177
394	SERVICEMASTER Downers Grove, Ill.	3,458.3	245.1	279	1,846.8	449
395	PACIFIC MUTUAL LIFE INS. Newport Beach, Calif.	3,454.2	113.1	370	26,215.8	101
396	WILLAMETTE INDUSTRIES Portland, Ore.	3,425.2	192.1	310	4,720.7	310
397	JEFFERSON SMURFIT St. Louis	3,410.0	112.0	371	2,688.0	399
398	WASHINGTON MUTUAL Seattle	3,408.5	114.3	365	44,551.9	63
399	SOUTHWEST AIRLINES Dallas	3,406.2	207.3	300	3,723.5	340
400	TIMES MIRROR Los Angeles	3,401.0	206.4	301	3,529.9	350

STOCKHOLDERS' EQUITY		MARKET VALUE 3/14/97		EARNINGS PER SHARE		1986–96 annual growth rate		TOTAL RETURN TO INVESTORS		1986–96 annual rate	
$ millions	Rank	$ millions	Rank	1996 $	% change from 1995	%	Rank	1996 %	Rank	%	Rank
1,047.8	373	6,196.2	217	7.32	1.7	19.5	38	44.1	77	15.5	149
811.2	400	1,658.5	403	1.57	25.1	3.7	240	22.1	220	14.1	192
1,384.0	330	3,348.5	323	3.23	9.1	9.4	153	15.2	275	11.5	250
417.3	460	1,086.7	433	2.06	182.2	4.2	236	37.1	122	13.9	198
2,315.3	230	12,628.9	111	1.57	13.4	15.8	60	16.5	265	18.4	93
2,595.2	207	6,265.8	216	0.69	(59.9)	(13.1)	324	18.8	245	9.6	292
866.9	389	2,294.2	374	2.54	182.2	—		(26.6)	438	—	
238.1	472	296.7	453	(7.27)	—	—		(36.7)	447	—	
122.0	481	118.7	458	(2.93)	—	—		33.3	143	—	
1,460.5	323	4,049.0	293	4.04	11.0	10.6	129	22.8	211	15.6	146
3,421.0	170	7,362.0	191	2.17	(74.5)	—		31.7	149	21.7	53
186.1	479	201.3	457	0.89	4,350.0	—		146.2	7	—	
1,481.7	320	15,160.4	95	(0.23)	(113.4)	—		31.5	151	32.7	13
1,968.9	262	2,602.2	362	2.05	25.8	(7.4)	319	25.2	196	(1.5)	372
381.2	463	2,778.0	355	2.00	(3.4)	4.6	228	50.1	54	15.2	158
1,676.9	291	4,924.6	265	4.14	27.0	18.5	45	38.5	111	21.7	52
603.6	433	1,784.6	400	1.70	41.1	6.9	199	26.7	182	10.8	265
2,015.0	259	3,074.7	338	2.39	(52.3)	8.5	172	26.5	185	11.2	254
796.8	407	3,845.7	299	1.70	17.5	19.1	40	33.4	142	28.0	21
815.2	399	N.A.		N.A.		—		—		—	
1,976.3	260	3,492.6	312	3.48	(62.7)	9.0	160	26.3	187	15.9	139
(375.0)	492	1,540.0	409	1.01	(53.9)	—		69.1	30	—	
2,397.9	224	7,089.4	195	0.85	(68.3)	(8.7)	320	54.0	52	23.4	35
1,648.3	297	3,408.3	319	1.37	11.4	14.8	68	(4.2)	390	17.4	108
1,498.8	317	5,401.6	246	1.55	(84.5)	—		48.1	60	—	

RANK 1996	COMPANY	REVENUES $ millions	PROFITS $ millions	Rank	ASSETS $ millions	Rank
401	**SONAT** Birmingham, Ala.	**3,394.9**	**201.2**	305	**3,774.7**	338
402	**OLSTEN** Melville, N.Y.	**3,377.7**	**54.6**	428	**1,439.2**	465
403	**AMERICAN FAMILY INS. GROUP** Madison, Wis.[8]	**3,328.0**	**97.6**	386	**7,514.9**	247
404	**NASH FINCH** Minneapolis	**3,322.7**	**20.0**	449	**945.5**	484
405	**TURNER CORP.** New York	**3,317.8**	**(1.7)**	458	**894.6**	488
406	**KELLY SERVICES** Troy, Mich.	**3,302.3**	**73.0**	414	**838.9**	492
407	**PENN TRAFFIC** Syracuse, N.Y.[1]	**3,296.5**	**(41.4)**	465	**N.A.**	
408	**HARCOURT GENERAL** Chestnut Hill, Mass.[2]	**3,289.9**	**190.9**	313	**3,326.2**	362
409	**BEVERLY ENTERPRISES** Fort Smith, Ark.	**3,281.0**	**50.3**	430	**2,525.1**	412
410	**REPUBLIC NEW YORK CORP.** New York	**3,279.2**	**418.8**	194	**52,298.9**	55
411	**MBNA** Wilmington, Del.	**3,279.2**	**474.5**	175	**17,035.3**	139
412	**ALLMERICA FINANCIAL** Worcester, Mass.	**3,274.7**	**181.9**	319	**18,997.7**	132
413	**COLUMBIA GAS SYSTEM** Reston, Va.	**3,269.8**[E]	**221.6**	291	**6,004.6**	266
414	**RICHFOOD HOLDINGS** Mechanicsville, Va.[28]	**3,250.9**	**37.1**	440	**564.3**	497
415	**CINERGY** Cincinnati	**3,242.7**	**334.8**	223	**8,848.5**	223
416	**MASCO** Taylor, Mich.	**3,237.0**	**295.2**	245	**3,701.7**	341
417	**AVERY DENNISON** Pasadena	**3,222.5**	**175.9**	324	**2,036.7**	439
418	**FLORIDA PROGRESS** St. Petersburg	**3,221.1**	**224.4**	289	**5,348.4**	282
419	**YORK INTERNATIONAL** York, Pa.	**3,218.5**	**147.9**	344	**2,074.8**	436
420	**HEALTH SYSTEMS INTL.** Woodland Hills, Calif.	**3,204.2**	**73.6**	412	**1,211.9**	477
421	**SHAW INDUSTRIES** Dalton, Ga.	**3,201.0**	**34.0**	444	**1,980.4**	441
422	**ESTÉE LAUDER** New York[3]	**3,194.5**	**160.4**	332	**1,821.6**	450
423	**ALLTEL** Little Rock	**3,192.4**	**291.7**	248	**5,359.2**	281
424	**DARDEN RESTAURANTS** Orlando[6]	**3,191.8**	**74.4**	411	**2,088.5**	434
425	**ENGELHARD** Iselin, N.J.	**3,184.4**	**150.4**	342	**2,494.9**	415

STOCKHOLDERS' EQUITY		MARKET VALUE 3/14/97		EARNINGS PER SHARE				TOTAL RETURN TO INVESTORS			
				1996 $	% change from 1995	1986–96 annual growth rate %	Rank	1996 %	Rank	1986–96 annual rate %	Rank
$ millions	Rank	$ millions	Rank								
1,584.4	306	4,417.3	278	2.33	4.0	—		48.3	59	20.1	72
769.3	413	1,412.0	416	0.70	(49.6)	10.1	138	(42.9)	450	11.3	252
2,556.3	213	N.A.		N.A.	—	—		—		—	
232.9	474	205.6	456	1.81	13.1	3.0	249	21.5	223	5.5	339
60.1	484	65.6	461	(0.66)	—	—		22.4	217	(3.8)	377
516.9	447	939.4	442	1.92	4.9	7.1	196	0.1	368	4.7	346
N.A.		75.0	459	(3.81)	—	—		(75.8)	456	(15.9)	383
1,033.5	374	3,365.4	322	2.62	21.3	4.5	230	11.9	297	10.6	271
861.1	390	1,526.9	410	0.50	—	(3.4)	309	20.0	234	(2.3)	374
3,306.6	173	5,241.3	250	6.97	49.6	8.9	162	34.5	133	10.6	270
1,704.3	286	11,151.4	129	1.33	29.5	—		72.9	26	—	
1,724.7	283	1,823.6	398	3.63	36.0	—		24.9	199	—	
1,553.7	311	3,302.0	324	4.12	—	8.5	170	46.7	66	6.3	332
199.6	478	1,059.2	434	1.19	0.0	—		35.9	129	—	
2,584.5	209	5,380.8	247	2.12	(4.5)	(0.6)	290	15.1	277	14.5	175
1,839.8	272	5,936.8	228	1.84	—	1.7	264	17.7	254	4.6	347
832.0	393	4,454.8	277	1.68	24.4	10.6	128	43.8	81	16.1	134
1,924.2	265	2,910.2	347	2.32	(7.2)	(0.6)	292	(0.4)	373	9.3	298
780.4	411	1,973.9	390	3.37	—	—		19.7	236	—	
365.0	465	1,436.8	415	1.52	(16.9)	—		(23.0)	433	—	
671.7	426	1,842.2	395	0.25	(34.2)	3.6	243	(17.6)	425	18.9	86
394.2	462	5,944.8	227	N.A.	—	—		46.8	65	—	
2,097.1	251	6,458.4	208	1.53	(17.7)	10.9	123	10.1	309	18.0	100
1,222.6	350	1,179.3	428	0.47	—	—		(25.7)	435	—	
833.2	392	3,416.5	318	1.05	9.4	10.4	134	(10.6)	412	15.7	144

RANK 1996	COMPANY	REVENUES $ millions	PROFITS $ millions	Rank	ASSETS $ millions	Rank
426	**OFFICEMAX** Shaker Heights, Ohio[1]	**3,179.3**	**68.8**	419	**1,867.3**	448
427	**BRUNSWICK** Lake Forest, Ill.	**3,160.3**	**185.8**	317	**2,802.4**	389
428	**ALUMAX** Norcross, Ga.	**3,159.3**	**250.0**	274	**3,298.7**	366
429	**BALTIMORE GAS & ELECTRIC** Baltimore	**3,153.2**	**310.8**	235	**8,551.0**	228
430	**LONG ISLAND LIGHTING** Hicksville, N.Y.	**3,150.7**	**316.5**	229	**12,209.7**	187
431	**ECHLIN** Branford, Conn.[13]	**3,128.7**	**142.2**	349	**2,130.8**	432
432	**WHITMAN** Rolling Meadows, Ill.	**3,111.3**	**139.4**	352	**2,409.4**	418
433	**OLIN** Norwalk, Conn.	**3,109.0¶**	**280.0**	256	**2,339.0**	421
434	**PITTSTON** Glen Allen, Va.	**3,106.6**	**104.2**	380	**1,812.9**	452
435	**CENTEX** Dallas[20]	**3,103.0**	**53.4**	429	**2,337.0**	423
436	**INACOM** Omaha	**3,102.1**	**18.7**	450	**847.6**	491
437	**HORMEL FOODS** Austin, Minn.[2]	**3,098.7**	**79.4**	405	**1,436.1**	466
438	**READER'S DIGEST ASSOCIATION** Pleasantville, N.Y.[3]	**3,098.1**	**80.6**	403	**1,904.1**	444
439	**RELIANCE GROUP HOLDINGS** New York	**3,090.6**	**48.2**	432	**10,591.1**	203
440	**OXFORD HEALTH PLANS** Norwalk, Conn.	**3,075.0**	**99.6**	385	**1,346.7**	469
441	**MCGRAW-HILL** New York	**3,074.7**	**495.7**	166	**3,642.2**	342
442	**WESTVACO** New York[2]	**3,074.5**	**212.2**	295	**4,437.5**	317
443	**YELLOW** Overland Park, Kansas	**3,072.6**	**(27.2)**	461	**1,227.8**	475
444	**COMERICA** Detroit	**3,069.7**	**417.2**	195	**34,206.1**	81
445	**U.S. BANCORP** Portland, Ore.	**3,068.5**	**478.9**	172	**33,260.4**	82
446	**CONSECO** Carmel, Ind.	**3,065.4**	**267.7**	264	**25,612.7**	104
447	**MERCANTILE STORES** Fairfield, Ohio[1]	**3,030.8**	**121.5**	362	**2,142.5**	430
448	**BAKER HUGHES** Houston[15]	**3,027.7**	**176.4**	322	**3,297.4**	367
449	**OWENS & MINOR** Glen Allen, Va.	**3,019.0**	**13.0**	454	**679.5**	496
450	**EL PASO NATURAL GAS** Houston	**3,010.1**	**38.2**	439	**8,712.0**	224

STOCKHOLDERS' EQUITY		MARKET VALUE 3/14/97		EARNINGS PER SHARE				TOTAL RETURN TO INVESTORS			
				1996	% change from	1986–96 annual growth rate		1996		1986–96 annual rate	
$ millions	Rank	$ millions	Rank	$	1995	%	Rank	%	Rank	%	Rank
1,063.6	372	1,778.8	401	0.55	(47.1)	—		(27.9)	440	—	
1,197.7	353	2,854.2	352	1.88	42.4	3.6	242	2.2	356	6.3	333
1,640.8	298	2,187.7	381	5.19	2.8	—		9.4	314	—	
3,067.1	183	3,968.6	296	1.85	(8.4)	(1.3)	294	(0.7)	374	8.4	313
2,587.0	208	2,883.7	350	2.20	4.8	0.3	281	49.7	55	14.6	173
1,008.9	376	2,168.3	382	2.30	(11.5)	7.6	181	(10.8)	413	8.8	306
642.2	428	2,423.6	370	1.31	4.0	—		0.1	369	7.9	322
946.0	381	2,225.1	378	5.34	94.2	12.3	99	4.3	344	10.7	266
606.7	432	1,504.6	411	N.A.	—	—		—		—	
722.8	419	1,129.8	431	1.83	(39.8)	3.4	245	9.0	317	10.2	281
176.8	480	268.5	454	1.76	54.4	15.8	61	183.2	3	—	
785.6	410	2,026.6	388	1.04	(33.8)	7.4	183	11.9	296	14.3	187
478.9	452	3,697.4	306	0.73	(68.9)	—		(18.0)	426	—	
676.7	424	1,313.7	422	0.41	(43.8)	(2.0)	301	10.2	308	6.6	329
598.2	435	4,923.1	266	1.24	73.4	—		58.5	40	—	
1,361.1	332	5,124.3	252	4.96	117.5	12.6	95	9.1	315	9.0	302
2,209.7	242	2,904.5	348	2.09	(24.8)	6.5	205	6.7	334	7.9	321
395.7	461	456.8	448	(0.97)	—	—		16.2	267	(6.5)	379
2,615.6	206	6,518.3	206	3.55	0.3	11.4	115	35.3	131	22.4	42
2,710.8	200	7,383.8	190	3.08	47.4	10.0	140	38.0	114	19.3	81
3,085.3	181	6,684.0	203	2.03	(13.5)	36.1	13	104.1	14	47.3	4
1,565.3	309	1,823.8	397	3.30	(1.5)	0.9	276	8.9	318	5.0	344
1,689.2	289	5,580.8	240	1.23	115.8	—		43.6	85	13.7	203
242.4	470	339.0	452	0.25	—	0.2	282	(18.3)	428	12.9	224
1,638.0	300	3,074.7	339	1.06	(57.1)	—		82.2	19	—	

RANK 1996	COMPANY	REVENUES $ millions	PROFITS $ millions	Rank	ASSETS $ millions	Rank
451	**HASBRO** Pawtucket, R.I.	3,002.4	199.9	307	2,701.5	397
452	**MAYTAG** Newton, Iowa	3,001.7	136.4	355	2,329.9	424
453	**GRAYBAR ELECTRIC** St. Louis	3,001.0	44.5	436	881.6	489
454	**CAROLINA POWER & LIGHT** Raleigh	2,995.7	391.3	204	8,369.2	231
455	**IMC GLOBAL** Northbrook, Ill.[3]	2,981.0	144.3	348	3,436.8	356
456	**HANNAFORD BROS.** Scarborough, Me.	2,958.6	75.2	410	1,183.7	479
457	**PETER KIEWIT SONS'** Omaha	2,934.0	221.0	292	3,548.0	347
458	**THERMO ELECTRON** Waltham, Mass.	2,932.6	190.8	314	5,141.2	292
459	**AID ASSOCIATION FOR LUTHERANS** Appleton, Wis.	2,924.1	129.7	358	16,671.0	146
460	**SILICON GRAPHICS** Mountain View, Calif.[3]	2,921.3	115.0	364	3,158.2	372
461	**SMITH'S FOOD & DRUG CENTERS** Salt Lake City	2,890.0	(164.2)*	483	1,786.0	454
462	**HARNISCHFEGER INDUSTRIES** St. Francis, Wis.[2]	2,887.6	114.2	367	2,690.0	398
463	**BRUNO'S** Birmingham, Ala.[43]	2,879.4	(52.5)	468	774.0	493
464	**INTERSTATE BAKERIES** Kansas City[6]	2,878.2	24.5	448	1,486.5	462
465	**NEWELL** Freeport, Ill.	2,872.8	256.5	270	3,005.1	377
466	**WESTERN DIGITAL** Irvine, Calif.[3]	2,865.2	96.9	389	984.1	483
467	**FLEETWOOD ENTERPRISES** Riverside, Calif.[28]	2,861.5	79.6	404	1,108.9	481
468	**CYPRUS AMAX MINERALS** Englewood, Colo.	2,843.0	77.0	406	6,786.0	252
469	**LONGS DRUG STORES** Walnut Creek, Calif.[1]	2,828.3	58.6	425	879.6	490
470	**SOLECTRON** Milpitas, Calif.[13]	2,817.2	114.2	366	1,452.2	463
471	**DEAN FOODS** Franklin Park, Ill.[6]	2,814.3	(49.7)	467	1,222.2	476
472	**PP&L RESOURCES** Allentown, Pa.	2,805.0[E]	329.0	226	9,636.0	215
473	**SONOCO PRODUCTS** Hartsville, S.C.	2,788.1	170.9	327	2,387.5	420
474	**KNIGHT-RIDDER** Miami	2,774.8	267.9	263	2,900.3	382
475	**BENEFICIAL** Wilmington, Del.	2,771.9	281.0	255	16,931.2	143

STOCKHOLDERS' EQUITY		MARKET VALUE 3/14/97		EARNINGS PER SHARE				TOTAL RETURN TO INVESTORS			
				1996 $	% change from 1995	1986–96 annual growth rate %	Rank	1996 %	Rank	1986–96 annual rate %	Rank
$ millions	Rank	$ millions	Rank								
1,652.0	296	3,793.8	302	1.52	(13.6)	2.9	250	26.7	183	12.5	232
574.0	438	2,110.2	383	1.34	—	0.4	280	0.2	366	2.0	360
213.7	476	N.A.		9.00	11.0	12.1	101	—		—	
2,834.3	191	5,507.8	241	2.66	7.3	3.0	248	11.2	303	13.7	202
1,156.3	360	3,142.3	333	1.56	(19.6)	—		(3.2)	384	—	
569.2	439	1,491.4	412	1.78	6.6	13.3	84	40.2	105	16.6	123
1,819.0	273	N.A.		N.A.	—	—		—		—	
1,754.4	277	5,374.0	248	1.35	21.3	18.6	44	19.0	243	23.4	34
1,093.1	366	N.A.		N.A.	—	—		—		—	
1,675.3	292	3,990.9	294	0.65	(49.2)	10.1	137	(7.7)	403	22.9	37
(122.2)	489	551.0	447	(8.42)	—	—		21.5	222	—	
673.5	425	2,284.7	376	2.42	95.2	—		46.4	68	14.0	195
(335.9)	491	340.7	451	N.A.	—	—		—		—	
460.2	454	1,809.2	399	0.70	(33.3)	—		123.8	10	—	
1,491.8	318	5,838.5	233	1.62	14.9	19.6	36	24.0	206	27.5	22
453.9	455	2,572.4	363	2.01	(21.5)	6.4	207	218.2	1	11.9	243
649.1	427	942.4	441	1.71	(6.0)	7.3	186	9.0	316	10.9	260
2,360.0	228	2,290.8	375	0.62	(45.1)	1.4	271	(7.1)	400	10.9	259
553.6	441	975.4	438	1.49	30.1	5.3	219	5.3	340	8.2	314
700.6	420	2,607.4	361	2.19	20.3	—		21.0	228	—	
507.7	449	1,287.6	423	(1.24)	(161.7)	—		20.7	231	8.0	319
2,916.0	189	3,407.9	320	2.05	0.0	2.8	252	(1.4)	376	9.8	289
920.6	383	2,374.5	372	1.81	5.2	11.8	107	0.9	364	13.7	200
1,131.5	362	3,803.6	301	2.75	72.4	8.6	168	25.3	194	7.6	324
1,694.8	288	3,965.3	297	5.08	86.8	—		40.6	101	13.2	217

RANK 1996	COMPANY	REVENUES $ millions	PROFITS $ millions	Rank	ASSETS $ millions	Rank
476	**BECTON DICKINSON** Franklin Lakes, N.J.[15]	**2,769.8**	**283.4**	253	**2,889.8**	384
477	**STATE STREET BOSTON CORP.** Boston	**2,744.4**	**292.8**	246	**31,523.9**	85
478	**ACE HARDWARE** Oak Brook, Ill.[25]	**2,742.5**	**N.A.**		**916.4**	486
479	**GENERAL AMERICAN LIFE INSURANCE** St. Louis[8]	**2,740.5**	**83.2**	398	**19,112.9**	131
480	**APL** Oakland[55]	**2,739.1**	**69.5**	418	**1,880.2**	447
481	**PHOENIX HOME LIFE MUTUAL INS.** Hartford[8]	**2,725.0**	**100.7**	384	**15,453.0**	152
482	**CALIBER SYSTEM** Akron	**2,718.1**	**(165.1)**	484	**1,432.2**	467
483	**LUTHERAN BROTHERHOOD** Minneapolis	**2,713.2**	**158.7**	335	**14,459.7**	161
484	**CALDOR** Norwalk, Conn.[43]	**2,698.4**	**(377.0)**	492	**1,310.8**	471
485	**ASARCO** New York	**2,696.7**	**138.3**	354	**4,120.3**	325
486	**GENERAL INSTRUMENT** Chicago	**2,689.7**	**(1.9)**	459	**2,706.9**	395
487	**STANLEY WORKS** New Britain, Conn.	**2,670.8**	**96.9**	388	**1,659.6**	458
488	**GOLDEN WEST FINANCIAL CORP.** Oakland	**2,656.5**	**164.7**	330	**37,730.6**	75
489	**NORTHERN STATES POWER** Minneapolis	**2,654.2**	**274.5**	259	**6,636.9**	254
490	**PAYLESS CASHWAYS** Kansas City[19]	**2,650.9**	**(19.1)**	460	**1,293.1**	473
491	**CONSOLIDATED STORES** Columbus, Ohio[1]	**2,647.5**	**83.9**	397	**1,330.5**	470
492	**OMNICOM GROUP** New York	**2,641.7**	**176.3**	323	**4,055.9**	327
493	**NATIONAL SEMICONDUCTOR** Santa Clara, Calif.[6]	**2,623.1**	**185.4**	318	**2,658.0**	402
494	**NEW YORK TIMES** New York	**2,615.0**	**84.5**	396	**3,539.9**	349
495	**WITCO** Greenwich, Conn.	**2,596.3**[¶]	**(315.1)**	491	**2,391.7**	419
496	**USG** Chicago	**2,590.0**	**15.0**	452	**1,818.0**	451
497	**PACIFIC ENTERPRISES** Los Angeles	**2,588.0**	**203.0**	302	**5,186.0**	289
498	**ROUNDY'S** Pewaukee, Wis.[25]	**2,583.5**	**N.A.**		**434.6**	498
499	**WESTERN ATLAS** Beverly Hills	**2,582.8**	**125.7**	361	**2,782.9**	391
500	**VENCOR** Louisville	**2,577.8**	**48.0**	434	**1,968.9**	443
	TOTALS	**5,077,370.6**	**300,911.7**		**11,546,466.8**	

STOCKHOLDERS' EQUITY		MARKET VALUE 3/14/97		EARNINGS PER SHARE				TOTAL RETURN TO INVESTORS			
				1996 $	% change from 1995	1986–96 annual growth rate %	Rank	1996 %	Rank	1986–96 annual rate %	Rank
$ millions	Rank	$ millions	Rank								
1,325.2	338	5,886.6	232	2.11	17.5	11.5	113	17.0	260	15.0	161
1,774.7	276	6,431.5	209	3.59	20.5	13.8	76	45.8	70	20.6	65
233.4	473	N.A.		N.A.	—	—		—		—	
997.8	377	N.A.		N.A.	—	—		—		—	
502.8	450	571.1	446	2.67	181.1	22.4	28	4.5	342	8.0	320
1,397.5	329	N.A.		N.A.	—	—		—		—	
538.6	446	851.6	443	(4.18)	—	—		(59.6)	454	(3.1)	375
811.0	401	N.A.		N.A.	—	—		—		—	
(82.2)	488	33.9	463	N.A.	—	—		(57.7)	453	—	
1,736.9	279	1,349.0	421	3.24	(19.0)	—		(20.1)	432	8.7	307
1,173.2	356	3,251.7	328	(0.01)	(101.0)	—		(7.0)	399	—	
780.1	412	3,482.3	314	1.09	63.9	1.6	265	7.6	330	11.2	256
2,350.5	229	3,970.6	295	2.84	(29.0)	(0.4)	289	15.1	278	14.5	178
2,376.3	226	3,263.3	327	3.82	(2.3)	2.1	260	(1.2)	375	9.4	295
289.7	469	74.9	460	(0.63)	—	—		(52.9)	452	—	
682.1	423	2,649.7	358	1.25	(5.3)	13.3	85	86.4	17	11.6	247
800.7	403	4,115.3	290	2.29	21.2	—		25.5	191	20.5	67
1,577.2	308	4,133.7	289	1.36	(32.7)	—		10.7	306	8.7	308
1,625.1	303	4,396.6	279	0.87	(37.9)	(6.1)	317	30.6	159	2.7	356
627.9	431	1,935.1	392	(5.54)	(399.5)	—		7.8	327	8.9	304
(23.0)	486	1,611.8	405	0.31	—	—		12.9	290	—	
1,440.0	325	2,636.5	359	2.37	11.8	5.9	213	12.9	291	1.1	366
103.7	482	N.A.		N.A.	—	—		—		—	
1,502.9	316	3,235.0	329	2.31	24.9	—		40.3	103	—	
797.1	406	2,489.7	364	0.68	—	—		(2.7)	382	—	
◄,872,314.1		5,697,351.6									

FOOTNOTES TO THE 1997 FORTUNE 500

N.A. Not available.

ᴱ Excise taxes have been deducted.

* Reflects extraordinary charge of at least 10%.

¶ Includes revenues of discontinued operations of at least 10%.

1-9

1 Figures are for fiscal year ended January 31, 1997.

2 Figures are for fiscal year ended Oct. 31, 1996.

3 Figures are for fiscal year ended June 30, 1996.

4 Name changed from Chemical Banking Corp. after acquiring Chase Manhattan Corp. (1995 rank: 112), March 31, 1996.

5 Name changed from Federal National Mortgage Association, January 6, 1997.

6 Figures are for fiscal year ended May 31, 1996.

7 Acquired Eckerd (1996 rank: 285), February 27, 1997.

8 A mutual company; the figures here, however, follow Generally Accepted Accounting Principles.

9 Acquired New England Mutual Life (1995 rank: 537), August 30, 1996.

10-19

10 All 1996 data are preliminary.

11 1996 figures are not comparable with 1995's because the company changed from statutory reporting to GAAP reporting.

12 Estimate.

13 Figures are for fiscal year ended August 31, 1996.

14 Name changed from Price/Costco, February 6, 1997.

15 Figures are for fiscal year ended September 30, 1996.

16 Figures do not include Boatmen's Bancshares (1995 rank: 415), acquired January 7, 1997.

17 Acquired U.S. Healthcare (1995 rank: 352), July 19, 1996.

18 Figures are for fiscal year ended Feb. 29, 1996.

19 Figures are for fiscal year ended November 30, 1996.

20-29

20 Figures are for fiscal year ended March 31, 1996.

21 Name changed from Alco Standard, January 23, 1997.

22 Acquired Turner Broadcasting (1995 rank: 363), October 11, 1996.

23 Acquired Southern Pacific Rail (1995 rank: 391), September 11, 1996.

24 Acquired Circle K (1995 rank: 348), May 30, 1996.

25 Cooperatives provide only net margin figures, which are not comparable with the profit figures on the list.

26 Acquired Duracell International (1995 rank: 560), December 31, 1996.

27 Name changed from Pacific Gas & Electric, January 1, 1997.

28 Figures are for fiscal year ended April 30, 1996.

29 Acquired First Interstate Bancorp (1995 rank: 274), April 1, 1996.

30-39

30 Acquired Conner Peripherals (1994 rank: 474), February 2, 1996.

31 Name changed from Melville, Nov. 20, 1996.

32 Ultramar merged with Diamond Shamrock (1995 rank: 418), December 3, 1996.

33 Name changed from USAir Group, February 21, 1997.

34 Figures are for fiscal year ended July 31, 1996.

35 Name changed from Associated Insurance, March 28, 1996.

36 Name changed from Lear Seating Corp., May 1, 1996.

37 Acquired BayBanks (1995 rank: 923), July 29, 1996.

38 Figures do not include OrNda HealthCorp (1996 rank: 581), acquired Jan. 30, 1997.

39 Name changed from FoxMeyer Health Corp., February 3, 1997.

40-49

40 Figures do not reflect acquisition of Thrifty Payless (1996 rank: 295), December 12, 1996.

41 Excludes discontinued operations of Allegiance (1996 rank: 313).

42 Excludes discontinued operations of Darden Restaurants (1996 rank: 424).

43 Figures are for four quarters ended October 31, 1996.

44 Acquired by J.C. Penney (1996 rank: 33), February 27, 1997. Data presented are for the fiscal year ended February 3, 1996.

45 Acquired Integra Financial (1995 rank: 812), May 3, 1996.

46 Acquired Caremark International (1995 rank: 511), September 6, 1996.

47 Acquired by Rite Aid (1996 rank: 262), December 12, 1996.

48 Acquired Meridian Bancorp (1995 rank: 741), April 11, 1996.

49 Acquired Bally Entertainment (1995 rank: 914), December 18, 1996.

50-59

50 Name changed from General Public Utilities, August 1, 1996.

51 Name changed from Allegheny Ludlum after merger with Teledyne (1995 rank: 478), August 15, 1996.

52 CSX (1996 rank: 130) and Norfolk Southern (1996 rank: 298) began discussions in 1997 to acquire and divide the company.

53 Name change from Consolidated Freightways Inc.; official on April 28, 1997.

54 Figure does not include discontinued operations of Consolidated Freightways Corp. (1996 rank: 582).

55 Name changed from American President, June 3, 1996.

THE 1997
FORTUNE 500 INDEX

◆◆◆

AMERICA'S MOST ADMIRED COMPANIES, 1997

◆◆◆

The 15th annual survey of America's most admired companies comprises 431 FORTUNE 1,000 companies, divided into 49 distinct industry groups. To determine the rankings, FORTUNE asked more than 13,000 senior executives, outside directors, and financial security analysts to rate the ten largest companies (or in some cases fewer) in their own industry by the eight key attributes of reputation: quality of management, quality of product or services, ability to attract, develop and keep talented people, value as a long-term investment, use of corporate assets, financial soundness, innovativeness, and community and environmental responsibility.

This year's survey includes two new industry groupings: recreation equipment and temporary help. We have divided insurance companies into two separate categories: property and casualty, and life and health. We have also eliminated ties in the rankings by carrying each company's score out to six decimal places and then rounding it off to two places.

COMMERCIAL BANKS

Rank	Last Year	Company	Score
1	1	J.P. Morgan	7.57
2	3	Citicorp	7.31
3	6	BankAmerica	6.85
4	5	NationsBank	6.74
5	4	Banc One Corp.	6.73
6	8	Chase Manhattan	6.52
7	7	First Union	6.42
8	•	First Chicago NBD	6.16
9	10	Bankers Trust New York	5.97
10	•	Fleet Financial Group	5.72

SAVINGS INSTITUTIONS

Rank	Last Year	Company	Score
1	2	Washington Mutual	7.06
2	1	Golden West Financial	6.96
3	5	Standard Federal Bancorp.	6.18
4	•	Charter One Financial	5.90
5	4	H.F. Ahmanson	5.75
6	3	Great Western Financial	5.57
7	6	Glendale Federal Bank	4.60
8	7	Cal Fed Bancorp	4.44

BROKERAGE

Rank	Last Year	Company	Score
1	1	Merrill Lynch	7.46
2	3	Morgan Stanley Group	7.23
3	2	Charles Schwab	6.93
4	3	Bear Stearns	6.25
5	•	A.G. Edwards & Sons	6.24
6	6	Salomon	5.31
7	5	Paine Webber Group	5.10
8	4	Lehman Brothers Holdings	4.74

INSURANCE: LIFE & HEALTH

Rank	Last Year	Company	Score
1	•	Northwestern Mutual Life	7.18
2	3	New York Life	6.80
3	•	Principal Mutual Life	6.44
4	4	Teachers Insurance & Annuity Assn.	6.35
5	•	Equitable	6.32
6	7	Metropolitan Life	5.88
7	6	Nationwide Insurance Enterprise	5.69
8	8	Cigna	5.68
9	9	Aetna Life & Casualty	5.26
10	10	Prudential Insurance of America	4.84

INSURANCE: PROPERTY & CASUALTY

Rank	Last Year	Company	Score
1	•	United Services Automobile Assn.	7.62
2	1	American International Group	7.58
3	•	General Re	7.32
4	•	Chubb	7.26
5	2	State Farm Group	7.08
6	•	Allstate	6.90
7	5	Travelers Group	6.70
8	•	ITT Hartford Group	6.60
9	9	Loews	6.10
10	•	Liberty Mutual Insurance Group	6.08

DIVERSIFIED FINANCIAL

Rank	Last Year	Company	Score
1	1	Berkshire Hathaway	8.18
2	2	Federal National Mortgage Assn.	7.45
3	4	Federal Home Loan Mortgage Assn.	7.30
4	5	Household International	6.95
5	•	Marsh & McLennan	6.76
6	6	American Express	6.74
7	7	Dean Witter Discover	6.66
8	•	Student Loan Marketing Assn.	6.40
9	•	College Retirement Equities Fund	6.20
10	8	American General	5.83

AEROSPACE

Rank	Last Year	Company	Score
1	1	Boeing	7.89
2	4	Lockheed Martin	7.17
3	2	AlliedSignal	6.94
4	6	United Technologies	6.91
5	8	Textron	6.78
6	7	McDonnell Douglas	6.38
7	5	General Dynamics	6.20
8	•	B.F. Goodrich	6.15
9	•	Sundstrand	6.11
10	9	Northrop Grumman	5.98

AIRLINES

Rank	Last Year	Company	Score
1	1	Southwest Airlines	7.39
2	2	AMR	6.94
3	3	UAL	6.58
4	4	Northwest Airlines	6.41
5	5	Delta Air Lines	6.09
6	8	Continental Airlines	5.86
7	6	Alaska Air Group	5.63
8	7	America West Airlines	4.73
9	9	USAir Group	4.13
10	10	TWA	3.42

MAIL, PACKAGE & FREIGHT DELIVERY

Rank	Last Year	Company	Score
1	1	United Parcel Service	8.31
2	2	Federal Express	7.16
3	3	Air Express International	5.84
4	5	Airborne Freight	5.69
5	4	Pittston	5.67

INDUSTRIAL & FARM EQUIPMENT

Rank	Last Year	Company	Score
1	2	Caterpillar	7.41
2	1	Deere	7.35
3	7	Parker Hannifin	6.61
4	6	Ingersoll-Rand	6.60
5	3	Dover	6.44
6	4	Black & Decker	6.42
7	5	Cummins Engine	6.41
8	9	American Standard	6.07
9	•	Case	6.00
10	10	Dresser Industries	5.93

RAILROADS

Rank	Last Year	Company	Score
1	1	Norfolk Southern	7.44
2	2	Union Pacific	6.95
3	3	CSX	6.88
4	6	Burlington Northern Santa Fe	6.85
5	5	Conrail	5.88
6	9	Southern Pacific Rail	4.58

TRUCKING

Rank	Last Year	Company	Score
1	3	Ryder System	6.85
2	•	Roadway Express	6.23
3	7	US Freightways	6.09
4	5	Landstar System	6.09
5	6	J.B. Hunt Transport Services	5.96
6	4	Consolidated Freightways	5.55
7	2	Caliber System	5.21
8	9	Yellow	4.59
9	8	Arkansas Best	4.46
10	10	Amerco	4.44

MOTOR VEHICLES & PARTS

Rank	Last Year	Company	Score
1	2	Chrysler	7.15
2	•	American Honda Motor	6.66
3	5	Johnson Controls	6.53
4	1	Ford Motor	6.52
5	7	TRW	6.42
6	3	Dana	6.41
7	6	Daimler-Benz NA	6.39
8	8	Tenneco	6.35
9	10	ITT Industries	6.13
10	9	General Motors	5.76

APPAREL

Rank	Last Year	Company	Score
1	1	Levi Strauss Associates	7.97
2	4	Liz Claiborne	7.23
3	2	VF	6.84
4	3	Russell	6.79
5	5	Warnaco Group	5.55
6	6	Kellwood	5.01
7	7	Fruit of the Loom	4.63

WHOLESALERS

Rank	Last Year	Company	Score
1	2	Cardinal Health	7.66
2	1	Sysco	7.21
3	5	Alco Standard	6.94
4	3	McKesson	6.89
5	4	Genuine Parts	6.79
6	•	Arrow Electronics	6.73
7	7	Bergen Brunswig	6.54
8	6	Supervalu	6.30
9	8	Fleming	5.47
10	9	Merisel	4.73

FURNITURE

Rank	Last Year	Company	Score
1	2	Herman Miller	7.78
2	1	Leggett & Platt	7.37
3	3	HON Industries	7.10
4	5	Kimball International	6.52
5	6	Furniture Brands International	6.13

SPECIALIST RETAILERS

Rank	Last Year	Company	Score
1	1	Home Depot	7.99
2	3	Circuit City Stores	6.60
3	2	Office Depot	6.58
4	4	Toys "R" Us	6.54
5	5	Lowe's	6.44
6	7	Limited	6.13
7	8	PriceCostco	5.92
8	6	Tandy	5.42
9	9	Melville	5.33
10	10	Woolworth	4.72

FOOD & DRUG STORES

Rank	Last Year	Company	Score
1	1	Albertson's	7.41
2	3	Walgreen	7.30
3	2	Publix Super Markets	7.10
4	4	Safeway	6.95
5	6	Kroger	6.60
6	7	American Stores	6.25
7	5	Winn-Dixie Stores	6.12
8	8	Food Lion	5.96
9	9	Southland	4.92
10	10	A&P	4.77

FOOD SERVICES

Rank	Last Year	Company	Score
1	1	McDonald's	7.95
2	2	PepsiCo	6.95
3	4	Brinker International	6.62
4	3	Wendy's International	6.49
5	5	Aramark	5.82
6	6	Ruby Tuesday	5.47
7	7	Shoney's	4.67
8	10	Foodmaker	4.58
9	9	Family Restaurants	4.47
10	8	Flagstar	4.07

GENERAL MERCHANDISE

Rank	Last Year	Company	Score
1	1	Wal-Mart Stores	7.24
2	2	Nordstrom	7.06
3	6	Sears Roebuck	7.05
4	4	May Department Stores	6.63
5	3	J.C. Penney	6.56
6	5	Dayton Hudson	6.32
7	7	Federated Department Stores	6.05
8	9	Dillard Department Stores	5.86
9	•	Fred Meyer	5.31
10	10	Kmart	3.82

SOAPS, COSMETICS

Rank	Last Year	Company	Score
1	1	Procter & Gamble	8.18
2	•	Estée Lauder	7.01
3	3	Clorox	6.89
4	4	Colgate-Palmolive	6.82
5	6	Unilever U.S.	6.74
6	2	International Flavors & Fragrances	6.71
7	5	Avon Products	6.28
8	9	Helene Curtis Industries	5.69
9	8	Alberto-Culver	5.53
10	6	Dial	5.04

HEALTH CARE

Rank	Last Year	Company	Score
1	2	Columbia/HCA Healthcare	7.11
2	1	United HealthCare	7.07
3	8	PacifiCare Health Systems	6.74
4	4	U.S. Healthcare	6.32
5	3	Tenet Healthcare	5.81
6	•	WellPoint Health Networks	5.54
7	•	Health Systems International	5.18
8	5	Humana	5.09
9	7	FHP International	4.99
10	10	Beverly Enterprises	4.31

FOOD

Rank	Last Year	Company	Score
1	•	Campbell Soup	7.18
2	1	General Mills	7.14
3	1	Sara Lee	7.13
4	3	ConAgra	7.06
5	•	Nestlé	6.99
6	4	CPC International	6.89
7	4	H.J. Heinz	6.84
8	4	RJR Nabisco Holdings	6.15
9	9	IBP	5.85
10	10	Archer Daniels Midland	5.11

BEVERAGES

Rank	Last Year	Company	Score
1	1	Coca-Cola	8.87
2	3	Coca-Cola Enterprises	7.38
3	2	Anheuser-Busch	7.36
4	4	Adolph Coors	6.14
5	5	Brown-Forman	5.21
6	6	J.E. Seagram	5.15
7	7	Whitman	4.55
8	•	Canandaigua Wine	4.03

TOBACCO

Rank	Last Year	Company	Score
1	1	American Brands	7.49
2	7	Philip Morris	6.76
3	2	UST	5.47
4	3	Universal	5.02
5	5	Dimon	4.78
6	6	Standard Commercial	3.76

ELECTRIC & GAS UTILITIES

Rank	Last Year	Company	Score
1	1	Southern	7.22
2	2	FPL Group	7.14
3	4	American Electric Power	6.50
4	3	Pacific Gas & Electric	6.40
5	5	Edison International	6.40
6	6	Texas Utilities	6.37
7	7	Entergy	6.16
8	8	Public Service Enterprise Group	5.65
9	9	Consolidated Edison of N.Y.	5.44
10	10	Unicom	5.35

MINING, CRUDE OIL

Rank	Last Year	Company	Score
1	3	Freeport-McMoRan	7.30
2	•	Freeport-McMoRan Copper & Gold	7.22
3	4	Cyprus Amax Minerals	6.80
4	5	Vulcan Materials	6.72
5	6	Mitchell Energy & Development	6.71
6	10	Oryx Energy	6.31
7	9	Asarco	6.15

PETROLEUM REFINING

Rank	Last Year	Company	Score
1	1	Shell Oil	7.57
2	3	Mobil	7.45
3	2	Exxon	7.40
4	4	Amoco	7.07
5	5	Chevron	6.87
6	•	BP America	6.53
7	6	Texaco	6.52
8	7	Arco	6.47
9	8	Phillips Petroleum	6.28
10	9	USX	5.51

PIPELINES

Rank	Last Year	Company	Score
1	1	Enron	7.89
2	2	Williams	7.27
3	3	PanEnergy	7.10
4	4	Sonat	6.76
5	•	NGC	6.70
6	•	KN Energy	6.67
7	5	Tejas Gas	6.41
8	6	Equitable Resources	5.84
9	9	NorAm Energy	5.64
10	7	Enserch	5.49

ENGINEERING, CONSTRUCTION

Rank	Last Year	Company	Score
1	1	Fluor	7.20
2	5	Halliburton	6.45
3	•	Jacobs Engineering Group	6.41
4	3	Foster Wheeler	6.41
5	2	Centex	6.38
6	4	Pulte	6.37
7	6	Peter Kiewit Sons'	6.09
8	•	Fleetwood Enterprises	5.76
9	7	Turner Corp.	5.43
10	10	Morrison Knudsen	4.05

METAL PRODUCTS

Rank	Last Year	Company	Score
1	1	Gillette	7.91
2	7	Tyco International	7.10
3	2	Illinois Tool Works	6.92
4	5	Stanley Works	6.38
5	3	Newell	6.17
6	4	Crown Cork & Seal	5.97
7	8	Masco	5.79
8	•	U.S. Industries	5.70
9	10	MascoTech	5.63
10	9	Ball	5.49

BUILDING MATERIALS, GLASS

Rank	Last Year	Company	Score
1	1	Corning	8.03
2	2	Armstrong World Industries	7.17
3	3	Owens-Corning	6.31
4	4	Owens-Illinois	5.75
5	5	USG	5.68
6	•	Schuller	5.28

METALS

Rank	Last Year	Company	Score
1	1	Alcoa	7.38
2	2	Nucor	7.09
3	3	Phelps Dodge	6.67
4	•	AK Steel Holding	6.41
5	4	Reynolds Metals	6.38
6	5	Alumax	6.25
7	7	LTV	5.36
8	6	Inland Steel Industries	5.22
9	8	Maxxam	4.95
10	10	Bethlehem Steel	4.67

PHARMACEUTICALS

Rank	Last Year	Company	Score
1	2	Merck	8.34
2	1	Johnson & Johnson	8.27
3	3	Pfizer	8.23
4	4	Abbott Laboratories	7.24
5	5	Eli Lilly	7.19
6	6	Schering-Plough	7.05
7	8	American Home Products	6.92
8	7	Bristol-Myers Squibb	6.83
9	10	Warner-Lambert	6.36
10	•	Pharmacia & Upjohn	5.94

TEXTILES

Rank	Last Year	Company	Score
1	1	Unifi	7.05
2	3	Springs Industries	7.03
3	2	Shaw Industries	6.96
4	4	WestPoint Stevens	6.48
5	•	Cone Mills	6.29
6	5	Burlington Industries	6.13
7	8	Mohawk Industries	6.08
8	7	Collins & Aikman	5.83
9	9	Triarc	5.20
10	6	Fieldcrest Cannon	5.06

RUBBER & PLASTIC PRODUCTS

Rank	Last Year	Company	Score
1	1	Rubbermaid	7.81
2	2	Goodyear Tire & Rubber	7.64
3	3	M.A. Hanna	7.52
4	4	Premark International	6.96
5	•	A. Schulman	6.83
6	5	Cooper Tire & Rubber	6.76
7	8	Bridgestone/Firestone	6.19
8	6	Mark IV Industries	6.10
9	9	Raychem	6.05
10	10	Foamex International	5.11

CHEMICALS

Rank	Last Year	Company	Score
1	1	Du Pont	7.48
2	2	Dow Chemical	7.12
3	3	Monsanto	7.03
4	4	PPG Industries	6.48
5	5	Bayer	6.32
6	6	Union Carbide	6.17
7	7	Hoechst Celanese	6.07
8	8	BASF	6.05
9	10	W.R. Grace	5.12
10	9	Occidental Petroleum	5.11

FOREST & PAPER PRODUCTS

Rank	Last Year	Company	Score
1	1	Kimberly-Clark	7.49
2	3	Weyerhaeuser	6.48
3	4	Mead	6.47
4	2	International Paper	6.45
5	•	Union Camp	6.42
6	5	Georgia-Pacific	5.64
7	6	Champion International	5.23
8	10	James River Corp. of Va.	4.91
9	8	Boise Cascade	4.77
10	9	Stone Container	4.49

ADVERTISING, MARKETING

Rank	Last Year	Company	Score
1	3	Omnicom Group	7.56
2	2	Interpublic Group	7.50
3	1	CUC International	7.17
4	4	ADVO	6.67

PUBLISHING, PRINTING

Rank	Last Year	Company	Score
1	1	Dow Jones	7.06
2	5	Gannett	6.98
3	3	Tribune	6.97
4	6	Knight-Ridder	6.54
5	7	New York Times	6.45
6	8	American Greetings	6.45
7	4	Reader's Digest Association	6.38
8	2	R.R. Donnelley & Sons	6.36
9	9	McGraw-Hill	6.18
10	10	Times Mirror	5.85

ENTERTAINMENT

Rank	Last Year	Company	Score
1	1	Walt Disney	7.97
2	4	Turner Broadcasting System	6.66
3	3	Viacom	6.08
4	5	Time Warner	5.80

HOTELS, CASINOS, RESORTS

Rank	Last Year	Company	Score
1	1	Mirage Resorts	8.44
2	3	Marriott International	7.24
3	8	Hilton Hotels	6.94
4	5	Circus Circus Enterprises	6.92
5	4	Host Marriott	6.69
6	•	Harrah's Entertainment	6.54
7	•	ITT	6.29
8	10	Bally Entertainment	5.49

RECREATIONAL EQUIPMENT

Rank	Last Year	Company	Score
1	•	Brunswick	6.87
2	•	Polaris Industries	6.40
3	•	Coleman Holdings	6.14
4	•	Outboard Marine	4.94

COMPUTER & DATA SERVICES

Rank	Last Year	Company	Score
1	1	Microsoft	8.29
2	2	Oracle	7.46
3	5	First Data	6.67
4	4	Computer Associates International	6.66
5	3	Automatic Data Processing	6.60
6	6	Computer Sciences	6.33
7	9	Comdisco	5.88
8	10	Dun & Bradstreet	5.74
9	8	Novell	5.54
10	10	Unisys	4.80

COMPUTERS, OFFICE EQUIPMENT

Rank	Last Year	Company	Score
1	1	Hewlett-Packard	8.06
2	3	Sun Microsystems	7.32
3	2	Compaq Computer	7.15
4	4	International Business Machines	7.04
5	5	Dell Computer	6.70
6	6	Seagate Technology	6.43
7	7	Pitney Bowes	6.05
8	•	Canon U.S.A.	5.94
9	9	Digital Equipment	5.11
10	8	Apple Computer	4.87

SCIENTIFIC, PHOTO & CONTROL EQUIP.

Rank	Last Year	Company	Score
1	1	Minnesota Mining & Manufacturing	8.14
2	2	Xerox	7.35
3	5	Eastman Kodak	7.16
4	3	Honeywell	6.88
5	4	Thermo Electron	6.45
6	6	Becton Dickinson	6.18
7	8	Baxter International	6.00
8	7	EG&G	5.81
9	10	Bausch & Lomb	5.67
10	9	Polaroid	5.66

TELECOMMUNICATIONS

Rank	Last Year	Company	Score
1	1	SBC Communications	6.86
2	3	BellSouth	6.35
3	8	Sprint	6.29
4	4	Ameritech	6.22
5	6	MCI Communications	6.17
6	5	Bell Atlantic	6.09
7	7	GTE	5.64
8	2	AT&T	5.61
9	9	US West	5.31
10	10	Nynex	4.88

ELECTRONICS, ELECTRICAL EQUIPMENT

Rank	Last Year	Company	Score
1	1	Intel	8.27
2	3	General Electric	7.92
3	2	Motorola	7.61
4	4	Emerson Electric	7.35
5	5	Texas Instruments	6.75
6	7	Rockwell International	6.45
7	6	Siemens	6.39
8	8	Raytheon	6.21
9	9	Whirlpool	5.81
10	10	Westinghouse Electric	5.03

TEMPORARY HELP			
Rank	Last Year	**Company**	**Score**
1	•	**Manpower**	**7.34**
2	•	**Olsten**	**7.06**
3	•	**Kelly Services**	**6.18**
4	•	**CDI**	**5.97**
5	•	**Volt Information Sciences**	**5.95**